PEOPLES OF ROMAN BRITAIN

General Editor: Keith Branigan
Professor of Prehistory and Archaeology
University of Sheffield

THE
CATUVELLAUNI

Keith Branigan

Professor of Prehistory & Archaeology
University of Sheffield

ALAN SUTTON
1987

First published in 1985
Reprinted in 1987
by Alan Sutton Publishing Limited
30 Brunswick Road,
Gloucester

ISBN 0 86299 255 9

Typesetting and origination by
Alan Sutton Publishing Limited
Printed in Great Britain

Contents

Jack Head
in memoriam

Preface

In writing this volume for the series I have been particularly aware of two problems. The first has been the quantity of material (the size of the data-base) available for the study of the civitas of the Catuvellauni, which probably outstrips that available for any other civitas in the province of Britain. The problem of compression, which all the authors in this series face, has thus been a particularly difficult one to handle and compression has inevitably led to the omission of material and topics which some readers may feel should have been included. At the same time I have felt constrained by the need to maintain the uniformity of the series by adopting broadly the same kind of treatment of the main topics under discussion. As a result, many of the present fundamental controversies in Romano-British archaeology – about the nature of towns in the fourth century, the nature of the market economy, the types of marketing systems in operation, the use of locational models in the study of urban and rural settlements, and so on – are only mentioned in passing or are but briefly discussed. Nevertheless, I hope that the volume will prove a useful basis on which to pursue these controversies elsewhere, at least as far as they relate to the Catuvellauni.

The difficulty of researching so much material has been greatly eased by the willing help of many good friends, amongst whom I should particularly mention Gareth Davies, Mike Farley, Roy and Liz Friendship-Taylor, David Miles, David Neal, Ros Niblett, Chris Saunders and David Smith. I have also been helped by the staff of the Oxford and Bucks County Museums, and those of the Verulamium

Museum. For the preparation of line drawings I must thank Simon Probert and Wayne Sheedy, for photographic work I am grateful to Trevor Corns, and for making my typescript presentable I owe much to Dorothy Cruse and Sheila Wallace. The problem of providing interesting illustrative material has been greatly alleviated by the kindness of Professor Sheppard Frere, Mr D.F. Mackreth, Mr. B.F. Rawlins, Dr. David Smith, Dr. Ian Stead, Dr. Graham Webster, the Society of Antiquaries and the Nene Valley Research Committee. That the volume was written at all owes much to the University of Sheffield who provided me with two periods of study leave to research and then write the book, and to the patience and understanding of my family who made sure that their demands on my time were minimal. To Nong, especially, I am grateful for also reading and checking my typescript.

Keith Branigan
14th February 1985

List of Illustrations

Line drawings by Simon Probert and Wayne Sheedy.

1
Tribal Territory and the Pre-Roman Iron Age

The territory occupied by the Catuvellauni and administered as a 'civitas' during the period of the Roman occupation of Britain is thought to have extended for about 80 miles northwards from the Thames, and about 60 miles east-west between the valleys of the Lea and Stort in the east and that of the Cherwell in the west. The north of this area is largely occupied by limestones and sandstones, which form the broken hill country of Northamptonshire in the north-west, and a dissected plateau, pierced by the valleys of the Welland and Nene in the north-east. Across the centre of the region stretches the Oxford Clay from south-west to north-east, with the low hills of east Bucks and west Beds flanked to the west by the Vale of Aylesbury and to the east by the flood plain and terrace of Beds and Cambridge. To the south, the chalk scarp of the Chilterns and the East Anglian Heights mark an abrupt geological and pedological change. The chalk scarp dips south-eastwards, its hills covered by clay-with-flints and its narrow valleys floored with alluvium and gravels. Beyond lie the gravel terraces of the Thames Valley blanketed with alluvium, and to the east of the Colne, marshy, undrained claylands.[1] The whole territory covers about 4,000 square miles, most of which seems to have been densely occupied throughout the Roman period, and represents one of the best explored areas of Roman Britain.

The Emergence of the Catuvellauni

The origins of the tribal kingdom which was to form the

basis of the Roman civitas are still poorly understood and, in recent years, much debated. The most promising point at which to begin the enquiry is with Caesar's campaigns in Britain in 55 and 54 BC. Caesar himself, in his description of Britain at that time, claims that in the decades before his invasion, the coastal areas of southern Britain had been occupied by 'Belgic' peoples coming from the continent, many of whom had retained the same tribal names they had borne in their home territory. (De Bello gallico V, 12). Earlier, in his account of operations in Gaul, (ii, 4) Caesar lists some eleven 'Belgic' tribes, but the name of the Catuvellauni is not amongst them, and nor is it mentioned by Caesar in his account of events in Britain. Furthermore, recent detailed studies of 'Belgic' pottery and coinage suggest that it is difficult to date the earliest distinctively Belgic pottery *before* Caesar and that the distribution of Gallo-Belgic coins may reflect trade and exchange rather than emergent Belgic states. Taken together, these observations are sufficient reason to question whether the Catuvellauni were themselves a Belgic tribe, and whether they existed as a tribe at all in 55/54 BC.

Given the ambiguous archaeological evidence, Caesar's description of events in 54 BC has to be carefully considered, not least because it is contemporary comment on the situation north of the River Thames. By the time Caesar had advanced half-way through Kent, the British tribes had agreed that their resistance should be led by a man named as Cassivellaunus. Although he is not called a king by Caesar, and he is not said to lead any specific tribe, Caesar does say that his 'territory' is separated from the maritime tribes by the Thames and lies about 70 miles from the sea. Since, subsequently, Caesar crossed the Thames at what he describes as the only fordable point, and by so doing entered the territory of the British leader, it is difficult to avoid the conclusion that Cassivellaunus held sway in the southernmost part of the area later occupied by the Roman civitas of the Catuvellauni. Furthermore, from what we know of Celtic society and from the attribution of certain territory to him, it is difficult to follow the view that, even though he had been selected to lead the British resistance,

Cassivellaunus was not a king (or at least a tribal chieftain). If it was possible to identify the 'oppidum' 'of great natural strength and excellently fortified' (De Bello Gallico V, 2) in which Cassivellaunus and many of his forces were congregated after their defeat at the Thames, it might help to locate his territory more precisely. Unfortunately, despite many suggestions, we still have no outstanding claimant for the title. The native site at Wheathampstead was excavated by Wheeler,[2] who claimed that its position,' defences and date all suited its identification with Cassivellaunus' oppidum. Even if one does not accept a recent view that there is no enclosure here at all because two of the 'earthworks' are natural,[3] there is certainly no evidence that the site was occupied before Caesar's time.[4] Other suggested identifications are no more persuasive – Ravensburgh seems too far north, Wallbury too far east, Braughing is completely unfortified as far as we know, and The Aubreys is undated. However, since we are not necessarily looking for Cassivellaunus' capital, but rather one of several strongholds,[5] our failure to locate it need not exercise us too much. More important is to understand from Caesar, the general political geography of the area north of the Thames in 54, and the nature of the politics that were emerging there at that time. Just as south of the Thames, Caesar refers to four kings where by the reign of Augustus there was but one, so in this area Caesar names five tribes in addition to the un-named tribe we must assume Cassivellaunus to lead. Cassivellaunus, so we are told, had been continually at war with other tribes before Caesar's intervention, and significantly none of the five tribes mentioned by Caesar (except perhaps the Cenimagni) ever re-appear on the stage of history. At the same time, Cassivellaunus had also tangled with the Trinovantes, whom Caesar describes as 'probably the strongest tribe in the area' and who we know occupied the county of Essex. Taking all of these scraps of information into account, it may be suggested that from Caesar we get a brief but valuable glimpse into the process of early state formation in southern Britain, as small tribal units engage in warfare in order to assert themselves and extend both their territory and presumably their economic base. In Essex the process was well advanced with a single powerful tribal kingdom, probably already engaging in cross-channel trade. Further inland, the struggle for power was at an earlier stage, and in 55/54 BC at least, it was being won by Cassivellaunus.

This need not mean that it was from the growing power of Cassivellaunus that the tribal kingdom of the Catuvellauni finally emerged. The struggle against Caesar might have reduced his wealth, power and, most important, his prestige, and he may either have been removed by his own kinsmen, or have been overwhelmed by one or other of his neighbouring enemies. Certainly we hear no more of him after 54. An alternative line of development has been proposed by Goodburn and Partridge,[6] based partly on Allen's[7] discussion of the British LX coin series. It is suggested, largely on the basis that it was they who were able to betray the location of Cassivellaunus' stronghold to Caesar, that the tribes named as the Cenimagni, Segontiaci, Ancalites, Bibroci and Cassi by Caesar, were actually located in the area between the Trinovantes of Essex and the territory held by Cassivellaunus. This would place them in east Herts, and Cassivellaunus in west Herts and south Bucks. Since the whole hypothesis hinges on this assumption or deduction, it is worth making brief comment on it before taking the argument further. It seems a reasonable assumption that these tribes were to be found north of the Thames, and that they were close neighbours of Cassivellaunus. There is less reason to suppose that they were all to be found squeezed into east Herts. If the suggestion that the Cenimagni are the same tribe (or even part of the same tribe) later known as the Iceni, then the nearest they could reasonably be placed to a Cassivellaunian territory in west Herts would be around the south-west fringes of Cambridgeshire. It is just possible that the Segontiaci, in contrast, may have held sway on the western flank of Cassivellaunus' territory. A dedication from Silchester to Hercules Saegon(tio) suggests that the deity perhaps implied in the first half of the tribal name was at home in the Upper Thames valley. On the whole, it seems a reasonable assumption that only one or two of these tribes did in fact occupy east Herts (and south Beds?). If that is so, then some interesting observations follow. The first concerns the distribution of the LX coins, and their date. Allen argued that they probably belong in the period c. 45–20 BC, and noted that they are found mainly in Bucks, Herts and Beds. He further suggested that the various types within the overall series were issued by several tribes rather than one, and that they stand ancestral to the issues of Tasciovanus from c. 20 BC. Partridge follows this suggestion, and identifies the tribes concerned with Caesar's five tribes; he goes further and notes that the Welwyn-type wealthy burials, containing imported amphorae and other goods, are found in the same areas as the LX coins, with a marked concentration in west Herts and Beds rather than in the heart of Trinovantian territory (around Colchester) or in Catuvellaunian territory (around St. Albans). This counters the arguments put forward by Peacock[8] and followed by Dunnett[9] that the distribution of Dressel Ib amphorae indicates the territory occupied by the Trinovantes after Caesar. Instead, we have a picture of these small tribes gradually coalescing and growing wealthy, perhaps as a result of a treaty and consequent trade with Rome, in the period c. 50–20 BC.

With certain reservations, this reconstruction of events can be supported. Hodder[10] has rightly pointed out that imported pottery distributions are dangerous grounds on which to identify tribal territories, and that they represent an economic rather than a tribal distribution. We should accept that the Dressel Ib amphorae therefore do not indicate the territorial extent of the Trinovantes or other tribes, but they do indicate that the occupants of east Herts and Beds, as well as the Trinovantes, were acquiring trade goods from the Roman world in the post-Caesarian period. Although some trade goods were penetrating further west to the St. Albans area, the contrast with the Welwyn area in both volume and quality is marked and suggestive of an economic 'barrier' between these adjacent areas.

The whole of the area between Essex and Oxford appears to have been brought into a single cultural and economic grouping in the period around 20 BC. The cultural unity of the area has been recently demonstrated by Thompson's[11] study of grog-tempered Belgic pottery. This pottery is notable in being almost entirely wheel-thrown, grog-tempered, and made in a range of new shapes. Some of the forms appear to be developed from local pottery of the immediately preceding period, and Thompson goes so far as to claim that 'here we are seeing the emergence of 'Belgic' pottery'. For our purposes her zone 7 group is the most interesting, for it occurs in quantity on many sites in Herts, Bucks and south Beds. It is in the same region that the coins of Tasciovanus now become widespread, although they are certainly found further afield, in Northants, Cambridgeshire and Essex as well as south of the Thames. Tasciovanus seems to have emerged, from an unknown background, as the pre-eminent ruler of the area later to be the heartland of the Catuvellaunian canton. The appearance of the names of three or four other kings or chiefs on various issues of Tasciovanus may reflect the initially federate nature of this emerging state. The focus of the new policy was clearly at Verulamium (St. Albans), where most of Tasciovanus' coins were minted and where, from about 15 BC, we have evidence from a large cremation cemetery of both a ranked society and a new wealth which enabled trade goods from the Roman empire to be acquired in quantity. To summarise, the origins of the tribe of the Catuvellauni are obscure, and there are several conflicting interpretations of the ambiguous evidence available. The most coherent interpretation, I suggest, sees the Catuvellauni as emerging from a number of small tribes occupying the chalklands of south Bucks and south Herts at the time of Caesar's invasion. These tribes shared a common material culture and probably a common ancestry. Under Tasciovanus they were united into a single political unit centered on Verulamium, but controlling all of Herts, south Beds, most of Bucks, and Oxfordshire west of the Cherwell. Such a history is not unlikely to judge from what we know of developments in the same period elsewhere in Britain. The Cantiaci of Kent, as we have already noted, were comprised of at least four tribal groups, and the Brigantes of northern England were certainly a federal tribe.

The Iceni, the Coritani, the Durotriges and the Parisi have all been suggested, by various scholars, to have emerged as tribal units from a number of smaller septs or tribes.

Cunobelin and Catuvellaunian Supremacy

Both the imported Roman trade goods and the classicizing types found on the reverses of the coins of Tasciovanus suggest that he established regular economic contact with Rome. To such commercial exchanges we can be sure political ones were added. His successor, Cunobelin, followed a similar policy to judge by increasing quantities of imports at his new capital at Camulodunum and by continued use of an ever-wider range of Roman motifs on his coinage. It has even been suggested that the size and quality of his gold coinage might reflect a Roman subsidy.[12] Be that as it may, it is clear from the quantity and quality of the coinage, from its widespread distribution, from events just before the Claudian invasion, and from the title Rex Britannorum bestowed on him by Suetonius (the only British king so to be called) that Cunobelin greatly enhanced the power, wealth and territory of his kingdom. Surprisingly, what is not established beyond all doubt is which particular kingdom that was!

The orthodox view is that Cunobelin was king of the Catuvellauni, but Rodwell[13] has challenged that view, suggesting instead that he was a Trinovantian. It is possible to hold this view because nowhere in the Roman sources is Cunobelin explicitly described as king of the Catuvellauni, and his first coin issues were minted at Camulodunum rather than Verulamium. Furthermore the harsh treatment accorded the Trinovantes following the Claudian conquest in AD 43 contrasts with the support and encouragement given to the Catuvellauni at this time (see below p. 38). One might conclude from this that it was the Trinovantian kingdom which led the resistance to the Roman conquest; if that were the case, then it would lead to the inescapable conclusion that Cunobelin's kingdom was that of the Trinovantes.

In fact, the one clue provided by the contemporary

written sources points firmly in the opposite direction. Dio Cassius describing the surrender of a tribe called 'the Bodunni' during the advance to the Thames, refers to them as 'tributaries of the Catuvellauni'. The implication is that the forces led by Caratacus and Togodumnus (described as sons of Cunobelin) are those of the Catuvellauni. Indeed the information that in AD 43 the Catuvellaunian kingdom not only survived but also held other tribes in tribute confirms that Cunobelin's kingdom was that of the Catuvellauni, since it is clear that he controlled the territory previously occupied by both the Catuvellauni and the Trinovantes. Only one or the other kingdom could have survived and Dio makes it clear that it was the Catuvellauni; the Trinovantes are nowhere mentioned in his (or any other) account of the invasion.

Cunobelin's rise to power within the Catuvellaunian kingdom appears to have been swift; he was minting coins at Camulodunum before AD 7, and at Verulamium by around AD 10. The coins circulating in Herts and Bucks frequently carry the name of Tasciovanus on the reverse and some explicitly proclaim TASC.FIL. – son of Tasciovanus. Whether or not Cunobelin was really the son of Tasciovanus, or even an adopted son and heir, there is no way of knowing, but the distribution of the coins carrying this claim is so heavily focussed around the Verulamium region that these issues were clearly intended to strengthen (or legitimise) his hold on this territory. It is significant that unlike the coins of Tasciovanus, those of Cunobelin carry the names of no other leaders, so that in the space of ten years, Cunobelin appears to have emerged as sole leader of the Catuvellauni and also to have united into a single powerful state, the kingdoms and territories of the Catuvellauni and the Trinovantes. How this was achieved is uncertain, but it was the culmination of a process begun by Tasciovanus. Within the Catuvellaunian kingdom he had emerged as the undisputed leader, and he had already laid some claim to Trinovantian territory around 15 BC by briefly minting coins carrying the mint mark of Camulodunum. Whilst it is unlikely that Tasciovanus himself completed the conquest of the Trinovantes[14] it is possible that he had formed a client-relationship with them.[15] In any event Cunobelin was established in Camulodunum by AD 7, whether by force of arms or dynastic marriage, and it was probably after Tasciovanus' death that he made his move to incorporate the two kingdoms into one and issued his Verulamium-minted coins around AD 10.

The political history of Cunobelin's kingdom from this point until his death around AD 40 can be traced only in its broadest outlines, but it would seem to justify Suetonius' use of the term King of Britain in that Cunobelin came to directly control a substantial part of southern England, and exerted political and economic influence over an even greater area. Although one cannot write political history from the changing distribution of inscribed coinage, the common appearance of Cunobelin's coinage in Beds, Cambridgeshire, Northants, Oxon and north Berks (as well as in Essex, Herts and Bucks) and the almost total absence in these same areas of the coinage of any other monarch or tribe must surely reflect Catuvellauni domination of these areas. That his influence reached still further afield is suggested by the appearance of his coins in Sussex, Hants, Gloucestershire and Norfolk. His coins are sufficiently common in north Kent for some scholars to suggest that he seized direct control of at least part of the kingdom of the Cantiaci.[16] It is indeed possible that he installed one of his sons, Adminius, in Kent[17] just as one of his brothers, Epaticcus, seems to have been given control of the northern part of the Atrebatic kingdom. Ironically, Adminius and Epaticcus were to be responsible for bringing about the destruction of Cunobelin's kingdom by the forces of Rome. In AD 39 Adminius fell out with his father and fled to Gaul, where he sought and obtained the help of Gaius Caligula to intervene in British affairs. Although the planned invasion was aborted, Gaius made much of the affair in Rome and revived Roman interest in the possibility of occupying Britain. Three years later as Catuvellaunian pressure on the remainder of the Atrebatan kingdom increased the Atrebatan king, Verica, fled to Rome and begged the new emperor, Claudius, to intervene on his behalf. The

Claudian invasion followed, and within twelve months, the kingdom which Tasciovanus and Cunobelin had so skilfully established over a period of fifty years had been swept away by the legions of Rome. It is probably significant that the crucial events fell in the years either side of Cunobelin's death around AD 40. At the beginning of his reign Cunobelin appears to have established reasonably good relations with Rome; it is difficult to see how he could have seized control of the Trinovantian kingdom had it been otherwise. Caesar had guaranteed Trinovantian independence in 54 BC, when it was threatened by Cassivellaunus, and the last Trinovantian king, Dubnovellaunus, duly fled to Rome when his kingdom fell to Cunobelin. It is likely that Cunobelin was amongst the British kings who Strabo tells us sent embassies to Augustus and won his friendship. His diplomatic dealings with the Romans may be reflected in the Roman motifs on his coinage[18] and his adoption of the Latin title Rex. Equally his promotion of trading contacts with the Roman empire and the British goods and customs dues that the Romans thus acquired were no doubt appreciated by the Roman government – indeed, Strabo says as much.

Although Strabo provides a valuable list of British exports – corn, cattle, gold, silver, iron, hides, slaves, hunting dogs – Catuvellaunian trade with the Roman empire during the reigns of Tasciovanus and Cunobelin is more vividly represented by the imported goods which flooded into Essex, Herts and Bedfordshire. Initially, in the early years of Tasciovanus, the imports seem to have consisted mainly of Italian wine and related bronze and silver vessels – jugs, bowls, strainers and goblets. The amphorae and other vessels have been found mainly in wealthy burials in Herts and Beds, though the amphorae also occur on settlement sites. In the last decade of the first century BC and the opening ones of the next century, a wider range of goods were brought in from the continent and turn up in quantity at settlements like Braughing and Verulamium as well as in isolated rural burials apparently associated with farmsteads. Alongside wine came amphorae from Spain, containing olive oil and fish sauces, and large quantities of Gallo-Belgic tableware. (fig. 1) Excavations in and around Braughing, for example, have already yielded remains of over 500 such vesels, as well as smaller quantities of samian ware from both northern Italy and southern Gaul.[19] Other imports included glassware and jewellery. Although the majority of these imports are concentrated at large and important settlements such as Camulodunum, Verulamium and Braughing, they are widely if thinly spread throughout most of the eastern part of Cunobelin's kingdom. Only in the west, beyond Verulamium, are they rarely found, a distribution which reflects both the relatively undeveloped settlement pattern in the Chilterns and its distance from Camulodunum, the port through which most of this continental trade was now channelled.

The acquisition of Camulodunum and its port by Cunobelin was a vital event in the growth of both the Catuvellaunian kingdom and Cunobelin's personal power and prestige. Whether or not he now directly controlled a fleet of merchant ships is unknown, but one of his coin-types minted at the new capital portrays a high-sided, rather flat-bottomed vessel with mast, yard and stays.[20] What is quite certain is that he could now exert close control over the flow of trade goods to his own, and probably other tribes, and that he could use this control to further his own position. It is by no means certain that Tasciovanus had exercised similar economic power. The earliest wealthy burials as noted above, are found in Essex, in the Welwyn area and in Bedfordshire and Cambridgeshire – all to the east and north of Tasciovanus' capital at Verulamium. Such burials are absent from Verulamium itself, and although the large cemetery at King Harry Lane, used from about 15BC up to the time of the Roman invasion, contained a number of wealthy graves their wealth does not compare to that of the Welwyn graves.

Society and Administration

Both the Welwyn type burials and the Verulamium cemetery, however, provide a reasonably clear picture of the social structure of the Catuvellauni. The Welwyn type

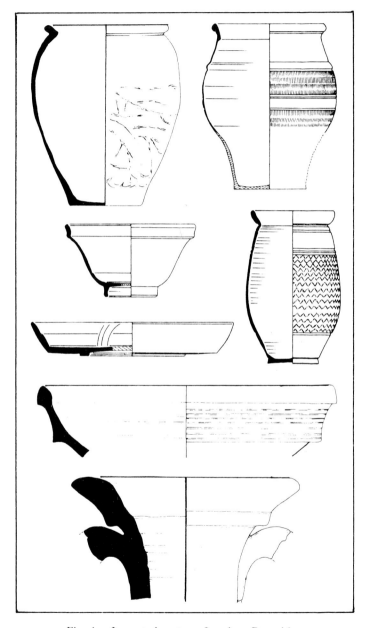

Fig. 1. Imported pottery found at Braughing.

burials are cremations accompanied by an ostentatious display of wealth commonly including several wine amphorae, fire-dogs and bronze or silver vessels. About fifteen examples are known to date, none of them from the site of a major Belgic settlement and mostly discovered and recorded a long time ago. A burial found at Panshanger, Welwyn in 1965, however, was carefully excavated and due care was paid to its surroundings.[21] This revealed that the burial was not in complete isolation; it was surrounded by at least six further cremations all of which were notable for their lack of grave-goods. In contrast, the main burial was accompanied by five amphorae, thirty-six other vessels, a silver cup, bronze serving dish and strainer, and a set of twenty-four glass gaming pieces. (fig. 2) It is difficult to

Fig. 2. The Panshanger burial group.

avoid the conclusion that here we see the two classes of Celtic society to which Caesar referred, the *equites* (literally knights, perhaps better translated nobles) and the peasants or possibly even the slaves. The juxtaposition of wealthy and unfurnished graves is repeated on a large scale in the Verulamium cemetery. About four hundred and fifty cremations were found here. Some were inside rectangular ditched enclosures, with a wealthy burial in a large grave at the centre and between ten and forty simple cremations arranged in a rough circle around it. At least six such enclosed groups were found and another three similar groups without enclosures. (fig. 3) The principal burials were not as richly equipped as those of the Welwyn-type burials, but they still produced imported samian pottery and brooches, silver mirrors and coins, and contrasted with the poverty of the surrounding burials. The same social dichotomy is represented, and since the cemetery had a life of only about fifty years, we may conclude that the burials are broadly contemporary and represent the burial plots of several noble families who lived in the oppidum at Verulamium in the period around 10 BC–AD 45.

Although Camulodunum had become Cunobelin's capital,[22] it is clear that Verulamium remained an important settlement in his kingdom. Some of his coinage, including the important series naming Tasciovanus, were minted at Verulamium, so that it played an administrative role of some sort in the organisation of the kingdom. The imported goods found both in the cremation cemetery and elsewhere in the settlement equally suggest that Verulamium continued to function as an economic focus in the western part of the kingdom. Some further light has been thrown on both the functions and form of the oppidum of Verulamium by excavation and fieldwork over a period of half a century. Wheeler's excavations in the 1930's seemed to indicate that the focus of Belgic occupation was in Prae Wood south-west of the later Roman city, but that view had undergone drastic revision. Although the absence of a series of enclosing dykes makes it difficult to define the area of the Belgic oppidum, excavation and field survey reveal a concentration of occupation in an area of about 500 hectares (1250 acres),

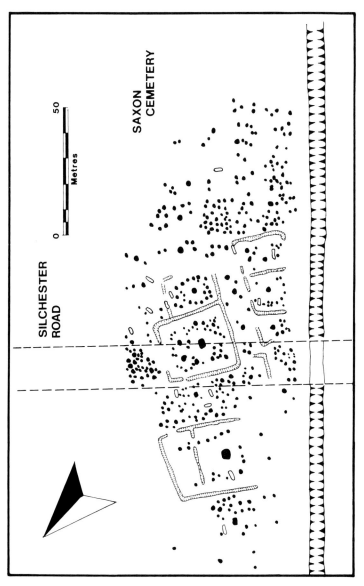

Fig. 3. The Belgic cremation cemetery at Verulamium.

mainly to the west of the River Ver.[24] The north-western limits of the oppidum are probably marked by the Devils Dyke, a 10m wide ditch, which runs west from the River Ver and is linked, by a second dyke running south, to the earthworks in Prae Wood. Recent work by Hunn[25] reveals that these have a complicated history, but occupation here and at Gorhambury (by Devils Dyke) begins no later than the reign of Tasciovanus. By the time of Cunobelin enclosures, droveways and occupation sites have been well-developed in both areas, and extensive occupation of the lower slopes west of the river has taken place. Under Cunobelin, the oppidum can be seen to comprise a number of functional zones. At Gorhambury and Prae Wood there are farmsteads. That at Gorhambury[26] develops from an initial rectangular enclosure into a double enclosure, the inner of which contained a circular living hut and a granary, and the outer one or two rectangular outbuildings. Beyond this lay a large area of enclosed meadowland. Prae Wood may well have been very similar, and there are hints that other farmsteads were to be found along the whole of the western edge of the oppidum. (fig. 4) Immediately east of the Prae Wood enclosures, and well within the oppidum, was the large cremation cemetery already described. Other cremation cemeteries also existed within the settlement – at Verulam Hill Fields and close to the site later occupied by the forum of the Roman city. It was in this latter area that Cunobelin's mint was probably to be found. Mint moulds and crucibles have been found at five locations in this vicinity, in one instance closely related to a timber-framed building with rammed chalk floors.[27] Other traces of houses have been found beneath the Roman city on the lower slopes above the river, including one building 9m × 5m with two rooms, one containing a hearth and the other perhaps used for weaving. Although the Belgic structures known from the levels beneath the Roman city are fragmentary and dispersed, there is an impression both of relative density of settlement in this area and of buildings which were both more substantial and more sophisticated than those found in the farmsteads. The focus of the oppidum seems to lie broadly in the area occupied later by the Roman forum, and

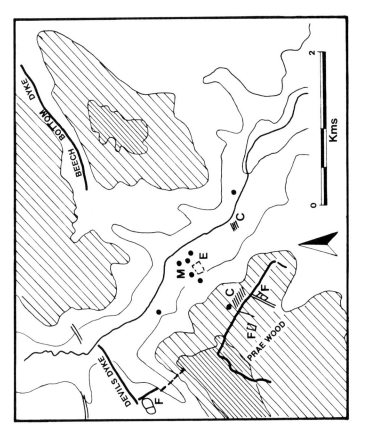

Fig. 4. The oppidum of Verulamium – a schematic plan

KEY

M – Coin Moulds
E – Enclosure
C – Cemetery
F – Farmstead

it may indeed have lain precisely under that structure. Traces of a large rectangular enclosure, surrounded by a very substantial ditch, were located beneath the forum; it appears to have been over 2 hectares (5½ acres) in size but its interior is totally unexplored. Nevertheless the subsequent location of the Roman forum over it, its size, and its nearness to the minting area, all suggest it was an important feature of Verulamium shortly before the Roman conquest. It may have been a temple enclosure, comparable to that at Gosbecks (Camulodunum), or perhaps a royal administrative and residential enclosure, like that recently excavated at Thetford (Norfolk) and tentatively identified as the enclosure of Prasutagus, king of the Iceni. In any event, the overall impression of pre-conquest Verulamium is that despite the removal of the Catuvellaunian capital to Camulodunum, Verulamium remained, and was probably deliberately maintained, as a major settlement in the kingdom.

More problematic is the role of Braughing, though the settlement's importance has been clearly established by recent excavations. A defended enclosure of about 3 ha (7½ acres) was established here, at Gatesbury, in the pre-Belgic era and possibly as early as the third century BC. It was only much later, around 20 BC, that there was a dramatic development in the area of occupation here. At that time settlement spread down to the river Rib, and then across the river to Wickham Hill; excavations and field-survey suggest a total area of not less than 100 ha (250 acres) so that we are clearly dealing with a major settlement. There is indeed sufficient evidence to justify describing it as an oppidum. Like Verulamium it has no artificial defences, but it is well protected by marshy ground to the north and south and by heavy forest to the west and east. The south-eastern approach to the original nucleus of settlement is also protected by two bournes. During Tasciovanus' reign some parts of the interior of the settlement were quite densely occupied by rectangular timber buildings arranged in an orderly manner.[28] (fig. 5) Evidence for craft activity is provided by iron-working debris and carpenters' tools, but the most significant material is a collection of fragments of

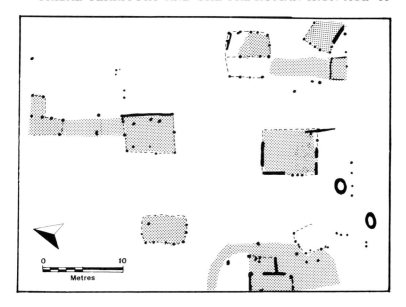

Fig. 5.   Part of the pre-conquest settlement at Braughing.

coin-moulds from Gatesbury. Analysis has shown that they were probably used for casting flans for silver coinage. Thus Braughing must be recognised as the site of a mint, although for which king remains uncertain. It might be possible to link these moulds with the British LX series which precede Tasciovanus and for which Rodwell[29] has suggested a mint at Braughing. The only mint mark carried by Tasciovanus' own issues is Verulamium, but another possibility is that the coins issued with the names of both Tasciovanus and one of his associates on them, might have been minted at Braughing; Partridge suggests the coins of Andoco may have been minted here.[30] The issue is unresolved, but the administrative and economic importance of Braughing to which the mint debris attests, is underlined by the concentration of trade goods here. In the reign of Tasciovanus these include Gallo-Belgic platters, cups and beakers from the Moselle region, mica-dusted jars from the Rhone-Loire area, samian from northern Italy, wine amphorae from southern Italy and probably early examples of Spanish oil amphorae. These together with occasional coins of the Coritani, Iceni and Trionovantes, suggest that Braughing's rise to prominence during the reign of Tasciovanus may have been due to its location on or near the boundary between the kingdom of the Trinovantes and that of the Catuvellauni. Initially, at least, this importance continued under Cunobelin and the number and variety of imported vessels grew rather than diminished. The discovery of graffiti on half a dozen sherds of this period, including a terra rubra platter inscribed Graecus, has been taken by Partridge[31] to indicate the presence at Braughing of foreign traders, and he may well be right. Whether or not the importance of Braughing continued undiminished throughout the reign of Cunobelin is uncertain. Some of the central areas of the settlement seem to have been at least partially abandoned in the period around AD 30–40, but elsewhere occupation continued.

Just as it is clear that a major settlement co-existed with Verulamium less than thirty kms to the north-east at Braughing, so it has been demonstrated that occupation at Wheathampstead, only eight kms north of Verulamium, also continued through to the Claudian conquest. For many years, Wheathampstead was identified not only as the stronghold of Cassivellaunus against Caesar, but it was also regarded as the predecessor of Verulamium which was abandoned when Tasciovanus established the latter as his capital. Although Wheathampstead was certainly established before Verulamium, probably around the time of Caesar's invasion, recent excavations there have shown that occupation not only continued through to about AD 50, but that the area of occupation was probably extended during the reign of Cunobelin.[32] Unlike Verulamium and Braughing, Wheathampstead was defended, at least to east, west and south-east by massive 'dykes'. Devils Dyke on the west was 12m deep and 40m wide, flanked by banks; The Slad on the east and south-east has not been excavated and some doubt its artificial nature, but man-made or natural it provides effective defence. The latest excavations show that the total area occupied may have been as much as 70 ha (175 acres) but they have revealed little of the nature of the occupation apart from pits, ditches and gullies. Nevertheless, in demonstrating that the low-lying land by the river Lea was occupied from about AD 5 into the early years of the Roman conquest, they have placed Wheathampstead firmly on the map of Cunobelin's kingdom as yet another major settlement.

Outside the heartland of Cunobelin's kingdom, it is difficult to locate any settlements comparable to those in Hertfordshire. One may exist at Dorchester on Thames, territory which was probably added to his kingdom early in Cunobelin's reign. The promontory fort there, defended by a loop of the Thames and by impressive earthworks to the north, is well known from aerial photographs but little is known about the history of its occupation. Flanked as it is by an earlier hillfort half a mile to the south at Whittenham Clumps, and by the small walled Roman town of Dorchester a few hundred metres to the north, it is difficult to resist the temptation to associate the fort and its crop marks with Belgic pottery and coins found in some abundance in the vicinity.[33] In size, the settlement of 46 ha (114 acres) is large enough to be called an oppidum, but we know nothing of the functions which it served. Its internal organisation is perhaps partly revealed by aerial photographs, showing a substantial rectangular ditched enclosure in the north-west corner, outside of which there is relatively dense occupation by circular huts, in addition to further ditch systems and enclosures. It may well be that in many respects Dyke Hills was similar to Verulamium, but until much more is known about the nature and date of the features seen as cropmarks, it would be unwise to speculate.

In the clay vale of Bucks and Beds, and in the hill country and dissected plateau of Northants, oppida-like settlements are at present lacking, and there is little evidence to indicate any major re-occupation or continued use of the earlier hillforts. The political and economic administration of Cunobelin's kingdom, therefore, was focussed very heavily on its south-east quarter in the territory between Camulodunum and Verulamium, with the possibility of an outlying subsidiary centre at Dorchester. How control was exercised over such a large area we do not know, but the effects of this arrangement may be imagined. The south-east quarter of the kingdom would have been something of a magnet to which the agricultural and other wealth of the kingdom as a whole would have been drawn in tribute and trade. To the same area would have come the manufactured goods and luxury foods imported from Roman Europe, to pass by trade or other forms of exchange into the hands of the tribal nobility and petty chiefs living in either the nucleated settlements or on the farming estates in the countryside around them.

Agricultural Settlements

The scattered Welwyn-type burials have long suggested that by the time of Tasciovanus, the upper echelons of Catuvellaunian society had established themselves on thriving farms, often at a distance from the nearest oppidum. Some of the earliest of these farms are found clustered in the Welwyn area where local archaeologists have been particularly active, and it is from these sites that we get confirmation of the link between the Welwyn-type burials and the farms. Some of the sites, like Crookhams and Broomhall Farm,[34] have produced sherds of imported Italian wine amphorae like those found in the burials. At Grubs Barn[35] traces of a contemporary farmstead were found only 150m east of the Panshanger 'chieftain' burial described above and at Baldock, further north-east, two contemporary settlements were found only 200–300m from two other Welwyn-type burials.[36] Investigation of these and other similar sites shows that they are usually ditched oval enclosures, often with a palisade inside the ditch. Recog-nisable hut structures have yet to be found in the enclosures around Welwyn, but there can be no doubt that the enclosures were for occupation since ovens, hearths and occupation debris are found in them. Circular timber huts were probably constructed to judge by similar huts found in the earliest phases of occupation at farmsteads nearer Verulamium such as Park Street and Gorhambury.

The farms in the vicinity of Verulamium appear, on current evidence, to be founded perhaps a little later than those around Welwyn. Park Street, the most extensively explored of the rural sites,[37] was probably founded early in the reign of Cunobelin at which time at least one circular hut stood on the site. Later this was replaced by a more substantial rectangular hut, about 8m x 3.5m, with a rammed chalk floor in the centre of which was a hearth, and on which was found a coin of Cunobelin. Close by was a smaller, oval hut, and an adjacent pit from which was recovered a slave-chain. This sequence is similar to that already briefly described from Gorhambury within the area of the oppidum, but at present we have no evidence for a rectangular enclosure at Park Street to match that at Gorhambury. At Beaumont Hall just north of Verulamium, and at Foxholes, just south of Hertford, bi-partite rectangular enclosures like Gorhambury have been discovered, and a further rectangular enclosure with two circular huts has been discovered at Baldock, so that there do seem to be two distinct enclosure-types in the region – oval around Welwyn and divided, rectangular ones elsewhere. The difference may be chronological, but it could possibly be related to the type of farming activities carried out on these farms. Elsewhere in the southern part of the tribal territory, pre-conquest farms seem to be found only along the natural routeways of the Thames, the Chiltern scarp and the valley of the Colne.[38] Little is known about most of these sites, except that several of them underlie later Roman villas in the same way as Park Street, Gorhambury and Lockleys. In the heart of the western Chilterns this pattern is repeated, with at least six villa sites producing late Belgic pottery, but this is probably of post-conquest date and the creation of farming estates in the valleys of the western Chilterns appears to take place after the Roman invasion.

Beyond the chalk country on the Oxford Clays, Belgic occupation in the period of Cunobelin appears to have been much less dense than in the region to the south, although it is in the clay-lands of central Bedfordshire that the outliers of Welwyn-type burials are found at Maulden Moor, Old Warden and (post-conquest) at Stanfordbury. Even these, however, appear to locate on or close to discrete areas of

greensand. Beyond central Bucks and Beds, in the valley of
the Ouse, Belgic farmsteads are much more numerous,
although the combination of the river gravels and active
archaeological groups may have led to a disproportionate
rate of discovery. Pre-Belgic farmsteads within enclosures
ranging from circular and oval to polygonal and rectangular
appear little different to those of the early first century AD,
but rarely occur on the same site. Whether Belgic settlers
from the Catuvellaunian heartland moved northwards and
took over the better agricultural land here is uncertain;[39] we
may be looking at the results of acculturation and economic
change rather than colonisation. Certainly some of the
farmsteads here appear to be exceptionally well organised
agricultural units. At Odell, for example, the farmstead
established at the end of the first century BC included not
only an oval enclosure for the two living huts (fig. 6), but a
large arable enclosure and possibly cultivation plots to the
east, and a series of pastoral enclosures served by a ditched
droveway and timber-lined wells, to the west. Just beyond
the living enclosure there were two small cremation

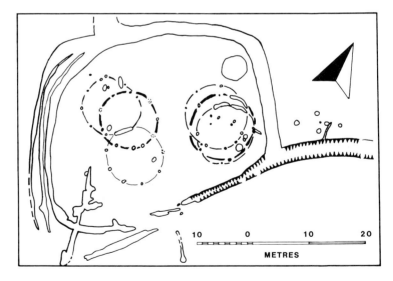

Fig. 6. The Belgic farm at Odell.

cemeteries.[40] Occupation here and at other sites appears to continue uninterrupted after the Roman invasion, and at Odell a small stone-founded timber farmhouse or villa was eventually constructed late in the Roman period. Villas succeeded Belgic farmsteads at Stanton Low, Bancroft and Newnham too, but though the transition here took place in the second century, there is nothing to match the speedy transition from Belgic farm to Roman villa that we shall see taking place in the later first century in the southern part of the tribal territory. Nor do these farms produce any tangible evidence of the acquisition of Roman trade goods during the reign of Cunobelin.

The same is true of native farms in the low hill country of Northamptonshire, where distinctively Belgic farmsteads are few. Some of the 'pre-Belgic' farms may indeed continue to be occupied into the Belgic era further south, but farmsteads of certain Belgic date occur sporadically. That at Moulton Park replaced a pre-Belgic farm, first with a single hut inside a circular enclosure, and subsequently with a rectangular enclosure containing four huts. Little remained of the huts, so that we cannot be sure whether they were built for a variety of functions or whether the population of the settlement, and presumably its productivity, increased in the years before the Roman invasion. Production of a different kind was attested at Quinton where the Belgic hut was associated with contemporary pottery kilns, anticipating the industrial importance of the northern part of the tribal territory in the Roman period. The same may be said of Wakerley too, on the northern fringes of the Catuvellaunian kingdom.[41] Here, two phases of occupation preceded that of the early first century AD when a trapezoidal enclosure was built. Within this stood a circular timber hut, and perhaps an animal pen in the opposite corner. Although arable farming was practised, pastoralism was probably the most important part of the farming economy with both cattle and sheep reared on the sloping meadowland surrounding the site. But the farmers at Wakerley clearly exploited local sources of ironstone to smelt and smith iron; pieces of ore, furnace lining and various slags were found in pre-Belgic and Belgic levels.

There were many hearths and furnaces excavated too, and although some of these were certainly built and used in the Roman period, others appear to belong to the late Iron Age occupation of the site.

In contrast there is nothing to suggest that the major Roman pottery industry in the lower Nene Valley around Peterborough was preceded by a significant Belgic industry. Rather a cluster of Belgic settlements on the Fen edge appear to be related to pastoral activities. At Orton Longueville[42] the occupation enclosure was joined to a second large rectangular enclosure with no traces of occupation or buildings within it, and which seems likely to have been a stock enclosure. Similar enclosures served two farmsteads at Longthorpe,[43] the larger of which was approached by a droveway. The Orton farmstead boasted three contemporary circular huts, each between 10.5m and 12m in diameter, and the enclosed farmstead at Fengate[44] may have had four or five huts of slightly smaller size in contemporary use, so that both may have been occupied by extended families. But family farms, like that excavated at Werrington,[45] and probably those at Longthorpe, suggest that in the last decades before the Roman conquest social patterns may have been varied in this remote corner of the Catuvellaunian kingdom.

The tribal boundaries

It is certainly possible that some of the settlements in the vicinity of Peterborough were not within the canton of the Catuvellauni during the Roman period, even though coins of Cunobelin and Tasciovanus are found north of the Nene. There has been much discussion in recent years of the extent to which the distribution of Iron Age coinage can be used to identify tribal boundaries, but fortunately this problem need not concern us too greatly. Our task is to suggest the most likely boundaries which were set for the civitas of the Catuvellauni when it was established in the late first century AD by the Roman government. The existence of the civitas is confirmed by an inscription found not in Hertfordshire but at Howgill on Hadrian's Wall, which records repair work carried out by draft labour supplied by the 'civitate Catuvellauni'.[46]

Whilst tribal boundaries probably changed and shifted constantly in the Iron Age, and some areas may never have been 'fixed' in any sense, in the Roman period we should expect the boundaries between civitates to be firm and for the most part enduring. The Roman government required the civitates to collect taxation and to maintain roads in their territory, and for these purposes clear boundaries between the tribal cantons were necessary. For the same reason, we might expect that wherever possible the boundaries selected would be prominent features of the landscape, whether natural or man-made. The framework within which the boundaries of the Catuvellaunian canton must be sought is that provided by the surrounding civitates. Within that framework we shall look for prominent natural boundaries, and seek to find supporting evidence for the lines suggested from occasional documentary and archaeological evidence. Given the generally discrete distributions of the pre-Roman tribal coinage, we would be foolish not to bear it in mind as supporting evidence.

The southern boundary of the Catuvellaunian canton can hardly be other than the river Thames, beyond which lay the territories of the Cantiaci and Atrebates. The city of Londinium will have formed a small independent enclave on the north bank of the Thames, probably established (about the same time as the civitas of the Catuvellauni) in the late first century when London may have become a *municipium*.[47] Rodwell has suggested that a 'town-zone' or territorium can be identified around Londinium,[48] stretching for about 5 kms. to east and west and perhaps rather less to the north, but totalling about 2,500 ha (over 6,000 acres).

At what point the tribal boundary left the Thames to run northwards is open to argument. Few coins of Cunobelin are found west of the Cherwell, and few of the Dobunni east of it, so that the boundary between the cantons may be fixed on this river. The rivers Evenlode and Glyme a little further west would have made much less distinctive boundaries, and their orientation would have carried the boundary unacceptably too far westwards towards the Cotswolds.

Some support for the Cherwell line may also come from the location of the important shrine at Woodeaton, overlooking the Cherwell just north of modern Oxford. Rivet has pointed out that in Gaul shrines are sometimes found on tribal boundaries where they provide both sanctuary and market places.[49] The many small finds and 2,700 coins from Woodeaton suggest it may indeed have acted as a market place. North of Banbury, the boundary becomes more controversial, since there are few natural features which make obvious territorial markers. At this point, the neighbouring tribe would change from the Dobunni to the Coritani, with their tribal capital at Leicester. The only tentative pointers to the possible line the boundary took in this area are the location of the small town and posting station of Bannaventa (Whilton Lodge) on Watling Street and the Roman building inside Borough Hill camp (most likely a temple) both of which may lie close to the tribal boundary. From here we follow the line of the hills northwards to Market Harborough and the Welland. It is widely agreed that the northern boundary of the canton lay somewhere along the line of the Welland, the Nene, or the strip of land between them.[50] The distribution of coinage supports this view, but since there is inevitably an overlap of Coritanian and Catuvellaunian coins in this area, it does not allow us to make the important distinction between the two river valleys, or the area which separates them. If we take the combination of a clear boundary, and of rural shrines as valid indicators, then our preference must be for the river Welland, since the shrines at Brigstock and Colley Weston both lie just to the south of it. Certainly it is difficult to take the Nene as the boundary, since so much of what went on at the town of Durobrivae was clearly and closely linked with the pottery works and villas on *both* sides of the river. This would have made for administrative difficulties in terms of taxation and census returns.

Where the Welland reaches the Fens, the boundary must have swung southwards, since when the civitas was created drainage and reclamation work was only beginning in the Fens and this area clearly saw a very different pattern of development to that found in the surrounding tribal cantons of the Iceni, Coritani and Catuvellauni. The boundary may have followed the Car Dyke and then swung to meet Ermine Street which would have been by far the clearest marker along the Fen edge south of Peterborough. At God-manchester the boundary could then have either followed Ermine Street again, or swung eastwards along the road to the town at Cambridge (Duroliponte). There is no strong supporting evidence for either line, but we follow the road to Cambridge. We do this partly because Tasciovanian coins reach considerably beyond the Cam and suggest that the pre-Cunobelin kingdom may have included this area, and partly because the northern boundary of the Trinovantes appears to follow the Fen edge westwards to Great Chesterford.[51] This being so, to take the Catuvellaunian boundary along the line of Ermine Street, south of God-manchester, would leave an awkward wedge of territory west of Cambridge either in the hands of the Iceni – from whose other territory it was separated by Fens – or else unattached to any tribal canton. From Cambridge the clearest boundary would then be the river Cam itself, with Great Chesterford as a Trinovantian border settlement. There was clearly an important Belgic settlement here, with ritual importance, which lends support to this view;[52] a Romano-Celtic temple continued the religious significance of the site. South of Great Chesterton, the valley of the Cam leads almost directly to the valley of the Stort, and a further important Iron Age and Roman shrine site at Harlow, where coins of Catuvellaunian and Trinovantian kings have been found in quantity. From this point, the boundary must then follow the river to its confluence with the river Lea, and thence down the Lea to the Thames.

It would be foolish to claim that our suggested boundaries follow closely those actually in use in the Roman occupation, but equally it is difficult to justify moving very far from those which we have suggested. The greatest areas of uncertainty, or dispute, are along the northern and eastern borders but even here the scope for movement is relatively small. Overall, the territory of the civitas of the Catuvellauni seems to cover about four thousand square miles. Its greatest north-south extent may have been 140 kms (90 miles), and its east-west extent about 100 kms. (65 miles). This is certainly a much smaller area than that over which Cunobelin exerted direct or indirect control in the years before the Roman invasion, and may well reflect the kingdom established by Tasciovanus.

After Cunobelin

Cunobelin died around AD 40/41, shortly after his son Adminius had been expelled by his father from the Kentish kingdom he had given him. He was succeeded by two further sons, Caratacus and Togodumnus, whilst his 'brother' Epaticcus continued to expand his control of Atrebatic territory. We have no direct evidence to suggest the nature of the arrangement between Caratacus and Togodumnus, but it is arguable that they divided Cunobelin's kingdom into two separate states rather than attempted any dual kingship. The only clues we have that this may have been the case are that the handful of extant coins of Caratacus do not mention Togodumnus' name, in the way that the coins of Tasciovanus for example had carried the names of other princes, and that the Roman invasion forces met and defeated the two kings separately according to Dio Cassius.

If there was a division of the kingdom, then the most likely divide would be along the old boundaries between the two original kingdoms which Cunobelin had united. The most recently acquired territory, in Kent, would probably have gone with the Trinovantian kingdom, so that although this would have been the smaller of the two, it would have had the advantage of controlling the cross-channel trade. It seems likely that the older of the two sons would have held this eastern, maritime kingdom, which apart from its valuable trade also possessed the oppidum at Camulodunum, presumably with the kingdom's principal religious centre and other important buildings. But neither Tacitus nor Dio Cassius, tell us which son was the elder. Caratacus' protracted and skilful struggle against Rome makes it easy to think of him as the natural successor to Cunobelin, the new 'strong man' of the Catuvellaunian kingdom, but it may be a misleading impression since

Togodumnus' early death robbed him of any chance to emulate his father's victories. The only hint, and it is no more, that it was Caratacus who took the eastern half of the kingdom, including Kent, is that when Aulus Plautius advances inland from the bridgehead at Richborough, his first encounter is with Caratacus. It may well be that the Catuvellaunian princes had decided to split their forces in two and that this explains why Togodumnus was not involved in the first battle, but it is perhaps more plausible that Caratacus and his force faced the Romans first and alone, because Togodumnus and his army were still on the march from the western kingdom. Whether or not one accepts this reconstruction of events following the death of Cunobelin, we know that within two to three years of his demise circumstances largely beyond the control of his successors had led to the Roman invasion and the destruction of his kingdom.

2
History: A.D. 43–367

The initial opposition to the Roman invasion of AD 43 was led by the two sons of Cunobelin, Togodumnus and Caratacus, but the direct involvement of the tribe of the Catuvellauni seems to have lasted no more than a few weeks. Our only source of information for the events of the summer of AD 43 is Dio Cassius;[1] Suetonius and Tacitus give only the briefest of accounts and the information recorded on the triumphal arch erected for Claudius in Rome may not all refer exclusively to AD 43. When Aulus Plautius led the Roman army inland from Richborough he appears to have met first Caratacus and then Togodumnus in separate engagements. The initial defeats suffered by the two kings led to at least one defection from their forces, for according to Dio the 'Bodunni', who were tributaries of the Catuvellauni, now took the opportunity to make terms with the Romans. This otherwise unrecorded tribe are probably to be identified with the northern Dobunni centred in Gloucestershire and west Oxfordshire, who were ruled by a king called Boduoc(us); it is easy to see how Dio may have confused king and tribe and arrived at 'Bodunni'. British forces had meanwhile withdrawn westwards and taken up positions on the west side of a large river which can only have been the Medway, and probably in the vicinity of Rochester. The Romans took two days to force a successful crossing of this river and this would suggest a substantial British force opposing them, but we are not told by Dio whether the forces of the two kings were now united into a single army or not. In any event, after the defeat at the Medway, a retreat to the Thames was inevitable, and here, perhaps in the area now occupied by the City of London, the British again prepared to defend the heartland of the two Catuvellauni kingdoms from the invader. Again, the skill, discipline and might of the Roman army forced them to give ground, although Dio's reference to the Roman's losing large numbers of men in the 'swamps' may be a veiled reference to heavy casualties inflicted by determined defenders. The British themselves lost at least one of their leaders at this time. We are told Togodumnus, who we have suggested earlier (p. 31) may have inherited the western part of the kingdom focussed on Verulamium, died shortly after the defeat at the Thames, though we are not told how. With the British in some confusion, and the north bank of the Thames in Roman hands, Plautius now inexplicably called the advance to a halt and sent for Claudius. Dio claims that the losses Plautius had suffered and the difficulties he still faced led to this decision; but Claudius was no general, and any troops he brought with him can have been little more than escorts – his arrival added nothing significant to the Roman strength. It is widely agreed, therefore, that Claudius' involvement was pre-determined and was undertaken for political rather than military reasons. When Claudius arrived he immediately marched on Camulodunum. Dio says he engaged the British, whilst Suetonius says he fought no battles, and Claudius' own triumphal arch says he conquered the British 'without any loss'. We may surmise that little more than skirmishes took place in the advance on Camulodunum, and this immediately raises the question of the whereabouts of Caratacus. He is not mentioned at all after the initial engagement of the war; we do not know if he fought at the Medway or the Thames, nor if he made any attempt to defend Camulodunum. Six or seven years later he re-emerges, leading the Welsh resistance to the Roman conquest, but at what point in the summer of AD 43 he made his escape westwards we do not know. By the time Camulodunum fell, the Catuvellauni appear then to have been kingless if not leaderless. Representatives of the kingdoms of Caratacus and Togodumnus were presumably amongst those who submitted to Claudius before he left the island to return to Rome, leaving Plautius behind to carve out a province and organise its military garrison.

Military occupation of the Catuvellauni

Despite the opposition which the Catuvellauni had offered the invading army, Roman military occupation of Catuvellaunian territory in both the eastern and western kingdoms was on the whole brief and scattered. A legion was based at Camulodunum, and four or five forts established in southern Essex.[2] The western kingdom, the area to become the civitas of the Catuvellauni, appears to have been occupied by only four or five forts and a vexillation fortress holding perhaps 2000 men. Webster, in his recent study of the invasion period,[3] has suggested that the Roman preference in newly conquered territory was for forts about a day's march apart, placed to control important routes, crossings, and native settlements. Within the boundaries we have set ourselves in this volume, this model strictly applied would produce a total of some 22 auxiliary forts and a garrison of about 11,000 men. This would amount to about a quarter of the invasion force, and would be a quite unacceptable concentration in an area well to the rear of the emerging frontier. The Romans simply could not afford this number of men to garrison the canton of the Catuvellauni, and as they pushed westwards the pressures to remove whatever garrison the canton was given would increase. As far as it goes, this is what the archaeological evidence seems to confirm although the evidence is woefully inadequate. A fort at Verulamium should come as no surprise and has been confirmed by the excavation of its timber north-east gate[4] and part of its rampart,[5] as well as the discovery of many items of military bronzework. It appears to have been of irregular design (like some other mid-first century forts in Britain), but might have been about $3-3\frac{1}{2}$ acres in size. Amongst the bronzes found in or near the fort site are those of both legionaries and cavalry.[6] The fort presumably housed a mixed garrison of about 500 men, and since it was abandoned before AD 50, it was probably part of the initial deployment, established in AD 43–44.

Northwards, another fort was established at God-manchester on the line soon to be occupied by Ermine Street.[7] Its structural details have been compared to those of Great Casterton, and its south-east gate is almost identical to two of those at Casterton.[8] Whether, as its excavator suggests, it was about the same size as Casterton (6 acres) we do not know, nor do we know its garrison although it is essentially an auxiliary fort. Beyond Godmanchester northwards, a further fort of 5 acres was established at Water Newton.[9] Without excavation we can say nothing of its garrison, but it must surely belong to the early years of the Claudian invasion since from about AD 48 to AD 65 a much larger fort or fortress stood less than three miles to the east at Longthorpe. There would have been no need for a fort at Water Newton during this period, and by the later sixties, military units had been moved north and west in preparation for further campaigns in Wales and the north.[10] In all likelihood then, the fort at Water Newton was occupied in the period c. AD 43–48.

North-west from Verulamium a fort may have been established at Little Brickhill, on the line of Watling Street.[11] Two overlapping ditch systems can be seen here on aerial photos, and trial excavations on one have revealed a ditch with Neronian samian pottery, overlain by a fill containing early Flavian pottery. If this is a fort it therefore appears to have been founded in the aftermath of the Boudican revolt of AD 60/61, and this suggests that the other 'fort' seen on aerial photos is probably pre-Boudiccan, and part of the initial deployment of troops in AD 43–44. The only other fort for which any structural remains can be offered is one at Dorchester on Thames, where traces of its defences have been identified on aerial photos and exca-vations have revealed timber-framed buildings demolished in the later first century, some time after AD 78.[12] A fort occupied as late as AD 80 is an anomaly in this part of the province and we should perhaps treat it with some suspicion until excavation of its defences has been undertaken.

A number of other locations have been suggested for forts, but in most cases the evidence is thin, however strong might be the strategic arguments for them. (fig. 7) Isolated

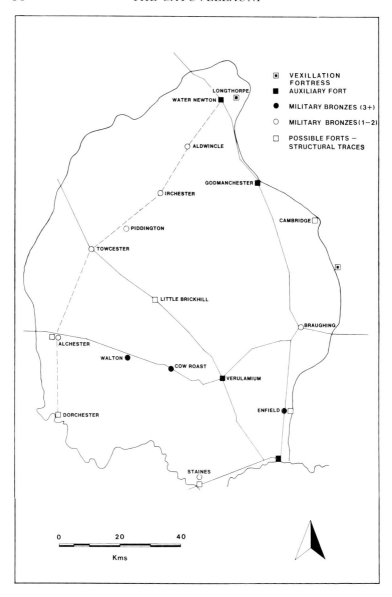

Fig. 7. Military sites in the canton.

finds of military bronzes from Aldwincle, Braughing, Enfield, Staines and Irchester are insufficient evidence on which to place forts at any of these sites. The same is probably true of Alchester from which at least two cavalry bronzes have been recovered, but Rowley has also argued a case for identifying traces of a demolished mid-1st century turf rampart here, which if correct could only be plausibly associated with a fort.[13] Other potential fort sites are at Walton Court (Aylesbury) and Northchurch in the valley of the Bourne, west of Verulamium. Walton Court produced four military bronzes and a spearhead, whilst recent excavations at the Cow Roast site have added five military bronzes and a pilum head to the Claudian legionary helmet found here early in the nineteenth century (Goodburn, 1976, 338–9), as well as copies of Claudian coins.[14]

In trying to interpret the little evidence we have for the military occupation of Catuvellaunian territory in the years immediately after the invasion we should bear in mind the broader military context. It is clear that by AD 47 the Roman army controlled all of England south and east of a line from the mouth of the Severn to the Trent at Newton and possibly to the Humber. By the mid-fifties it had pushed further west.[15] In these circumstances the governor of Britain would want the bulk of his troops well to the west and north of Catuvellaunian territory. The initial disposition may have seen forts only at Verulamium, Little Brickhill, Water Newton, Godmanchester and possibly Northchurch. If a fort existed at the latter site, it may very soon have been replaced by one further west on Akeman Street at Walton or Alchester. The number of troops deployed in Catuvellaunian territory between AD 43–48 may therefore have been of the order of 2000–2500, and these would have been essentially a winter garrison, since in the campaigning season they would have been required in the east and west Midlands.

With the move westwards which took place in the governorship of Scapula between AD 48 and 51 changes were made in the deployment of troops in south-east England. The best known example is the removal of the XXth legion from Colchester to the west country in AD 49, and the evidence from Verulamium strongly suggests that the fort there was abandoned in AD 48–49, presumably as part of the same redeployment. We have already noted that the fort at Water Newton is unlikely to have been occupied after c. AD 48, and Godmanchester would also seem superfluous with the foundation of the vexillation fortress at Longthorpe at this time. Given the general picture of a wholesale movement of troops westward it seems likely that any forts which may have existed at Alchester and Little Brickhill would also have been vacated.

This was not the end of military occupation in the Catuvellaunian territory however, for at about the same time a vexillation fortress was established near the northern borders of the Catuvellauni at Longthorpe.[16] This fortress was excavated by Frere and St. Joseph, who suggest that it was built in response to the Iceni rebellion of that year. Certainly its location would suit such an interpretation, and subsequent events showed that the Iceni were indeed likely to foment further trouble. The most likely garrison of the fortress, to judge from its partially excavated plan and the finds made within it, is three cohorts of about 2400 men. (fig. 8) Situated at Longthorpe, a garrison of this sort could intimidate the Iceni whilst still being available for operations on the frontier in the east midlands.

The municipium of Verulamium

At about the same time as these redispositions were taking place, the settlement at Verulamium also saw major redevelopment. Up to that time we have no evidence that the Roman occupation, and the building of an auxiliary fort here, had made any material impact on the extent, layout and architecture of the native settlement. In the years between AD 48–60 Verulamium was transformed. The sprawling Iron Age oppidum of perhaps 500 ha (1250 acres) was replaced by a town of up to 48 ha (116 acres) eventually enclosed with an earth rampart fronted by a ditch 6m wide and half as deep.[17] The area inside these defences was at least partially divided into insulae by gravelled roads laid out in a rectilinear grid, through which Watling Street

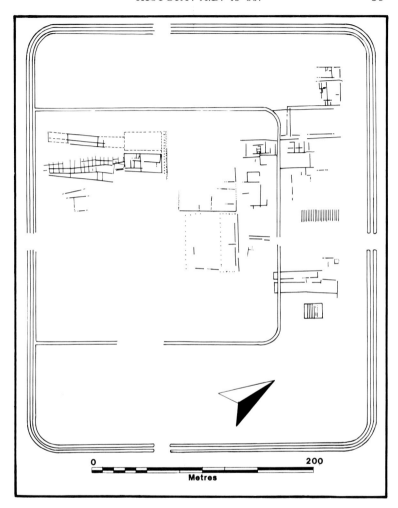

Fig. 8. The vexillation fortress at Longthorpe.

sliced diagonally, following its original line to the gate of the fort. Traces of occupation have been recovered from ten insulae, mostly associated with timber-framed buildings erected on sleeper beams and provided with clay, gravel or mortar floors. In insula XVII a timber building of unusual sophistication for this period was found, measuring 17m by

12m and provided with tiled roof, plastered walls and glazed windows.[18] More remarkable still was the block of shops erected on a prime site on Watling Street, just across the road from the gateway of the now-demolished fort.[19] The building measured at least 46m long and was 10m wide, fronted by a timber verandah and colonnade. (fig. 9) A detailed study of its measurements has suggested that it was either built with 'army surplus' timber – perhaps from the demolished fort – or that the army were involved in its construction. It contained nine shops, two apparently belonging to bronzesmiths and another probably a tavern, and all contained under a single roof with no alleyways providing separate access to the individual units. The shops were therefore in all probability the property of a single owner and were leased out by tenant craftsmen. Apart from these timber buildings, pre-Boudiccan Verulamium has produced evidence for at least two masonry buildings. One, in insula XIX, had painted plaster on its walls and was probably a bath-house whilst the other, found below the later forum, is potentially the more significant by reason of its location though we know little about it.[21]

All of the structures described appear to have been built after about AD 48 and before AD 60, with the defences and the masonry building in insula XIX as probably the latest of them. They point very clearly to the rapid and extensive Romanisation of the community at Verulamium in the years immediately following the withdrawal of the Roman garrison. Apart from architecture with distinctive Roman features (tiled roofs, masonry foundations, plastered walls, glazed windows, and verandahs), the commercial Romanisation of the native people is represented by the row of shops, the abundance of imported samian ware from southern Gaul, and the discovery of over two dozen Republican and Claudian coins in the levels within the shops. In terms of administration and social organisation, the changing pattern of life is emphasised by the provision of defences and the construction of a grid-system of streets. The process of Romanisation at Verulamium is notable, particularly in comparison to other British settlements, for its speed and its breadth.

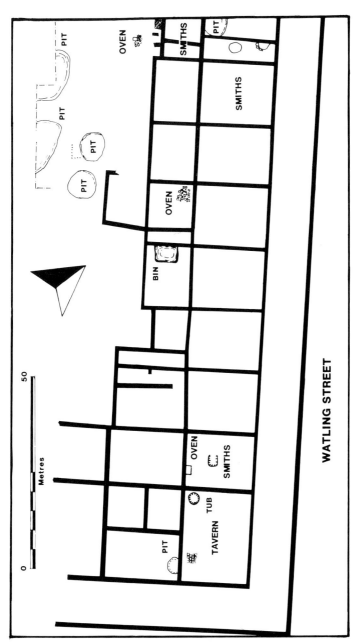

Fig. 9. Claudian shops at Verulamium.

It is reasonable to relate this anomalous development at Verulamium to some form of official encouragement, and the possibility of an official foundation here in the years around AD 50. In AD 49 the Romans had founded the *colonia* at Colchester, the heart of Cunobelin's kingdom; is it possible that at the same time they founded another Romanised town in the other tribal capital at Verulamium? This seems to be the clear implication of Tacitus who describes the Verulamium destroyed by Boudicca as a *municipium* – that is, a chartered town.[22] Although argument has raged as to whether Tacitus was using the term loosely, or whether he was anachronistically applying Verulamium's status in his own lifetime to that of the town some sixty years before, it is difficult to reject this evidence. Frere has discussed the problem at length and argues convincingly for the accuracy of Tacitus' terminology in this context, and for the supportive evidence from Dio and Suetonius.[23] As we have seen, the archaeological evidence too suggests that Verulamium was selected for special treatment in the years around AD 50, and the coincidence of historical and archaeological evidence cannot be lightly set aside. In all probability, Verulamium was created a *municipium* by Claudius c. AD 50.

The Boudiccan Revolt and Its Aftermath

Claudius' gesture may have sealed the fate of Verulamium ten years later, when the Iceni and the Trinovantes rose in rebellion against the Romans. The early events of the revolt took place outside the Catuvellaunian canton, culminating in the capture and destruction of the *colonia* at Colchester. At this point, according to Tacitus, a mixed legionary and cavalry force led by Cerialis, the legate of the Ninth Legion, attempted to intervene, but was heavily defeated and Cerialis retreated with the cavalry to a 'castra' or camp. Almost certainly the Roman force in question was the garrison of the fortress at Longthorpe, possibly augmented by auxiliary units from other forts in the region. It also seems likely that it was to Longthorpe that the beaten force retreated, since although the fortress built at Longthorpe c.

AD 48 can scarcely be described as a 'camp', around AD 60/61 it was greatly reduced in size by the rapid construction of new, simpler defences, which cut across the line of existing buildings.[24] This has all the appearances of a temporary measure, taken in a time of emergency, and appears to confirm that Cerialis retreated back to the base from which he had set out. Meanwhile, the Boudiccan forces had turned west and attacked and burnt Londinium; next they turned northwards, presumably moving along Watling Street, and this brought them inevitably to Verulamium. Despite its defences, Verulamium had no garrison and it received no help from the powerful force – thought to be a thousand cavalry – which Cerialis commanded at Longthorpe. It suffered the same fate as Colchester and London, presumably a mixture of retribution from the Iceni and Trinovantes who had suffered at the hands of Cunobelin, and a hatred for all things Roman, amongst which the wealthy *municipium* was clearly numbered. The archaeological evidence for the Boudiccan destruction at Verulamium is clear and unequivocal. Destruction debris has been found in eight different insulae, especially those close to Watling Street, and the shops in insula XIV and the sophisticated building in insula XVII were all razed to the ground. Outside the town, the nearby farms at Park Street and Gorhambury were destroyed by fire, and evidence that the rebellion's consequences were felt more widely in the Catuvellaunian canton may be recognised in the destruction of settlements at Staines and Godmanchester around AD 60.

The near loss of the province, and the destruction of a colonia, municipium, and the seat of the fiscal administration, were a major setback for the Roman government. Equally, the canton of the Catuvellauni had suffered a devastating blow with the razing of Verulamium and the destruction of farms and settlements elsewhere in the region. Any hope that the Catuvellauni might progress swiftly to the status of a *civitas* was abruptly crushed. Here, as elsewhere, the immediate aftermath of the rebellion saw retribution against its perpetrators and the return of troops to the tribal territory. The reduced fortress at Longthorpe continued in occupation and a new one of about 14ha (35 acres) was probably established further south on the eastern borders of the tribe at Great Chesterford.[25] Tacitus describes how 2,000 legionaries, eight auxiliary cohorts and a thousand cavalry from Germany were brought into Britain as reinforcements.[26] The auxiliaries, he says, were placed in new winter quarters. It is possible that these quarters were at Great Chesterford. Longthorpe and Chesterford were clearly aimed primarily at the Iceni and Trinovantes, but smaller forts may have been re-introduced to other areas of the Catuvellaunian territory. A possible fort of about 2ha ($5\frac{1}{2}$ acres) at Little Brickhill yielded Neronian pottery from its lower ditch fill and was perhaps established in the aftermath of the Boudiccan revolt.[27] It was apparently abandoned in the Flavian period, and it perhaps invites comparison with the fort identified at Dorchester on Thames, the suggested timber buildings of which were also abandoned in the Flavian era. Whilst Longthorpe and Great Chesterford were abandoned by the mid 60's, the continued occupation of one, perhaps two, forts elsewhere in the canton emphasises that civilian recovery from the rebellion was much slower than has sometimes been assumed. This is true of London and Colchester,[28] and it is certainly the case at Verulamium. The debris of the block of shops on Watling Street was partly carted away and the remainder raked over, but neither here nor in adjacent insulae is there yet any evidence of new buildings erected during the 60's. Some parts of the town may have escaped destruction in 60/61 and their houses continued in occupation, and certainly coins and pottery of the period c. AD 60–75 point to continued activity in the town. It is not impossible that a military unit was stationed here again in the aftermath of the revolt, which might account for the relatively high numbers of Neronian coins of the period c. AD 63–69, and might help to explain the mixture of military bronzes – from legionary, cavalry and auxiliary infantry found at Verulamium, often in residual contexts. Timber buildings erected alongside Watling Street but outside the defences may have housed some of the population displaced from the destroyed areas of the town, but for fifteen years or thereabouts the level of civilian life at Verulamium was much below that before the Boudiccan revolt. It was not until the later 70's, when the problems of the Welsh and northern frontiers had apparently been resolved, that the imperial government were able to offer the incentives and assistance which were needed to revitalise both the Catuvellauni and their tribal capital.

The civitas of the Catuvellauni

Although Wacher has argued that the Catuvellauni were granted civitas status c. AD 50, that view is not widely shared and the establishment of the civitas is usually placed in the mid 70's and related to the fragmentary inscription recovered from the Forum.[30] The inscription, recording the completion of the forum, is dated to AD 79 and suggests that the decision to build a forum and basilica was taken no later than about AD 75. (fig. 10) The creation of a civitas of the Catuvellauni at this time would fit into a wider framework of similar grants of local self-government to six or seven other tribal territories in southern Britain in the 70's and 80's. Such grants appear to be the result of a favourable combination of circumstances – enlightened emperors and governors, the apparent solution of the frontier problems in Wales and northern England, and the decision to advance into Scotland. The success of the military policy in the north was partly dependent on the success of the new civilian policy in the south, since despite reinforcements the garrison would be stretched to the limits with the conquest of Scotland. Tacitus, in describing the governorship of his father-in-law Agricola, who arrived in Britain in AD 78 in time to have his name included on the Verulamium inscription, makes it clear that official encouragement was given to the new civic authorities.[31]

At Verulamium there is no clear indication of any government assistance in the provision of either public or private buildings, but the forum and basilica were certainly of unusual type and scale in a Romano-British context. They were followed within the next two decades by a market-hall and at least one, perhaps two or three, temples

Fig. 10.   Fragments of the forum inscription at Verulamium.

of Romano-Celtic type. Around these masonry public buildings, timber shops and houses were built in impressive numbers and increasing quality in the Flavian period. The shops burnt down by Boudicca on the Watling Street frontage in insula XIV were replaced, around AD 75, by the same number of new shops, still under one roof, and presumably therefore one ownership, but now largely occupied by bronze-smiths. One of the larger shops, however, appears to have sold samian ware and this, together with imported glassware of this period, suggests a growing market for imported luxuries. Equally, the private houses of the late first century begin to display features which point to an increasingly Romanised population – mortar and occasionally tesselated floors, painted wall plaster, plaster quarter-mouldings, and window glass. Further, the appearance of houses with between five and eight separate rooms, usually provided with independent access

from one or more corridors, points to the development of a
life-style modelled on Roman lines rather than native ones.
(fig. 11) The absence of any private bath-suites in the late
first century townhouses almost certainly points to the
existence of a contemporary public bath-house yet to be
discovered.

Certainly the Catuvellaunian land-owners had adopted
the practice of bathing Roman style by the later first
century. We can say this with confidence since we have

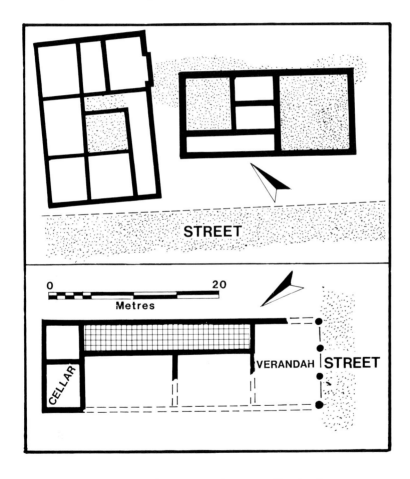

Fig. 11.   Late first century houses at Verulamium.

examples of Flavian bath-suites adjacent to early villas at Park Street and Gadebridge.[32] The villas themselves are small by comparison with later villa buildings but show the same signs of increasing Romanisation as the town houses of Verulamium. Indeed the villas occasionally reveal greater sophistication than their urban counterparts – stucco mouldings at Gorhambury, elaborate wall decoration at Boxmoor, perhaps a mosaic at Saunderton, the bath-buildings already mentioned at Park Street and Gadebridge, and in the majority of cases mortared stone walls rather than timber-framed ones. These early villas tend to cluster close to Verulamium, though examples are found further afield including a small number in Northamptonshire (Brixworth, Cosgrove, Mileoak, and Wood Burcote). Elsewhere in the canton timber-framed buildings of native type continue to be built, but there are some notable areas of increased settlement or even new colonisation, including that in the western Chilterns where several villas were apparently preceded by native-style farms founded in the late first century.[33]

The creation of the civitas, then, seems to have been accompanied or swiftly followed by the development of social and economic facilities at Verulamium, the building of modest Romanised homes both at Verulamium and in the countryside around it or close to Watling Street, and by an increase in the extent and density of rural settlement. The contemporary development of several minor towns or nucleated settlements throughout the canton – at Alchester, Braughing, Dorchester, Godmanchester, Staines and Towcester – was surely related to this buoyancy of agricultural settlement, for beyond the vicinity of Verulamium the minor towns provided both the marketing facilities and the potential consumers for the produce of the farms.

That the relationship was mutually beneficial and that Verulamium as the social and economic focus of the whole canton also benefited from the developments of the late first century seems clear. At Verulamium further public buildings were constructed in the early second century, most notably the theatre built towards the close of

Hadrian's reign. The flourishing economic life of the town is demonstrated by the increasing pressure on the shop frontage in insula XIV. By about AD 130 this valuable site seems to have been broken down into a number of separate holdings, with individual access ways to the rear of the properties. Although these alleys took up valuable space, the number of shops has increased from an original nine to ten or eleven; by AD 150 there were twelve or thirteen. (fig. 12) Nothing demonstrates better the success of commercial life at Verulamium between AD 75 and 150. Confidence in the future prosperity of the city appears to have determined the decision to erect new defences, replacing the now obsolete first century ones, and to take the opportunity to enclose a much greater area of land. Frere is surely correct in suggesting that the incomplete circuit represented by the Fosse Earthwork probably belongs to this period.[34] These defences represent a confident investment of resources in the future of Verulamium around AD 150.

Before the defences could be completed, Verulamium suffered a major fire which destroyed at least 20ha (50 acres) of the town centre focussed around the forum and along Watling Street; fortunately the fire failed to spread up the slope into the southern and south-western quarters of the town. Nevertheless many private houses and shops were razed to the ground, and the forum and market hall did not escape damage. There is no reason to think the fire was anything other than accidental, and it is indeed one of several urban fires that are known from Romano-British towns and from others elsewhere in the empire. Like the Great Fire of London, however, it turned out to be both a catastrophe and an opportunity.

The destruction of many of the smaller timber houses and shops and the change over to less combustible building materials which the fire encouraged, resulted in the construction of larger, more durable houses with better facilities. They were not all built at once, and the early replacement of houses in insulae III, IV, XIII and XXII, was not matched in insulae XXI, XXVI, XXVII and XXVIII where new buildings were not erected until twenty years or more after the conflagration. Since the shops in insula XIV,

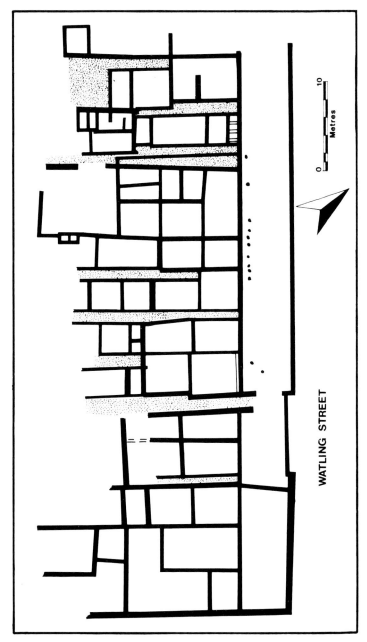

Fig. 12. Antonine shops c. AD 150 at Verulamium.

on a site which we have seen to be highly prized for commercial development, were not replaced until c. AD 275, one wonders if, following the fire, the whole of the space between the forum-basilica and the theatre and temple complex (i.e. insulae XIV, XXVII and XXVIII), was originally designated a 'development area' for public buildings which, in the event, were never provided. Other public buildings, however, were certainly altered and improved, one of the most significant changes being the addition of two temples of classical type to the forum complex.[35] Since it is widely agreed that these were probably dedicated to the Capitoline Triad and the Imperial Cult, they demonstrate not only the appearance of two examples of Roman, as opposed to Romano-British, architecture at Verulamium but also a notable degree of political awareness on the part of the local council. At the same time, changes taking place in the design of the theatre carry interesting implications. The construction of additional seating over much of the old arena-like orchestra suggest on the one hand that the theatre was now to be used only for dramatic and musical performances and on the other that the more popular sports and spectacles previously presented there were now perhaps, to be staged in a new amphitheatre. Although the amphitheatre at Verulamium has yet to be found, we know from the description of the martyrdom of St Alban that it possessed one, and that it stood outside the walled town.

Defending the Civitas

The alterations and additions to the civic amenities and private houses at Verulamium seem to have occupied the energies and the resources of the community for several decades, since there was no immediate attempt to complete the defences begun before the fire of c. AD 155. The date at which this important task was recommenced has been much debated and recently the weight of opinion has shifted for a later rather than an earlier date, with Frere suggesting c. AD 260–270.[36] As with the dating of the earthwork defences, there is no reason to closely associate the building of a stone wall at Verulamium with the provision of similar defences at other towns. (fig. 13) Most of the civitas capitals in southern

Fig. 13. The defence wall and corner tower at Verulamium.

Britain seem to have constructed stone defences at some time in the third century. Canterbury and Caerwent are probably of late third century date, but Winchester, Leicester and Chichester have all been placed in the earlier part of the century, and Cirencester has a *terminus post quem* of c. AD 220 for its walls. The best dated circuit is that of London, erected between AD 190 and 215.[37] There is no *a priori* reason why Verulamium should be much if any later than London, and one might expect it to at least match the developments at Chichester and Winchester for example.

The coin evidence available from Wheeler's excavations certainly appears to indicate a date no later than the first half of the third century. A coin hoard of c. AD 273, found in the debris of a wall-tower, sets a firm *terminus ante quem* of AD 275. From the same tower a smaller and less coherent hoard in which the latest issue is of AD 227–9 was found in a repair to the tower floor.[38] This would appear to favour a *terminus ante quem* no later than c. AD 230, and suggests that a date considerably earlier is possible. Professor Frere's 1955 section of the defences yielded pottery from the rampart which must be post c. AD 160, and a coin 'in mint condition' of c. AD 200–1 which was probably, but not certainly, incorporated in the rampart. In the 1981 section a mid-second century building was demolished and overlain by the rampart backing the stone wall; no pottery later than c. AD 170 was recovered from the excavated corner of this building. From the highest surviving level of the rampart in this section, however, came five sherds of a shallow bowl dated c. AD 220–70. These are probably significant, although it should be noted that we cannot be certain that this is a primary tip level within the rampart, nor that there is no contamination from the immediately overlying modern top-soil. The cumulative testimony of these deposits would point to a probable construction date after c. AD 220 but before c. AD 230, and any deviation from these dates must be backed by firm and positive evidence.

The evidence from Frere's trench A.III, which is used to argue for a date as late as c. AD 265–270 does not appear to fall into this category. This interpretation relies on the assumptions that the estimated position of the town wall was in fact followed by the wall at this point, and that the building found in A.III was demolished to make way for the wall.[39] These assumptions are probably correct, but the dating evidence which goes with them amounts to two sherds of coarse-ware and this is surely insufficient at present to set aside the other evidence we have considered. It is also significant that in seven sections through the defences not a single example of the ubiquitous coins of the period c. AD 259–94 has come to light, despite 'above average coin-loss' at Verulamium in this period.

On careful consideration of the evidence we also have to disagree with Frere's suggestion that the London and Chester gates were not contemporary with the masonry walls but belonged to the unfinished earthwork defences represented by the Fosse. Certainly the Fosse defences cannot be shown to have physically joined either gate. The arguments for associating these two gates with the Fosse are three-fold.[40] It is clear from the way in which the stone defence wall is butt-jointed to the London Gate that the gateway was built before the wall, and Frere notes that the foundations of the London Gate were cut to a deeper level than those of the wall. He also contrasts the design of the London and Chester Gates with that of the Silchester Gate, which he concedes 'must certainly be contemporary with the curtain-wall'. It should first be noted that these arguments, even if accepted, serve only to dissociate the London and Chester Gates from the building of the stone defences, they do not present any positive evidence for linking the gates with the Fosse earthworks. The butt-jointing of the masonry wall and the London Gate demonstrates that the gate was erected before the sections of wall on either side of it, but it provides no indication at all of the gap which occurred between the building of the gate and the erection of the adjacent lengths of defence wall, it may have been days, decades or even, as Frere suggests, over a century. As to the varying depth of the foundations of wall and gate towers, it is difficult to see any chronological significance in this. The gate-towers were almost certainly built to a greater height than the flanking walls (they would hardly be towers if they were not) and deeper foundations might therefore be expected. Furthermore Wheeler's section suggests that the gate builders dug down to place the towers' foundations directly onto the surface of the pre-gate road level.[41]

There remains the difference in design between the London and Chester Gates and the Silchester Gate. There is no reason to assume that a difference of design must imply a difference of date. One has only to look at the gates of Lincoln, all rebuilt to new designs in the early third century, to see how varied contemporary gates could be.[42] At Verulamium it is surely understandable that the two gates which spanned Watling Street – one of the major roads in the province along which, as we have seen, imperial and official couriers travelled – should be built in a more grandiose design than the other gates of the city. (fig. 14) One might suggest that the similar techniques of all the three gates and the masonry defence wall, namely tile-bonded flint and mortar, is suggestive of contemporaneity. Unfortunately close dating of the gates is difficult because Wheeler published very little of the pottery found in the various levels sealed by the gates, apart from a dozen profiles from various (unspecified) levels which 'antedated' the London Gate.[43] Amongst these are two flagon necks

Fig. 14.   Model of the London Gate, Verulamium.

which Frere's excavations show to be 'common in the period c. AD 140–180'.[44] Given that the precise relationship between the gate and the deposit containing these sherds is unknown, other than that it pre-dates the gate, these sherds are not inconsistent with a construction date for the gates of c. AD 220–230. A similar date, early in the third century, is firmly fixed for the double-portal Newgate at London and the East Gate at Lincoln which was remodelled along similar lines to the London and Chester Gates at Verulamium c. AD 210–230. Taking all the evidence into account, therefore, it appears that Verulamium was probably walled c. AD 220–230 and that it received its principal gateways at the same time.

Meanwhile, the minor towns of the civitas had acquired earthwork defences. Although the dating of the defensive ramparts of the towns at Dorchester, Irchester, Towcester, Fenny Stratford and Whilton Lodge is far from precise, the indications are that they were probably erected towards the end of the second century or possibly very early in the third. It would be possible to place the stone walls around Alchester and Water Newton in the early third century, although this is thought to be unlikely when seen in the general context of the defensive development of minor towns in Britain. The spate of defence-building to which the earthwork defences mentioned above appear to belong is usually attributed to the governorship of Clodius Albinus but Todd has rightly questioned this view.[45] There is no reason to think that Albinus had the inclination, nor the many towns involved the time, to build these defences in the period AD 193–196. More importantly, imprecise as the dating evidence is, it seems to indicate a broader chronological bracket for the earthwork defences than the governorship of Albinus. The crucial issue is whether or not the Roman administration gave a general, blanket permission for the towns to build defences. Permission there must have been, but there is no reason to assume that it must have been granted on a single occasion to all the towns of the province. Indeed, we have already seen that Verulamium had earthwork defences before the Boudiccan revolt, and there are other towns, admittedly thought to be exceptional cases, which constructed defences in the first century. In the mid second century Verulamium, and probably some other civitas capitals such as Exeter and Silchester, were constructing new earthwork defences. There is no evidence to suggest that the defences were built in a hurry; they were, in part at least, status symbols. The widespread building of earthwork defences in the later second century may as plausibly be seen as the result of a developing fashion for displaying civic pride and status as the hasty response to distant threats on the northern frontier or belated attempts to defend the cities of a province whose governor was about to abandon it.[46]

Continuity and Change in the Third and Fourth Centuries

The construction of urban defences in Britain in the later second century may perhaps be related to a more wide-spread tendency for towns to seek new and elevated status, as a *municipium* or even a *colonia*, at this time. One of the results of this was that some civitates were divided into smaller units. This almost certainly happened with the civitas of the Durotriges in south-west England,[47] and it is thought that the civitas of the Carvetii was carved out from a corner of that of the Brigantes. We have no clear indication of the time when the civitas of the Carvetii may have been created, but the division of the Durotriges had probably taken place by the early third century. It is possible that the Catuvellauni were similarly divided into two civitates although the evidence for this hangs heavily on a single milestone found outside Water Newton (Durobrivae) which demonstrates that distances were being measured from this town.[48] The town itself compares favourably in size with some of the smaller civitas capitals such as Caistor and Caerwent, and had very wealthy and extensive suburbs. Furthermore aerial photographs reveal a temple enclosure and at least two buildings which in size and design appear to be public rather than private.[49] Attempts to relate Water Newton to a Civitas Corielsoliliorum apparently referred to in a graffiti on a tile found at Caves Inn, Warwickshire, however, have never been convincing and have recently been firmly dismissed by Tomlin.[50] On present evidence we cannot confidently claim that a second Catuvellaunian civitas was established with its capital at Water Newton, but if such a decision was taken it may have been at the start of the third century.

There is no indication at Verulamium that it suffered economically or socially from any administrative changes in the early third century. Apart from the new defence walls and the impressive gateways that accompanied it, other public works of this period probably included the construction of two monumental arches, spanning Watling Street. Since they are located at the boundaries of the original municipium, as marked by the so-called '1955 ditch', Frere must surely be right in suggesting that they were erected to commemorate the ancient defences of the town at or shortly after the erection of the new, permanent defences. The excavation of the foundations of the northern arch produced evidence that it was probably to be dated no earlier than c. AD 220–230 but could have been somewhat later.[51] Whilst these public works were underway, private development continued too. One notable example of private enterprise, a block of corner shops, public latrine and private house in a single development, was built on the lane between the Forum and the theatre c. AD 215.[52] Two other houses were constructed at the edge of the town in insula XX perhaps as late as c. AD 240,[53] and one wonders whether there may have been a general development of these areas close to the new defence wall following its construction c. AD 220–230. In any event, the first half of the third century appears to have been a time of continuing vigour and prosperity at Verulamium, although the character of the town may have been undergoing a slow process of change with less emphasis on production and commerce and more on the provision of private and public amenities.

The situation in the later third century is less clear. Wheeler, on the basis of his excavations in the south-east quarter of the town was in no doubt that in the period c. 275–300 Verulamium suffered serious economic decline, presumably related to both the political and military uncertainty and the monetary inflation of the times.[54] Wheeler recorded in several houses in this part of the city pits dug through floors, walls in ruin, hypocausts and mosaics collapsed. Marble plaques from a public building, probably the southern monumental arch, were found as broken fragments in debris of the period c. AD 270–290, whilst the hoard found in the ruins of the wall-tower suggests that at least part of the defences had fallen into disrepair by around AD 275. Although the hoard from the tower may be re-interpreted, it is not easy to dismiss the other evidence presented by Wheeler, and Frere offers no specific rebuttal of these pieces of evidence in arguing that in fact the late third century town was largely unaffected by economic decline.[55] Certainly there were exceptions, of which the block of shops in insula XIV erected c. AD 275 is the most notable example, but they should not allow us to ignore the evidence elsewhere in the town.

Furthermore, the evidence of an increasing inability to fully maintain the fabric and facilities of Romanised houses is not confined to Verulamium. It appears too, in varying degrees, at villas such as Park Street, Boxmoor, Hambleden, Dickets Mead and Latimer.[56] At some sites rooms fell into disuse and decay, whilst at Latimer and Dickets Mead the effects were apparent throughout the villa buildings and led to abandonment, though Latimer was subsequently re-occupied and rebuilt. It may be significant, however, that all of these villas lie in the southern part of the canton and that all except Hambleden probably regarded Verulamium as their market town. Further afield in the territory of the civitas signs of decline and decay are scarce in both the minor towns and the villas. It may be that Verulamium and its hinterland suffered more from the economic problems of the late third century than did the small towns and the settlements and farms dependent on them. Certainly it is widely agreed that in the fourth century the minor towns flourished as never before, to some extent at the expense of the civitas capitals, and this development might be partly explained by their comparative resilience in the later third century.[57] Verulamium's vulnerability to the economic pressures of the time may have been due partly to the drain on public and private funds of financing public works and entertainments on the sort of scale expected of a *municipium* and civitas capital. At the same time, its economic basis may have been threatened by the disruption of trade with the rest of the empire. The minor towns, with few public buildings and an economy based mainly on local supply and demand, would have been much less severely affected by the political and economic problems of the period.

With the restoration of 'legal' Roman government in AD 296, the political problems at least were largely resolved, and there was an attempt (already begun by Carausius around AD 290) to improve the economic situation and to restore confidence in the coinage. Although Diocletian's Edict of AD 301, fixing maximum prices for all sorts of goods and services, was a failure there was undoubtedly a greater confidence in money and in the investment of capital in property than for several decades. At Verulamium additions and improvements were made to public buildings like the theatre, market-hall and principal temple, and a third monumental arch was erected over Watling Street at the centre of the town. In the southern quarter of the town new houses were erected and old ones renovated, and there were extensions and improvements to homes in other parts of the town too. Most of the minor towns of the civitas erected stone defensive circuits either in the late third century or in the early fourth, and there are signs of intensive occupation within these defences at several of the towns. Equally, villas throughout the canton testify to extensions, improvements and renovations in the early fourth century.

Given this evidence it is difficult to deny that the early fourth century saw a revival of urban and rural prosperity and activity in the civitas of the Catuvellauni. It is more difficult to be certain how long this lasted, as inflation once again took hold and attacks on the frontiers of the province became more frequent. There is little evidence from Verulamium or the villas for disruption or decline before AD 350. About this time, however, a group of villas around Verulamium appear to have been abruptly abandoned or gone into a rapid decline. The clearest example is Gadebridge Park, but Boxmoor, Latimer and perhaps High Wycombe appear to fall into this group too.[58] It is tempting to relate these events to those following the defeat of the usurper Magnentius in AD 353. The historian Ammianus Marcellinus records that Paulus, an imperial agent nicknamed 'the chain', was sent to Britain and carried out reprisals against those, both soldiers and civilians, who had supported Magnentius. Men were arrested, tried and condemned, and property was confiscated. Is it possible that some prominent Catuvellaunian land-owners had backed Magnentius and were victims of 'the chain'? It is, but of course there is no evidence which can prove a link between an abandoned villa and the events recorded by Ammianus, and the villas in question may have gone into abrupt decline for several other reasons. Certainly the disrepair noted in the temple at Verulamium after AD 350 need not be ascribed to Paulus. Following Constantine's conversion to Christianity, pagan temples in major cities had inevitably come under threat, and the closure of such temples had been decreed by his successors. In a town noted for its early Christian martyr, St Alban, we might expect such decrees to be more vigorously implemented than elsewhere. It follows from this that we should not necessarily assume that the fate of the temple automatically points to the impending collapse of urban life at Verulamium in the mid fourth century. As we shall see in the last chapter, there is evidence that the urban community at Verulamium was in fact remarkably tenacious even a century later.

3

Communications and Urban Settlement

In prehistoric times, including the pre-Roman Iron Age, the principal lines of communication through the area later occupied by the civitas of the Catuvellauni all ran broadly east to west. The southern border of the area was marked by the Thames Valley and the River Thames itself. North of the Chiltern valleys, the top of the scarp marked the line of the Icknield Way – a corridor of communication from East Anglia to Wiltshire from neolithic times onwards. Further north again, the rivers Ouse and Nene meandered from one side of the tribal territory to the other, providing routeways in areas where movement was otherwise difficult. Another line of communication may have lain along the watershed between the valleys of the Ouse and Nene. The extent to which these major routeways were supplemented by more localised trackways is much debated, but aerial photographs reveal ditched tracks running for short distances from and to apparently Iron Age settlement sites in parts of Bedfordshire and Northants, and there was probably a far more extensive system of trackways in existence at the time of the Roman conquest than is often imagined.[1]

Many of these minor tracks may well have continued in use during the Roman occupation, but the major lines of communication were abruptly re-oriented by the invaders. To supply the forces moving north and north-west, spearheaded by the IXth and XIVth legions respectively, the Romans surveyed and built two major roads, now known as Watling Street and Ermine Street. Ermine Street ran from London, via Ware to Braughing and thence through

Royston to Godmanchester, Sawtry and Water Newton before leaving tribal territory and heading for Lincoln. At Ware it was initially 12m wide, but at Godmanchester it was only 6m and just outside Water Newton it was 7–8m in width; excavations at Godmanchester confirmed that it was constructed in the first few years of the Claudian invasion.[2] Watling Street passed from London through Brockley Hill on its way to Verulamium, and then headed north-west through Dunstable, Towcester and Whilton Lodge on its course to cross the Fosse Way at High Cross and head for the legionary bases in the west Midlands, and eventually to Wroxeter and the River Severn. A third major road left Watling Street at Verulamium and ran in a more westerly direction through the valley of the Bulborne to Fleet Marston and then on to Alchester, across the Cherwell and via Wilcote to Cirencester. This road, now called Akeman Street, was almost certainly an early construction too, and perhaps served Claudian military sites at Cow Roast, Walton or Alchester.[3] Finally, a fourth early road skirted the southern edge of the canton, running west from London, through Brentford and Staines on its way to Silchester. At Brentford, excavations revealed two phases of use prior to the deposition of Neronian pottery, so that a Claudian date for its construction is quite certain.[4] These four roads were clearly to dominate movement through the territory of the future civitas, and their radial pattern focussed on London cut across the earlier prehistoric routeways in the area. In fact, this meant that from the first something approaching a communications network existed in the territory, with potentially important nodal points where Roman and major prehistoric routeways, including the Ouse and the Nene, crossed.

To these roads, others seem to have been added within the space of two to three decades. The important road linking the old tribal capitals of Camulodunum and Verulamium, known as Stane Street, is as yet undated but is unlikely to be later than other lesser roads of the Flavian period. Of these, one of the most important must have been the loop which ran from Ermine Street at Baldock to Sandy and thence, to join Ermine Street again at Godmanchester.

With the aid of a link road to Welwyn, this road provided the shortest route between Verulamium and the northern parts of the tribal territory and in particular the important town of Water Newton. By means of another road running from Cambridge through Sandy it also linked Verulamium to the town of Irchester. Both of these roads appear to belong to the later first century.[5] On the opposite side of the canton, a road was built to link Alchester (and Akeman Street) with Dorchester (and the Thames) at about the same time, most probably in the 70's, and an onward link to Towcester and Watling Street was provided, probably no later than c AD 80.[6] Roads such as these were apparently built for primarily civilian use and their construction confirms their local economic importance. The Towcester-Alchester road, for example, was found to be 8 to 10m wide, its gravel metalling laid directly on the sub-soil and flanked by successive drainage ditches. There were no doubt other roads of a similar nature providing important links between the towns of the canton, but their courses cannot be followed in any detail even where fragments of the system are known. This is particularly true of the road which left Verulamium heading through the Chilterns presumably for Silchester, and probably heading initially for the crossing of the Thames at Hedsor.[7] The many villas occupying the valleys of the western Chilterns from the mid second century onwards must provide a *terminus ante-quem* for this road but how much earlier it was constructed and where it ran is still largely a matter of conjecture. Equally the route and construction date of the Lower Icknield Way is uncertain, though it has been sampled by excavation at Dunstable and at Drays Ditches.[8] Unlike its prehistoric predecessor, it ran along the foot of the scarp, providing a vital link for the villas situated there with Dunstable and Verulamium in one direction and Dorchester and the Thames in the other. It appears to have varied between 4m and 7m in width and in some places had no gravel metalling but relied on the bedrock for its surfacing. Again, the foundation dates of villas along its line suggest it was in existence no later than the early second century. Elsewhere, roads were still being added to the system in the third century, and repairs and re-metalling were no doubt regular events, to which occasional dated milestones presumably refer.[10] The full extent of the system, however, is still very imperfectly understood and is much debated. The system identified by the Viatores is now generally agreed to have been a very optimistic interpretation of the evidence,[11] but it is equally true that what we can place on a map of the canton with any confidence is certainly only a fragment of the road system as it must have existed in, say, the fourth century AD. (fig. 15).

The secondary roads which are the focus of so much uncertainty were of great importance for the local economy, and to some extent for local administration but the work of the civitas council in Verulamium and its role in the wider administrative network of the province, was facilitated mainly by the arterial roads of military origin. This is clearly underlined by the evidence of the Antonine Itinerary, in which five of the official routes in use in Britain pass through the territory of the Catuvellauni. Two of them, Iters V and VII only touch the fringes of the area, with Iter V on its way from London to Carlisle passing along Ermine Street through Cambridge and Water Newton. Iter VII, from London to Chichester, uses the London-Silchester road, passing through Staines. The remaining three routes, however, pass through the very heart of the canton, and all utilise Watling Street on their route northwards. The relevant sections of the three iters are as follows:

Iter II	Iter VI	Iter VIII
Venonis	Tripontio	Vennonis
Bannaventa m.p. xvii	Isannavantia m.p. xvi	Bannavanto m.p. xviiii
Lactodoro m.p. xii	Lactodoro m.p. xii	—
Magiovinto m.p. xvii	Magiovinio m.p. xvi	Magiovinio m.p. xxviii
Durocobrivis m.p. xii	Durocobrius m.p. xii	Durocobrivis m.p. xii
Verolamio m.p. xii	Verolami m.p. xii	Verolamo m.p. xii
Sulloniacis m.p. viiii	—	—
Londinio m.p. xii	Londinio m.p. xxi	Londinio m.p. xxi

They can be seen to agree closely in all respects, although Lactodorum (Towcester) is apparently by-passed in iter VIII and Sulloniacis (Brockley Hill) appears only in iter II.

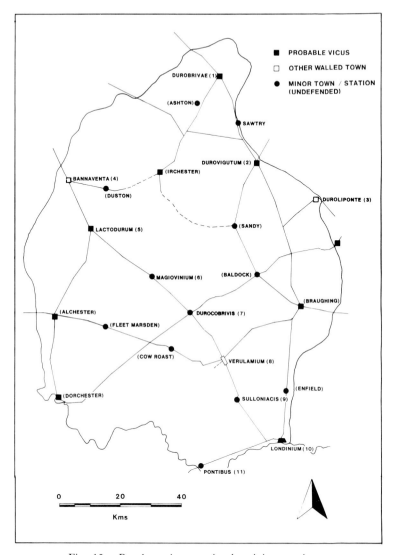

Fig. 15. Roads and towns in the civitas territory.

1. Water Newton
2. Godmanchester
3. Cambridge
4. Whilton Lodge
5. Towcester

6. Fenny Stratford
7. Dunstable
8. St. Albans
9. Brockley Hill
10. London
11. Staines

The information from the itineraries, is particularly valuable for confirming the identity and name of towns and posting stations in the canton.

The Tribal Capital

The Roman (and pre-Roman) names of St Albans are attested by several sources – Iron Age coins, Tacitus, Ptolemy, the Antonine Itinerary and Ravenna Cosmography, as well as later writers such as Gildas and Bede. Two problems remain, however. The first is the meaning of the name, about which there has been much speculation but no satisfactory conclusions at all. The second is its identification as the tribal capital of the civitas of the Catuvellauni. In none of the sources mentioned is the name of the town followed by a tribal suffix, as is the case with eleven of the remaining twelve major civitas capitals in Britain. It is widely agreed, however, that this probably confirms Tacitus' description of the town as a *municipium* rather than denying its role as a civitas capital.[12] We know that there was a civitas of the Catuvellauni,[13] that no other town within the probable boundaries of the canton was ascribed the tribal suffix or had the major public facilities required of a civitas capital, and that Verulamium did possess such facilities. There is simply no alternative to Verulamium as the capital of the civitas of the Catuvellauni.

The history of the pre-Roman and Roman town of Verulamium has already been covered in the previous two chapters. In summary, we have seen that the Iron Age settlement rose rapidly to prominence under Tasciovanus and that although it suffered some loss of status and prosperity when Cunobelin chose Colchester as his capital, Verulamium remained an important political and economic focus in the western part of the kingdom. After the death of Cunobelin it probably became the capital of the western kingdom and was considered important enough by Plautius to be garrisoned by Roman troops for five or six years. When the army moved on, the settlement became a town, probably in the strict sense of the word with a charter, but certainly in the broader sense as its streets were laid out, administrative buildings erected, and shops and private houses were built, very possibly with official encouragement. The Boudiccan revolt was a serious setback, even if the whole town was not razed to the ground, and it was not until the mid 70's that major rebuilding was underway. It seems almost certain that this activity coincides with the creation of the civitas and the choice of Verulamium as its capital. Public and private buildings were constructed, extended and improved over the next eighty years until a second, accidental fire, again destroyed the heart of the city. Once more recovery was not immediate, but once it began a decade later it was steady and sustained. By the middle of the third century the town had almost certainly acquired its masonry defences which enclosed 80ha (200 acres). In the political, economic and military uncertainties of the late third century, there are some signs that not all the inhabitants of Verulamium escaped unscathed. The first decades of the fourth century, however, saw renewed building activity on both public and private structures and a level of prosperity not matched perhaps since the later second century or early third century.

If we place the foundation of the city at c. AD 50 and the Roman withdrawal from Britain in c. AD 410, then the mid-point of Verulamium's existence as a Roman city came in c. AD 230. This is, in fact, a convenient point at which to look at the city as it was about then that the city was formally completed by the construction of its stone defences. (fig. 16) The defences erected at this time have never been examined in the detail that they require to satisfactorily elucidate either their history or their constructional details, and only a general description of them is possible. The outermost defence was a ditch, about 25m wide and 6m deep, behind which stood the wall. The wall was built of flint with tile bonding courses on a foundation almost 3m wide, narrowed by offsets to just over 2m, and backed by a substantial bank up to 15m wide at its base. Near the London Gate the wall survives to a height of 4m, with four bonding courses, and its full height, with crenellations, must have been between 7m and 8m. The London Gate, and its companion known as the Chester Gate

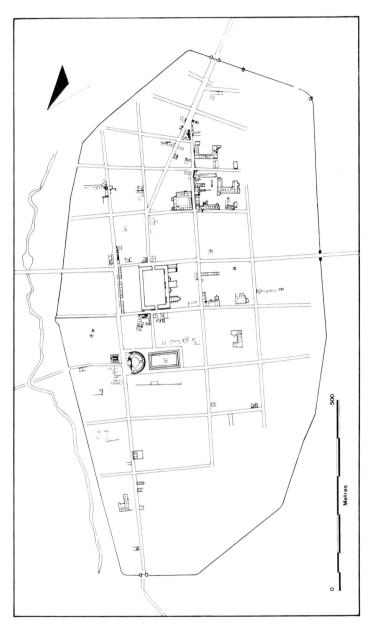

Fig. 16. Plan of Verulamium, c. AD 250.

on the opposite side of the town, were impressive structures and were clearly designed as symbols of Verulamium's status. Both gates were about 30m wide and the drum towers which flanked the double-portal and pedestrian passageways may have stood to 12m–13m in height. The south-west (or Silchester) gate was not built to the same lavish plan but was nevertheless a very substantial structure, about 22m wide and perhaps 11m high. It possessed a single portal, again flanked by pedestrian ways, and protected by square towers. All three gates were built in the same manner as the town wall, with flint and mortar bonded by regular tile or brick courses, but a fragment of oolite architrave found by the Silchester Gate suggests that they had been embellished with freestone.[14] Nothing is known of the other two gates which served the city, both set in its northern wall. Close to one of these five gates should stand a *mansio* to serve the needs of official guests and travellers, but at present there is no trace of such a building.

The principal public building was of course the forum and basilica, which altogether covered an area of about 2ha (5 acres). Although our knowledge of the forum and basilica is extremely fragmentary its broad outlines are clear. The basilica itself measured about 120m x 60m, with offices along its north-east side and a basilical hall occupying the major part of the building. Adjoining it on the south-west was the forum, 115m x 80m, the gravelled piazza of which was surrounded on all four sides by an ambulatory and was entered by two opposed entrances in the shorter sides. On the far side of the forum from the basilica, three substantial structures projected south-westwards into insula XXII. Even in outline, the Verulamium forum can thus be seen to be of quite different design to the fora found in most other Romano-British civitas capitals, which were of the 'principia' type. The Verulamium forum is better paralleled in major continental towns such as Trier, Paris and Augst.

Frere has attempted to make a rational reconstruction of the forum and basilica from the surviving remains, and has made a good case for an unusual basilica with two aisles on each side of the nave.[15] With columns estimated at a height of 10.7m, the total height of the nave would have been a full

29m. Yet this is not out of keeping with the overall size and magnificence of the forum and basilica. In the centre of the suite of offices on the north-west side of the basilica there must have been an *aedes* to house the principal cult statue and probably that of the emperor too. Flanking it there was probably a double row of offices, up to thirty of them, housing the administration of the civitas. The public approach to these, and to the basilical hall, was through two entrances in the north-west facade of the building, over one of which the inscription recording the completion of the complex had originally been displayed. The piazza of the forum was surrounded by ambulatories, probably two-storied, on all four sides. As originally designed, the centre of the side opposite the basilica was occupied by a large hall, 19m x 12m, flanked by two smaller rooms. This was probably the curia, or council chamber, and flanking offices of the magistrates. Probably no later than the early third century, two new buildings were erected flanking the curia. Their size and massive foundations almost certainly betray their functions as temples.[16] Built in such a prestigious position it is difficult to associate them with any cults other than the Capitoline triad of Juno, Jupiter and Minerva, and of the Imperial house. By the mid third century therefore, the forum and basilica at Verulamium was an extremely impressive complex which was the economic, administrative and religious focus of both the town, and the civitas (fig. 17).

Apart from the forum piazza, used for public markets, Verulamium was also provided before the end of the Flavian period with a *macellum* or market hall, fronting onto Watling Street in insula XVII. As built, it consisted of two rows of nine single-room lock-up shops facing each other across a central courtyard. Normally such structures were reserved for the sale of meat or vegetables but we have no indications of what commodities were sold in the Verulamium *macellum*.[17] Before the end of the second century the market hall was reduced in size but was remodelled and given a more impressive facade, so that there are no grounds for thinking that the changes reflect a drop in marketing activities in the town.

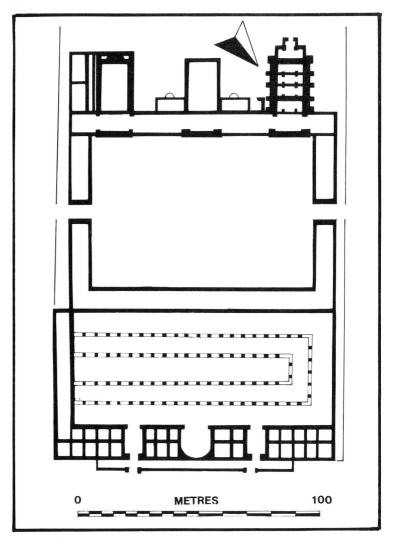

Fig. 17. Plan of the forum and basilica, Verulamium.

At the time that the market hall was first built, it was faced across Watling Street by an open area beyond which stood the oldest temple in the town.[18] The area seems to have been reserved for special use from the time of the town's foundation and it is possible that an early timber shrine stood here before a more substantial successor obliterated all trace of it. The first recorded structure on the site is a masonry temple built in the conventional Romano-Celtic manner with a square cella surrounded by an outer verandah or ambulatory. Muckelroy has argued that in this instance, the cella was surrounded by an enclosed ambulatory.[19] At the time it was built, probably around AD 90, it was enclosed within a low temenos wall only 0.5m wide but probably eye-catching nevertheless as it was constructed largely of squared chalk blocks and was buttressed every 4m. At a much later date, probably around AD 300, the temple was given a major face-lift, with the addition of two flanking rectangular annexes to the temple and inner and outer colonnades to the temenos wall. There are no indications to which deity the temple was dedicated, though Wacher has argued that the juxtaposition of temple and *macellum* c. AD 100 might suggest a temple dedicated to Mercury in his role as patron of trade and commerce.[20] Certainly there is no need to assume that the temple was jointly dedicated to more than one diety, like a good many rural temples appear to have been, since apart from the forum temples and this one, there were at least four further temples at Verulamium. Three of these are known only from aerial photos, and little can be said of them except that they are all of the same square Romano-Celtic type. Two stand adjacent to one another in insula XVII, and the other is in insula XXI close to the main road running between the Silchester and north-east gates. The remaining temple is that explored by Wheeler in the south-east quarter of the town and known as the triangular temple.[21] Its unusual form was dictated by its position in the fork of the road created by the junction of Watling Street and one of the main NW-SE roads of the street grid. The significance of this position was further enhanced by the line of the first century defences, which passed only 30m to the south-east where there must have been some form of gateway in the first century. The temple built in this prominent position took the form of a truncated triangle, its narrower end facing the gateway (fig. 18). A central courtyard was surrounded by a colonnaded

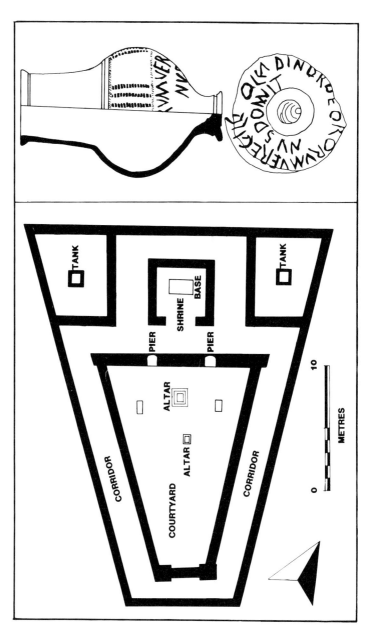

Fig. 18. The triangular temple, and an inscribed vessel from Dunstable.

ambulatory to the rear of which stood a central cella, flanked by two small rooms or possibly small yards in each of which was set a tank. Apart from a large plinth or altar base in the cella, four further bases were located in the courtyard, and here there were also nine pits containing charcoal and a variety of other material. Six further pits were found in the ambulatory and enclosed areas flanking the cella. There can be no doubt that all of these pits were ritual depositions, containing a mixture of animal and bird bones and miniature vessels. The discovery of the seeds and scales of cones from the Italian pine in two of the pits suggested to Wheeler that the temple was dedicated to Cybele in her role as patroness of cities, and the unusual position of the temple would certainly accord well with such a dedication. Confirmation that the cult of Cybele flourished in Verulamium has recently come from an inscribed pot found twelve miles away at Dunstable (see below p. 00).

In time, the approach to the triangular temple was made still more impressive by the construction of the southern monumental arch on the line of the first century defences 30m away. The arch itself, though found only as a massive masonry foundation, must have been an imposing structure for it was probably embellished with marble veneers, several panels of which were found nearby. Wheeler's plan suggests that the arch had two passages,[22] but Frere's careful discussion of the arch that he excavated at the opposite end of the town produces good reasons for supposing that that arch had but a single passage.[23] The evidence is indecisive but in each case favours the solutions proposed by respective excavators. A third monumental arch erected c. AD 300 across Watling Street between the *macellum* and the theatre is generally agreed to be of single-span design.

The theatre, like the forum, is of a type so far unique in Britain and with clear continental parallels.[24] It was probably built no later than c. AD 140 on an open area which appears to have been reserved since c. AD 50 for a major public building. As originally constructed, the theatre had a circular orchestra, flanked on the east by a small stage-building, and surrounded on the remaining sides by tiered timber seating set on an earth and clay bank retained by an inner and outer revetment wall, the latter strongly buttressed, and raised to a height of perhaps 8m. In such a cavea an audience of up to 1500 people may have been accommodated (fig. 19). That the optimism of those who

Fig. 19. The Verulamium theatre.

sponsored the work was not misplaced is confirmed by the extension of the seating within a decade or so into the area of the orchestra. At the same time the stage was embellished with three stone columns capped with Corinthian capitals, and various other changes were made in the design. The juxtaposition of temple and theatre, apparently planned from an early period, suggests that the performances in the theatre were at least partly related to ritual activities and religious festivals. Equally the setting for a cruciform timber structure in the centre of the orchestra suggests that in the first phase the arena-like area was used for animal baiting and other entertainments more normally associated with an amphitheatre. Indeed, the extension of seating into one half of the orchestra c. AD 150–160, which would have put an end to animal baiting and similar activities, may reflect the construction and completion of an amphitheatre itself at Verulamium. The account of the martyrdom of St Alban refers to the amphitheatre[25] and locates it outside the city wall and

across the river – that is to the east of the town – but no
trace of the structure has yet been discovered. The same
must be said of a third important public amenity, the baths,
which one would expect Verulamium to have possessed by
the end of the first century at the latest, on analogy with
other civitas capitals in the province. Indeed, we noted in
chapter 2 that a bath-house probably existed in pre-
Boudiccan Verulamium, and that building appears to have
been patched-up and re-used until it was demolished c. AD.
75–80, perhaps when a new bath-house was constructed.
One can only speculate as to the whereabouts of a Flavian
baths, but if it was to be reasonably near the river and also
connected to a main drain or sewer then insulae XXII and
XVII are likely locations.[26] There are indications of a
substantial structure, perhaps with apses, to the north of
the two Romano-Celtic temples in insula XVII, but only
excavation would reveal whether or not this was part of a
public baths.

The case for an early provision of public baths is greatly
strengthened by the lack of private bathing facilities in any
of the private houses which ante-date the Antonine fire.
Since many villas in the surrounding countryside had
bath-houses in the earlier second century, and some in the
late first, one might expect the curial class to have
demanded similar facilities in Verulamium. We still know
little of the earliest houses, as opposed to shops, of the
pre-Boudiccan town, although that partly discovered by
Frere in insula XVII shows that in terms of simple
embellishments such as plaster, window-glass and tiled
roofs, they were already an advance over the Belgic houses
of the pre-Roman era.[27] Houses erected in the last decade of
the first century continue to be mainly timber-frame structures, but their more complicated plans with several rooms
linked by a corridor, and the occasional appearance of
painted wall plaster, tesselated floors, quarter-mouldings
and cellars suggest they were not much inferior to
contemporary villas such as Park Street and Boxmoor.[28] One
Flavian house in insula XXVII was overlain in the mid-
second century by a new timber-framed house with perhaps
as many as twenty rooms. Next to it, within a few years, a

second house was erected with ten or a dozen rooms, seven of which had boasted tesselated floors. Both houses were burnt down by the Antonine fire of c. AD 155.

In the period following the Antonine fire, over a period of several decades, many new houses were built at Verulamium of superior construction, size and interior decoration to anything found previously in the town (fig. 20). Amongst the buildings excavated by Frere, houses XXI, 2 and XXVIII, 3 were both notable for fine mosaics and their elaborate wall plaster, all dating to the period c. AD 180.[29] The plaster carried imitation marble dados and panels, stone columns, and the more common candelabras and floral swags. In house XXI, 2 a large area of ceiling plaster was recovered from one room, decorated with a coffer-design enclosing birds and feline masks, and from the same house came a fine peopled scroll. (fig. 21) These houses, however, still lacked hypocaust-heated rooms and bath-suites, but Wheeler found houses with hypocausts in insulae III and IV, and house IV, 8 is interpreted by Wheeler as having a sumptuous bath-suite.[30] Other houses excavated by Wheeler in the south-east quarter, dating from the later 1st century onwards, have the appearance of shops rather than purely domestic dwellings.[31] Frere excavated an impressive sequence of shops in insula XIV, fronting on Watling Street and having a history which extended (with a long interval between c. AD 155 and 275) from AD 50 to the later fourth century. Other shops have been partially excavated elsewhere in the town, and still more can be identified on aerial photos. From the material found in them, a wide variety of tradesmen can be identified − bronzesmiths, blacksmiths/ironmongers, pottery shops, cobblers and carpenters, and taverns. Wheeler claimed that the building III, 1 was not merely a butchers but that more specifically it made sausages.[32] Other butchers may have had their shops in the *macellum*, although in the absence of rubbish pits full of animal bone a market-hall for fruit and vegetables is as likely. All in all, considering the limited excavation and study of private buildings at Verulamium, the evidence suggests a very lively commercial life in the town, neatly epitomised perhaps by the development on the corner of

Fig. 20. A later second century mosaic in a private house, Verulamium.

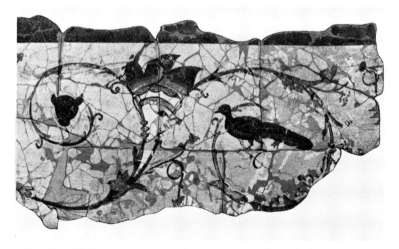

Fig. 21. Wall plaster decorated with a peopled scroll, Verulamium.

insula XXVIII, where a private house was attached to a corner block of shops, an office and a public latrine, for the use of which a charge would have been made (fig. 22).

This latrine gave directly into a major sewer which also ran along the side of the basilica and forum. Another major sewer ran along Watling Street, through the base of the monumental arch on its way through the Chester Gate. Smaller drains, including timber-lined examples of late first century date, have been partly sampled by excavation elsewhere. The earliest water mains yet recorded also belong to the late first century,[33] and throughout the town's history are made of wooden pipes with iron jointing collars.

It is clear from the results of excavations over the last fifty years that from an early date Verulamium exhibited a high level of Romanisation when compared to most other Romano-British towns. Initially this may have been due to official encouragement but later it must have been due to a certain civic pride and perhaps a more cosmopolitan or better-educated curial class. In particular the Gallic-style forum and basilica complex and theatre might argue for an acquaintance with urban life on the other side of the English Channel. Frere has also drawn attention to the exceptional

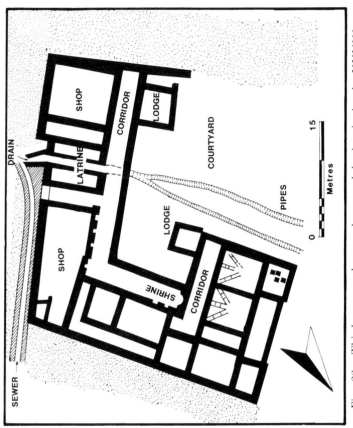

Fig. 22.   Third century house, shops and latrine in insula XXVIII, Verulamium.

number of cellars found at Verulamium and in nearby villas,[34] commenting on their relative scarcity in Britain compared to their frequency in northern Gaul. The level of Romanisation amongst the leading families at Verulamium is also reflected in the construction of two classical style temples and three monumental arches, and at a private level in the quality of their town houses from the mid second century onwards. In every respect, Verulamium formed a worthy focus for the civitas of the Catuvellauni.

Minor Towns – Vici

In a civitas territory as large as that of the Catuvellauni we should not be surprised to find that minor towns developed at some distance from the civitas capital to serve the administrative and economic needs of the canton. What is surprising, however, is their number; altogether there are between fifteen and twenty settlements which might be termed minor towns, although the use of the term to describe some of these settlements is arguable. Of these settlements, there are seven for which a combination of evidence – defences, spatial organisation, size, public buildings and inscriptions – suggests genuine urban status. It is tempting to suggest that a constitutional status was acquired by these towns and that they were accorded the title of *vicus*.[35] The term is still poorly understood, although Johnson has thrown some light on its usage. Johnson has also suggested that many towns which were given the status of *vicus* in the first or second century may have later been called *castrum* once they were walled in the later third century, and that this term may be reflected in the place-name element 'chester'.[36] This is an interesting suggestion since six of the seven towns we suggest may have been *vici* contain the element 'chester' or 'cester' in their modern place name; the exception is Braughing, which is also the only settlement of the seven which was apparently unwalled.

The only town of the seven for which we have evidence that it had achieved the status of a *vicus*, however, is Water Newton (Durobrivae).[37] This precious piece of information is recorded on a late second century mortarium stamped CVNOARDA FECIT VICO DVROBRIVIS. It is possible that two fragments of a limestone slab carrying inscribed letters 11 cms high found in the foundations of Peterborough Cathedral may be all that remains of a magisterial inscription from Durobrivae.[38] Our impression of Durobrivae, however, depends as much on what we know of the archaeological remains of the settlement as it does on epigraphic material (fig. 23). The town succeeded a fort and lay fair and square across Ermine Street. It was defended by a stone wall and contemporary earth bank, fronted by a ditch; the date of the defences is uncertain, though the archaeological evidence at present available would allow a date as early as the early third century. Rectangular towers or bastions project from the wall along the south-east and south-west sides of the town, and at least one is known on the north-east section of wall, but none of them are yet dated. The defences enclose 18ha. (44 acres) which aerial photos show to be heavily built up at the western half of the town, but possibly less so in the eastern half. Ermine Street forms a 'high street' through the town, and to the north of it a series of small lanes run off more or less at right angles to it; the roads or lanes to the south of Ermine Street are less regularly aligned. Ermine Street itself is flanked by at least three dozen long, narrow-fronted buildings which must surely be shops, and there are many similar structures alongside the lanes to either side of the high street. Buildings of any size or complexity are few, and the general impression is that the town was a thriving centre of commerce and craft activity rather than the home of fashionable residences. Three buildings stand out, even on aerial photographs, as public structures. Nearest to the centre of the town, but set back a little from Ermine Street is a courtyard building (B) about 60m x 45m. Since two roads, from the south gate and a postern gate a little further west, run close to this building, and it also lies just off Ermine Street, it is tempting to see this as a *mansio*, although it could also be interpreted as a *macellum*. A second large building (c) about 55m x 45m, stands immediately alongside Ermine Street just to the north of the first building, and with its

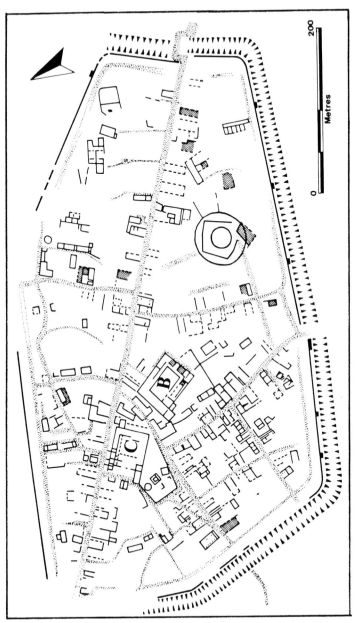

Fig. 23.   Water Newton (Durobrivae).

double forecourt and suite of single rooms fronted by a corridor or ambulatory, may have a stronger claim to be identified as a *mansio*. A walled enclosure attached to one side of it contains a square structure almost certainly a Romano-Celtic temple, flanked by a further square and one circular building, which may also be temples. Whatever the true functions of these various buildings, together with the walled area of 18ha they clearly pick out Durobrivae as something more than just a road-side settlement. Furthermore, beyond the walls stretch densely occupied suburbs which some have estimated as covering 100 ha (250 acres). Excavations in buildings outside the east gate revealed amongst the workshops and other structures fragments of carved bases, a capital, and a sculpture suggestive of buildings of high quality in the vicinity, and Blagg has argued that the town housed a mason's workshop in the third century AD. Whether or not it had by this time been elevated to a higher status than that of a vicus is uncertain, as we have noted in the previous chapter.

Some 30km (19 miles) south of Durobrivae on Ermine Street lay the much smaller settlement of Godmanchester (Durovigutum).[39] Like Durobrivae, the town succeeded a Roman fort and sat astride Ermine Street. Although there is evidence for Flavian occupation in timber huts, of both circular and rectangular plan, the settlement's claim to any sort of urban status can only date from the Hadrianic period. At this time, a substantial *mansio* 50m x 30m was erected east of Ermine Street (fig. 24). It possessed about thirty rooms and adjacent to it stood a separate bath-house, whilst immediately west of the *mansio* was a small temple dedicated to the god Abandinus. At about the same time as these amenities were provided, a ditch or dyke 3m wide and 2m deep was dug to form a straight-sided enclosure of about 8ha (20 acres), though there is no evidence that it was accompanied by an internal rampart. Several other second century structures have been excavated in the town, but they are all timber-framed or of cob-construction and provided only with clay or gravel floors. One or two may have been shops, and an iron-smith's workshop can be recognised both from its furnaces and the metalworking

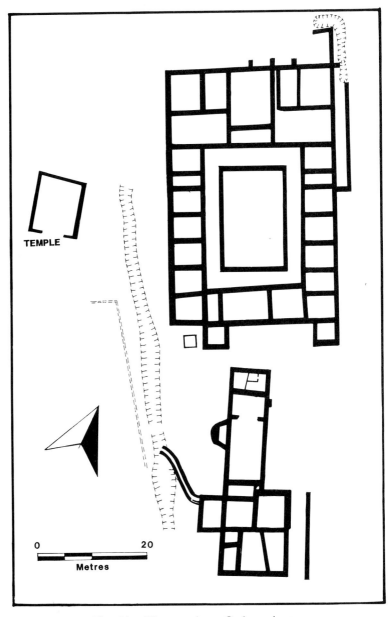

TEMPLE

0   20

Metres

Fig. 24. The mansio at Godmanchester.

debris, but many of these buildings appear to have been cottages occupied by peasant farmers to judge from agricultural facilities around them. This, together with the small population estimated for the settlement – about 200 persons – make the identification of Godmanchester as a 'town' at this time somewhat arguable, despite the provision of the *mansio* and a public shrine. However, in the early third century there were two significant developments, which were probably related. One was the re-alignment of Ermine Street in the middle of the enclosed area, which resulted in the creation of a gravelled area 67m x 30m at the town centre; this unusual arrangement is difficult to interpret as anything other than a market area. At the north end of this area a new public building was erected. Despite its unusual design, the building seems to have been a single-aisled basilica, fronted by a small enclosed court, the whole complex only occupying 24m x 21m. Yet apart from the design, the 2m wide footings suggest this was a building of some importance, as does its position at the very centre of the town alongside Ermine Street and at the head of the market area. The most sensible explanation seems to be that the town had achieved a measure of local government, presumably being given the status of *vicus*. In the late third century the town's status, if not its rank, was confirmed by the construction of a town wall, which now enclosed 11ha (27 acres). On present evidence it was after, rather than before, the defences were erected that the *mansio* and its bath-house were destroyed by fire, possibly as a result of hostile action, at the end of the third century, but the relationship between these events may yet be changed by further excavations of the defences. In any event the town continued to be occupied until at least the end of the fourth century.

About 50kms (30m) south of Godmanchester and a similar distance north of London on Ermine Street was the settlement of Braughing.[40] Its importance in the formative years of the Catuvellaunian tribal kingdom has been stressed in chapter 1, and with the coming of the Roman occupation it remained an important nodal point where Ermine Street and Stane Street crossed. Excavations at

Skeleton Green revealed a thriving settlement established here in the first decades of the conquest and although habitation was subsequently replaced by cemetery usage at this point, a major settlement appears to have developed on the eastern slopes of Wickham Hill, above the River Rib. Six or seven streets can be traced here, with the two major roads running off Ermine Street set at right angles to one another, and some of the minor streets running parallel to these, suggesting an element of town-planning. The nucleated area of occupation focusses around the two principal roads and probably covers between 25 and 30ha (60–75 acres), although there were outlying buildings. At the centre of the settlement were a good many rectangular stone built houses, known from aerial photographs and field-walking, and including at least one house of winged-corridor plan. Two buildings in this area, however, stand out as something different. One is known only from aerial photographs, but appears to be a courtyard house with an outer yard, the house measuring c. 30m × 25m, and the whole complex c. 65m × 30m. Both in plan and in size it can be generally compared to the mansio excavated at Godmanchester and that identified on aerial photographs at Durobrivae, and a similar function can be tentatively ascribed to this building at Braughing. Further east along the same road stands a complex of three buildings, two of which are again known only from aerial photographs and field-walking but were apparently substantial structures, each 20m–25m long. The third building of the group has been partly sampled by excavation, and measured c. 38m × 21m overall. Its detailed plan is still uncertain, though it appears to be L-shaped and to have had a portico fronting the road. It has been variously identified as a temple or *macellum*, but there is nothing to indicate its function, although it is widely agreed to be a public building of some sort. Finally, a bath-house providing a suite of basic accommodation has been completely excavated close both to the river and to the road coming from Great Chesterford, and must also probably be regarded as a public amenity rather than a building for purely personal and private use. All the indications are that Braughing was a town of some importance, providing services beyond those of purely local agricultural use, and similar in terms of facilities to Godmanchester. The only symbol of civic status obviously lacking is a defensive circuit, and it seems increasingly likely that Braughing never possessed either earth ramparts or stone walls.

The three towns discussed so far are placed along, or close to, the eastern boundary of the Catuvellaunian civitas, following the route of Ermine Street. Four further settlements with claims to urban status are spread around the western and northern fringes of the canton. South-west of Durobrivae and linked to it by road was the settlement of Irchester, for which we have no Roman name.[11] Nevertheless, the indications are that it was a town of some importance. Occupation certainly began in the mid first century, succeeding some Belgic occupation of the site. In the late second century an earth rampart was built enclosing about 8ha (20 acres), and a stone wall of good masonry was later inserted in front of this. Although there has been little modern excavation of the interior it is clear from earlier investigations that there were many stone built houses in the town, and others are known from recent work in the extensive suburbs south and east of the walled area (fig. 25). The street system is irregular but at the centre of the settlement stood a Romano-Celtic temple, set within its own temenos. Fragments of columns, an ornate capital and a torso of a nude youth probably come from this sanctuary. Another religious monument of substantial proportions and some pretensions is indicated by two pieces of a sculptured octagonal pier or drum, perhaps from a Jupiter column and a possibly octagonal temple is seen on aerial photographs in the western half of the town. These finds suggest that Irchester had some importance as a cult centre, and a role in the administrative system is hinted at but not confirmed by the tombstone of a *strator* found here in the 1850's. Since the age of this minor official on the governor's staff is not given on the stone we cannot tell, unfortunately, whether he died here during service or after retirement.

A *strator*, whose responsibilities included provision of horses for the governor and his staff, would have had a greater role to play in a town such as Towcester (Lac-

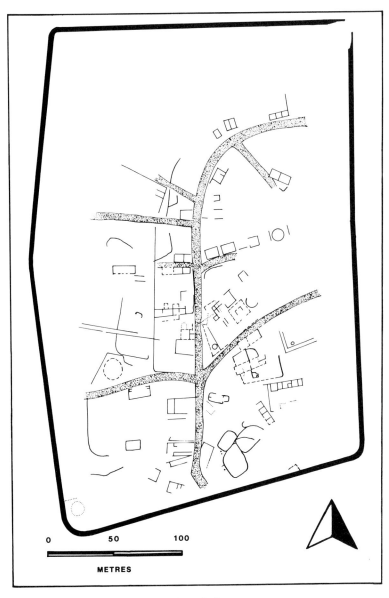

Fig. 25.   Irchester.

tordorum), which is situated about 30kms (19 miles) south-
west of Irchester on Watling Street.[42] Although the place-
name suggests a fort here, there is no clear evidence of a
Roman military presence yet occupation of the settlement
certainly began soon after the invasion. Coins and pottery of
the first century are numerous and both timber and stone
buildings were being erected here by the end of the century.
The earth rampart defences were probably erected in the
later second century. At one point the fronting stone wall is
said to be contemporary with the rampart but elsewhere it is
clearly a later addition. The defensive circuit enclosed
probably c. 14ha (35 acres). Here, as at Irchester, there were
suburban developments beyond the defences. Although
most of the recently explored buildings have proved to be
workshops, including at least two which were working
lead/pewter, there are certainly clear indications of
buildings of better quality. Sculptured stone fragments,
some re-used in the fourth century, include a column shaft,
two capitals, and pieces of a frieze and a plinth, and at least
one teselated floor is also recorded. More specific evidence
for Towcester's role as an urban settlement may be provided
by the remains of a masonry public building, erected
perhaps as early as c. AD 75, which the excavator suggests
may be a mansio.

Towcester was linked to Akeman Street and the town of
Alchester by a road which ran cross-country for about
30kms (19 miles). Alchester itself lies 700m south of
Akeman Street, and its military origins are still to be
proven, but there can be no doubt that it was established
early in the Roman occupation.[43] It has the clear impression
of a planned town in that it is neatly divided into six almost
equal insulae by its three main streets. In the first century
these were flanked by wattle-and-daub buildings, but these
were progressively replaced by stone structures from the
end of the first century. The town was enclosed by a wall
with backing rampart and fronting ditch at a date which
could be as early as the late second century on the evidence
available. The area within the defences was about 10ha (25
acres), but there were extensive suburbs which some have
claimed to cover as much as 40ha (100 acres). Stone shops

and houses can be seen on aerial photographs to line the streets, and a temple may be situated near the main cross-roads of the town. Near this point excavations in 1850 and 1892 found the remains of a large courtyard structure with a portico fronting the street; it may have been a *macellum*, whilst the substantial building inside a walled or ditched enclosure next to it seems likely to have been a temple. Beyond the west gate lay a large bath-house which one suspects may not have been an isolated structure but part of a hostel complex for travellers; certainly it seems too large to be a private bath-suite. In any event, it is clear that Alchester possessed at least two, perhaps three, public buildings of some pretensions. This fact together with its size, its regular street plan and early defences all suggest that it had urban status.

Finally, about 27kms (17m) south of Alchester was the town of Dorchester, to which it was linked by a road built no later than the Flavian era.[44] Dorchester may have been the site of a Roman fort, and was certainly the location of an important Belgic settlement, and there is ample evidence of its development as a civilian settlement in the later first century. Apart from Flavian buildings a gravelled area 35m square near the town centre and possibly a market place was established before the end of the century. The early buildings were timber-framed, and timber buildings were still being constructed here in the later third century, but by then stone-built houses were also in use, though only one tesselated pavement has yet been recorded from the settlement. An earth rampart was erected towards the end of the second century and fronted by a stone wall in the later third, the circuit enclosing a defended area of only 5.5ha (13.5 acres). The only hint of a public building at present derives from an altar dedicated to Jupiter and the Deities of the Emperors, presumably once standing in a temple. However, the altar has an added significance since it was erected by Marcus Varius Severus, who describes himself as a *beneficiarius consularis*. He would have been concerned with gubernatorial supplies and his dedication of an altar at Dorchester may indicate that the town had a role to play in the administrative system.

The evidence from the seven towns discussed is patchy and often unsatisfactory, yet in every case there is some reason to think that the settlement in question fulfilled functions other than those of purely agricultural marketing and that they probably had a role in the administrative system. The provision of defences at all but one of the settlements in the period either side of AD 200 is again suggestive that these settlements had all acquired urban status by that time, and it is reasonable to suggest therefore that they had become *vici*. As *vici* they would have elected magistrates to oversee local affairs, particularly commerce, and they would almost certainly have been expected to act as the administrative centres of the rural areas known as *pagi*. Rivet in fact has suggested that the shrine of Abandinus at Godmanchester was that of a *pagus* deity.[45] If one looks at the distribution of these towns on the map of the canton one can see how conveniently placed they are in this respect, occupying locations distant from Verulamium, but also almost equidistant from one another. It would be wrong to suggest that the location of the towns was determined by administrative considerations, but once the towns had begun to develop due to other factors, their subsequent development as secondary administrative centres may have been deliberately fostered according to their location.

Other Minor Towns

The other minor towns in the canton have so far failed to yield any sound evidence of urban status, although two of them do have stone defences; these are Cambridge[46] and Whilton Lodge. After much excavation and speculation there is still no good evidence for a Claudian fort at Cambridge, and the rectangular ditched enclosure of the period c. AD 60–80 is so small (c. 60 × 30m) that at most it can be little more than a 'police post', presumably established in the aftermath of the Boudiccan revolt. From the second century onwards occupation spread over about 16ha (40 acres), but it was generally unsophisticated, with small rectangular cottages set in gravelled and fenced yards, and

only iron-smithing and perhaps pottery-making representing craft activity. In spite of further extensive
occupation south of the river, there is little to suggest that
second century Cambridge had any claim to urban status.
Only in the early fourth century when the town is provided
with a wall and rampart enclosing 10ha (25 acres) are there
signs of commercial activity and affluence at a level which
one might associate with a town serving as both a market
centre and the focus of local administration, but although
the town may have been elevated to the status of a *vicus*, we
have as yet no evidence for public buildings to substantiate
the suggestion. All we know is that, as Duroliponte, it
appears in iter V of the Antonine Itinerary and at sufficient
distance from the two stations which flank it to suggest it
may have had a *mansio*. Of all the minor towns we are
considering in this section, this is perhaps the most likely to
have achieved *vicus* status. Whilton Lodge (Bannaventa),[47]
also appears in the Antonine Itinerary, in iters II, VI and
VIII, but its flanking stations at Towcester and High Cross,
are much closer and are more likely to have been the
location of *mansios*. Whilton Lodge may have been provided
only with a *mutatione*, providing a change of horses. Nevertheless it was clearly a settlement of some importance,
with occupation attested from the first century, and
earthwork defences provided by the later second or early
third. A stone wall was added to the front of the rampart in
the fourth century and two defensive ditches were cut.
Within the defences, however, no traces of stone-founded
buildings have yet come to light in recent excavations,
despite an early 19th century reference to many wall
foundations. For the most part the timber-framed buildings
seem unsophisticated with clay or pebble floors, but fragmentary traces of mortar floors and painted wall plaster
have been recovered near the centre of the settlement.
Further light on the status and function of the town must
await more extensive exploration.

    Further south along Watling Street, and also listed in the
Antonine Itinerary are the settlements at Fenny Stratford
and Dunstable. Fenny Stratford (Magiovinium)[48] should be
the location of a *mutatione* if we are correct in assuming

Towcester held a *mansio*. Like Whilton Lodge it was clearly established in the early years of the Roman occupation, initially with timber-framed buildings but later boasting stone-founded houses with tessellated floors and plastered walls. No recognisable public buildings are yet known, and the only craft activity for which there is evidence is iron-smithing. Before the late third century the settlement had been enclosed by an earth rampart and fronting ditch, but this was never replaced or strengthened by a stone wall. The publication of the most recent and extensive excavations by Neal may throw much-needed new light on this site. Dunstable (Durocobrivis)[49] remains something of an enigma. It was clearly a settlement of some significance and traces of Roman occupation are widespread and have been extensively explored over many years by the local archaeologists, yet we still know virtually nothing of the settlement itself. It was established in the mid first century and occupied until the end of the fourth, to judge from the quantity of material covering this period. Structural remains, however, are limited to pits, ditches, gullies and post-holes, and finds of roofing tiles and a few fragments of hypocaust tile. Evidence for craft activities is limited to iron- and bronze-smithing, and the many wells which are known (19 to date), the nine corn-ovens, and the finds of ploughshares and sickles give the impression the settlement may have functioned mainly as a nucleated agricultural settlement. There remains the possibility that the principal buildings, presumably along Watling Street, have been destroyed by later occupation. A further hint that the town was inhabited by skilled craftsmen as well as farmers is provided by the inscribed vessel found in one of the graves, apparently a burial gift by the guild of the Dendrophori to one of their members.[50] The Dendrophori (or branch-bearers) were associated with the cult of Cybele and their membership was drawn from the ranks of carpenters.

A string of minor towns similar to those along Watling Street are found along Ermine Street and the loop road which left it at Braughing and rejoined it at Godmanchester. Between Godmanchester and Water Newton there was probably a *mutatione* at Sawtry,[51] from where a fragmentary inscription perhaps referring to public property was found near a small group of rectangular buildings. There is nothing to suggest, however, the growth of a town here. Evidence of occupation is much more extensive at Sandy,[52] but in many respects it mirrors the situation at Dunstable. In spite of investigation over many years and a lot of material, including many burials, we still have little idea of what the settlement looked like. Occupation in the first century succeeded Belgic occupation, and continued until the late fourth century and beyond and perhaps covered an area of about 8ha (20 acres). Remains of floors, hearths, pits and ditches have been recovered but never in sufficiently large areas to allow their proper interpretation. The stray finds and some of the cemetery material suggest local residents of reasonable affluence – bronze mirrors and bowls, pewter vessels, fine glassware, and an occulist's stamp. There is also evidence for the usual local craftsmen working lead and iron and making coarse pottery. However, although building stone and tile hint at substantial buildings, not a single tessera or scrap of wall plaster has been found to suggest any level of sophistication. Furthermore, other discoveries such as querns, a coulter, cart fittings and a mower's anvil convey an impression of an essentially agricultural settlement. The evidence is thus somewhat confusing, but there is perhaps enough evidence of non-agricultural activity, together with Sandy's location on an important road, to suggest that it merits description as a minor town rather than a village. Whether or not the same may be said of Baldock, 16km (10m) further south along the main road is uncertain.[53] On the patchy evidence available it may have been not unlike Sandy. Certainly there was a late Iron Age predecessor to the Roman settlement, and two Welwyn type burials suggest that not all the inhabitants were peasant farmers. There are extensive cemeteries surrounding the Roman settlement, which seems to have been established soon after the conquest around the early Roman road and eventually covered about 20ha (50 acres). Circular and rectangular timber buildings of first and second century date are known, but stone foundations, flue tiles and plaster quarter-mouldings hint at buildings with Romanised amenities. Even more uncertainty surrounds the Roman settlement at Enfield,[54] which should be the location of a *mutatione* situated mid-way between Londinium and the *mansio* at Braughing. Traces of timber buildings along with hearths, pits and gullies have been found widely spread over an area of about 20ha (50 acres), but it is by no means certain that all of these structures belong to a single, let alone a nucleated, settlement. Again there are scraps of evidence pointing to some Romanised buildings within the area, and the quantity of coinage, glass, samian and amphorae all suggest a lively commercial activity here.

West of London an important road- and river-side settlement inevitably developed at Staines,[55] aptly named Pontibus by the Romans, since it must have possessed bridges over both the Colne and the Thames. An early military site seems likely here, and there is already evidence of a civilian settlement as well as military occupation by the time of Boudicca. Reconstruction after the Boudiccan destruction saw the erection of timber-framed shops and by the mid-second century stone buildings, tesselated floors and painted wall plaster are all attested. There can be little doubt that a *mansio* also stood here and probably private hostels as well. The quantity and variety of pottery from widely spread kilns in southern England as well as imports from Gaul, Italy, Spain and Germany suggest that Staines may have served as a secondary marketing centre upstream from London. Fragmentary as the evidence is, all the signs are that a small but important town of about 4–5ha (10–12 acres) prospered at Staines throughout the Roman period, despite no less than three extensive destructions by fire.

Along Watling Street, the equivalent settlement to Enfield and Staines was located at Brockley Hill (Sulloniacae), which features as a post in iter II of the Antonine Itinerary but not in iters VI and VIII.[56] With Verulamium only twenty miles from London, Brockley Hill can have served as no more than a *mutatione*, and its absence from iters VI and VIII might suggest it was not regarded as a significant station at all. Certainly its main function was as a production centre for the mortarium potteries and most of the extensive remains discovered here over a period of centuries have related to pottery production. Brockley Hill was essentially an industrial settlement and its other functions were strictly secondary.

There were other industrial settlements scattered through the Catuvellaunian canton, though none perhaps as committed to the production of a single commodity as Brockley Hill. At Cow Roast in the valley of the Bulbourne a settlement established in the early years of the occupation on Akeman Street was much concerned with iron-working to judge by at least eight bowl-furnaces found here, but it is difficult on present evidence to call it a town.[57] The same must be said of the settlement at Foxholes Farm near Hertford, where an area of 10ha (25 acres) may have been occupied by another community largely concerned with iron-working.[58] Over forty furnaces and ovens have been discovered here, in addition to four 'corn-drying' ovens. In Northamptonshire, Ashton appears to be yet another industrial settlement, possibly extending over 15ha (37 acres).[59] This well-ordered community began in the mid–first century and developed in the second century alongside a road from which side streets ran off at right angles. Workshops and other rectangular buildings flanked these streets and the main road, some of them devoted to metalworking, and one of them quite clearly a blacksmiths workshop. The discovery of a stone column shaft in the fill of a well suggests there may be more sophisticated buildings to be found and that the status of Ashton is best left undecided at present.

Ashton may be one of half a dozen large settlements, probably with industrial aspects, to be found in Northamptonshire. These include a very extensive area of settlement at Kettering, and others somewhat smaller at Titchmarsh, Higham Ferrers, Duston, Norton and Little Houghton.[60] These settlements are almost all larger than the walled towns in the area, such as Towcester and Irchester, but one suspects they are not so densely occupied and may not be nucleated settlements at all. Equally their functions are at present very uncertain, though industrial production is clearly amongst them. On balance, it would seem inappropriate in a Roman context to refer to them as towns.

Looking again at the map of the canton with all the nucleated settlements marked on it, we can see that most of those for which the term town seems likely to be appropriate provide useful intermediate points between Verulamium and the walled towns we have earlier suggested were *vici*. This is largely a function of their position on the communications systems, but it inevitably must have had an economic significance, making these settlements market-places not only for local agricultural produce but also for local craft goods and for other products entering the canton via the Thames and London, Staines and Dorchester, or via the Nene and Water Newton. In the absence of any suggestion of public buildings at these sites, however, and in view of the fact that almost all of them remained unwalled throughout the Roman period, it would be unjustified to suggest either that they were *vici* or that they played a role in the administration of the civitas. Further discoveries may of course call for a revision of that view for individual sites.

Even though we have denied *vicus* status to nine or ten settlements, it remains true that the canton of the Catuvellauni contained more towns than any other civitas territory in the province. We have suggested there were seven *vici* and between eight and ten other minor towns. This proliferation of urban sites may partly reflect the level of Romanisation which was achieved, apparently at an early date, by the native population of the area. It may also reflect the lively commercial activity which existed throughout the civitas area, and the important lines of communication which ran through the canton. But it must also be related in part to the size of the civitas territory and the flourishing agricultural industry which it supported, and for which local market centres were essential. It is appropriate therefore that we should move from the consideration of the minor towns to that of the rural settlements and farms.

4

Rural Settlement

Despite the abundance of urban settlements in the canton of the Catuvellauni there can be no doubt that the majority of the people of the civitas lived in the countryside. Just as the size and nature of the urban settlements varied considerably, so too did those of the rural settlements, ranging from isolated huts and farmsteads, through hamlets to villages and nucleated settlements which in size at least were as large, and indeed sometimes larger, than settlements which we have defined as towns. This variety reflects a complexity of social, tenurial and agricultural relationships which we can be quite certain existed, but which archaeological evidence alone makes it difficult to identify and almost impossible to understand. In addition there were important social, economic and administrative relationships between the urban and rural settlements, to which we will need to return in both this and the following chapter. This web of relationships, between people and between elements of the settlement pattern, make it highly desirable to approach their study in terms of entire landscapes rather than isolated settlements. Once again, however, the archaeological evidence is usually totally inadequate to allow such an approach to be made, although we shall look at small segments of landscapes later in this chapter where the available evidence is of sufficient quality and quantity to make such an approach worthwhile. Initially, however, we will find it easiest to organise and analyse our information about rural settlement if we consider the principal elements – villas and villages and farms – separately, as representing change and Romanisation on the one hand and continuity and the native tradition on the other.

The history and development of villas, and of the cultural phenomenon they represent, was principally determined not by agricultural considerations (and ultimately, therefore, by topographical and pedalogical factors) but rather by their spatial, social and economic relationships with the urban settlements. It is therefore intended here to attempt to study the development of villa estates in the civitas by relating them to their urban focus. Apart from Verulamium, it has been suggested (above p. 82–93) that there were seven other towns in the canton which provided a sufficiently wide range of services and amenities to have functioned as economic and social centres, and probably administrative centres too, for rural settlements in the region. In order to indicate which towns were most likely to have served as centres for which villas, we have constructed notional territories for each town by drawing Thiessen polygons on the map of the canton, based on the locations of these seven towns and of Verulamium. In constructing this network we have assumed all the towns exerted a broadly equal economic and social attraction with the exception of Verulamium and Durobrivae; the polygons have been weighted to make allowance for the additional 'pull' of these two important towns. It must be emphasised that the resulting map is not intended to identify any formal territories and in particular is not meant to indicate where local administrative boundaries lay. It is meant to show which town was most likely to have been the social and, more particularly, the economic focus for any individual villa. (fig. 26)

On the map, the sites of about one hundred and thirty *known* villas are recorded, and about one hundred further sites which were *probably* occupied by villas. The latter include mainly sites known from field survey which have yielded in addition to pottery and general building debris, material suggestive of relatively sophisticated buildings, such as tesserae and opus signinum, flue tiles and painted wall plaster. Evidence from the excavated buildings suggests that such features are normally associated with the type of Romanised farmhouse we call a villa, although they

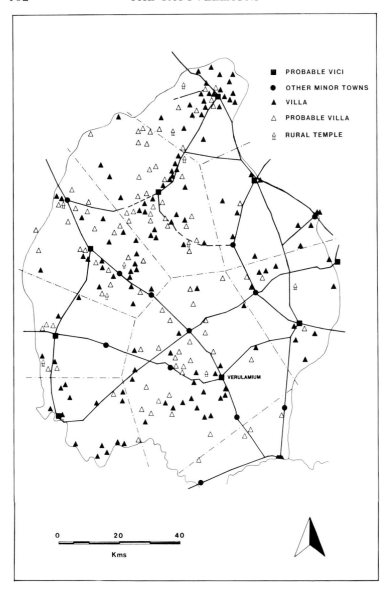

Fig. 26.   Towns and villas in the civitas territory.

also occur in rural temples. Only a small number of the total of one hundred 'probable' villa sites are likely to have been temples (one in twelve on analogy with known temples and villas), so that the general distribution and number of villas will not be seriously distorted by any erroneous attributions.

Villas in the Verulamium area

One of the largest concentrations of villas, not surprisingly, is that focussed on the civitas capital of Verulamium. Almost fifty villa sites are known or suspected in the area, and on present evidence they are located mainly to the west of Verulamium, in the Chilterns. The scarcity of villas to the east of Verulamium is difficult to explain, since the area is geologically similar to the western Chilterns, it was densely occupied in the century before the Roman conquest, and some of the Belgic occupants of the area were wealthier and better acquainted with Roman culture than those to the west of Verulamium. Furthermore there has been more archaeological survey in this area than in the Chilterns, so that the thin distribution of villas is not the result of archaeological inactivity. One possible explanation is that some of the land to the east of Verulamium was municipal land and was mainly farmed from the city. Alternatively, the estates of the Belgic nobility to which the Welwyn-type burials attest may have continued in existence after the conquest but the owners may have committed themselves to living in the new city of Verulamium, where we believe they would soon have had an important part to play in the affairs of the municipium, and later of the civitas. This raises the important issue of the continuity of ownership of land from the Belgic to the Roman period. Archaeological evidence of course does not allow us to prove or disprove continuity of ownership, and we may speak only of probabilities. In the territory around Verulamium we might expect a high level of continuity for two reasons. The first is that the focus of tribal society remained the same, namely the settlement at Verulamium. The second, and more important, is that all the indications are that the Romans treated the Catuvellauni generously at the time of the conquest and that they actively promoted and encouraged the rapid development of local government. We should not expect, therefore, widespread confiscations of the estates of the nobility. The evidence from the villas at Gorhambury, Park Street and Lockleys would seem to support this view. The remains of Belgic occupation at Lockleys and Park Street have been known and discussed for more than forty years and need little repetition here.[1]

Attempts to recognise a long hiatus, of up to one hundred and eighty years, between the two phases of Belgic occupation and the first small stone-founded villa at Lockleys have not been widely accepted,[2] whilst the general continuity from the two phases of occupation to the first pre-Boudiccan farmstead and finally the first, Flavian villa at Park Street is well established. This sequence has now been identified also at Gorhambury, where there may have been as many as five Belgic phases of occupation before the first Roman timber structure was built c. AD. 45.[3] Burnt down in the Boudiccan revolt, this house was later replaced by a circular one, before the first masonry villa was constructed about the turn of the century. At both Park Street and Gorhambury there is a hiatus of about fifteen years after the Boudiccan destructions, and it would be reasonable to argue that a change of ownership could have taken place during this period. On the other hand we have noted already that a similar hiatus occurs at Verulamium, and it is in fact common at other sites destroyed during the Boudiccan revolt,[4] so that we should not read too much into this interruption of occupation. At Park Street and Gorhambury the general impression is one of continuity, of progression from a comfortable Belgic farmstead to a semi-Romanised timber house immediately after the conquest, and then to the stone-founded villa in the later first century.

There may have been continuity from Belgic farmstead to villa at other sites too, but in general the evidence is too fragmentary to allow even reasonable certainty. In the Vale of Aylesbury Bierton and Terrick are possible examples, but in both cases we have insufficient information about the villa buildings and about the precise chronology of the Belgic and Roman occupations. To the west of Verulamium the evidence is better but on close examination it does not point to continuity from Belgic estates but to something rather different and potentially more interesting. In the valleys of the Gade and the Bulbourne the villas at Gadebridge Park and Boxmoor were found to be established in the later first century on sites which yielded no trace of Belgic occupation.[5] A third villa may have been built in the valley at this time at Northchurch.[6] In the next valley to the west, villa buildings appear at Latimer and Sarrat about two generations later, but beneath them are traces of earlier occupation using Belgic-style pottery. The indications are that this pottery is in fact post-conquest and belongs in the later first century AD. At Latimer a substantial timber building was associated with this pottery; in size and style it might be compared to the first post-conquest timber building at Gorhambury, but it appears to have been erected in the Flavian period. Further west again, in the valley of the Misbourne, the sites at Great Missenden and Shardloes produce Belgic pottery like that from Sarrat.[7] On present evidence therefore, the establishment of farms in the valleys west of Verulamium, where villa settlement was to become the norm, was perhaps begun on previously unoccupied land in the period c. AD 75–100. In the valley nearest to Verulamium, and already served by Akeman Street, villas were built immediately, whilst further west timber-built farms were constructed and Belgic-type pottery continued in use. The regularity of later villa settlement in these three valleys is such as to suggest a deliberate and controlled settlement policy here. Since the regularity of the pattern was first noted in 1968, three of the sites then listed as possible or probable villas have been confirmed by excavations, so that the distribution probably is as regular as was first suggested.[8] If there was colonisation of this land in the Flavian period, with estates of about 450–500 acres established here, then it is a matter for speculation as to who was settled here and why.

Subsequently the pattern of villa settlement filled out as further villas were built at Kings Langley, Moor Park and elsewhere in the early second century,[9] and at Latimer, Sarrat and High Wycombe in the middle of the century.[10]

Many of the unexcavated sites also probably belong to this period of development, to judge from surface material, and the only villa known to be much later is that at Dickets Mead, Welwyn, where its relationship to the earlier Lockleys villa still awaits satisfactory explanation.[11] The development of villas in the area centred on Verulamium can be seen to take place over a period of about 70–80 years, from the later-first century to the mid-second. Some Belgic farmsteads appear to have been developed into villa estates in the space of a generation, but other Belgic farmhouses east of Verulamium seem not to have been replaced by villas. This need not mean that the estates ceased to exist, or even changed hands, though that is possible. West of Verulamium settlement was extended into the Chiltern valleys and in time led to the appearance of many villa-based estates.

The villas around Verulamium are not the earliest known in Britain; some of the villas in Sussex, Kent and Essex precede them by a decade or two. On the other hand it has been suggested that at least some of the early villas in these three counties were the property of Roman officials, merchants or possibly retired soldiers. Such evidence as we have for the Verulamium area suggests that the early villas here were most probably built and occupied by native owners whose families in some cases had held these estates before the conquest. These villas attest the early Romanisation of the upper echelon's of Catuvellaunian society, a process no doubt speeded by the acquisition of Roman imports in the period before the conquest. The degree of Romanisation represented by these villas is perhaps more remarkable than the speed at which it took place. (fig. 27) The pre-Boudiccan timber buildings at Park Street and Gorhambury both reveal traces of the early impact of Roman architecture on the local Belgic tradition. The Park Street building had a timber verandah and was divided into at least two rooms; that at Gorhambury contained three or four rooms, probably in an L-shaped arrangement, and was linked to a further room or small building by a covered way or lean-to shed. When the villa proper was built at Park Street c. AD 75, it was constructed

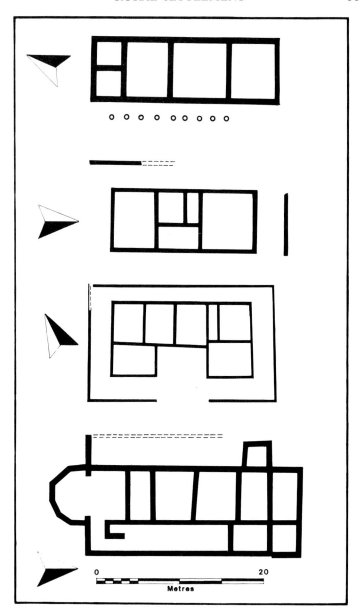

Fig. 27. Late first century villas at Lockleys, Park Street, Boxmoor, and Gorhambury.

on sound stone foundations, possessed five rooms, a cellar, and a verandah. In addition it had a free-standing bath-house. (fig. 28) An almost identical bath-house of about the

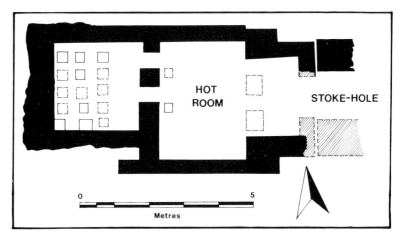

Fig. 28.   Late first century bath-house at Park Street villa.

same date was built at Gadebridge, almost certainly to serve a timber-built villa of which few traces survived, and at Boxmoor there may have been another first century bath-suite. The timber house built here at the end of the first century is notable for its winged corridor plan, and also for its painted wall plaster, which featured a *dado*, imitation moulding, rectangular panels and a candelabrum, in a combination of six colours. More elaborate wall decoration was found in the first stone built house at Gorhambury, where figured stucco was discovered. This building was similar in other respects to Park Street, with four rooms, a corridor and a cellar, and the late first century villa at Lockleys was of the same general type, though the five rooms here were fronted by a timber verandah and there was no cellar. Two rooms, however, were floored with tesserae. These various plans, embellishments and furnishings are an impressive collection at so early a date, and compare favourably with the domestic houses exca-vated in Verulamium. On present evidence, the creation of the civitas c. AD 75 led to a spate of public building at

Verulamium but private investment was initially greatest in country houses on estates close to Watling Street and Akeman Street and in close proximity to the city.

Only in the mid-second century, after the Antonine fire, did town houses catch, and indeed overtake, the villas in terms of size, amenities and furnishings. Though the first century villas were rebuilt or extended at this time, and new villas were built with ten or a dozen rooms from the first, the largest and best furnished private houses are now found in Verulamium. It is important to note, however, that the balance of the evidence suggests that examples of both extension and new constructions date *after* rather than before c. AD 155 and the Antonine fire at Verulamium. Only at Northchurch, abandoned c. AD 170, is there evidence that villa owners may have permanently moved to a town house. The developing demand for mosaics in the city no doubt encouraged their appearance in villas at Park Street, Boxmoor, Gorhambury, High Wycombe and Latimer, which are amongst the earliest villa mosaics in the province.[12] Subsequent developments on the villa estates around Verulamium show none of the dramatic expansion of the living accommodation and provision of sumptuous private quarters that we see in west country villas in the fourth century. In the late third century some villa-estates appear to have experienced economic difficulties, to judge from the signs of decay or decline which their villas display. Latimer villa appears to have been abandoned for a short period, Lockleys was in disrepair, and at Northchurch a pit and post-holes cut through existing floors, but sealed by early fourth century ones, suggests a marked decline in the quality of occupation. Other traces of disrepair have been noted at Gadebridge and Park Street, whilst at Boxmoor the villa was reduced in size and its walls buttressed in alterations made around the close of the third century.[13] This evidence is broadly in line with that noted by Wheeler in Verulamium and suggests that the modest wealth of the Catuvellaunian villa-owning class could not always cope with the increased burdens of taxation, the *annona militaris*, and inflation in the later third century.

Some estates seem to have recovered well during the early

fourth century, and Latimer and Gadebridge in particular were considerably extended and improved at this time. At Park Street new hypocausts were inserted into three rooms and the baths were extended, whilst at High Wycombe and Great Wymondley small swimming pools may have been built. These were dwarfed, however, by the huge pool (by Roman standards) built at Gadebridge, perhaps in the 320's. Elsewhere developments may have followed a different course. At Boxmoor an imperial lead seal was found amongst coins of the first half of the fourth century, and another seal of this type is known from Sarrat.[14] Their significance is uncertain, though they appear to imply at least some form of governmental control or interference in the running of these estates. Their appearance may indeed be related to the abrupt decline of the apparently prosperous villas at Latimer and Gadebridge in the period c. AD 350,[15] which has otherwise been attributed to the confiscations taking place in Britain following the unsuccessful usurpation of Magnentius in AD 353. Other villas in the area such as High Wycombe and Park Street also seem to either have been abandoned or seen a marked decline in the quality of occupation in the mid-fourth century. Although it would be rash to jump to the conclusion that all were victims of the events of AD 353, it is safe to say that the mid-fourth century was a time of change for the villas in the Verulamium region, and that it was a change for the worse.

Villas in the Dorchester and Alchester Area

In the western areas of the canton, in the areas focussed on Dorchester and Alchester, villas are relatively scarce. Indeed, within the catchment we ascribe to Alchester only four certain and five probable sites are known, although in the area around Dorchester fourteen certain examples are known, and two probables. It is a notable feature of their distribution that over half of the Dorchester villas are close to the Thames, and that all but one of the nine sites centred on Alchester are within 1.5kms. of a major Roman road. In this part of the canton, communications appears to have been a particularly potent factor in the location of villas.

The development of the villas in this region is difficult to trace because few of the villas have been excavated, but there is some evidence to suggest that some of the villas were established in the later first century, and in three cases that early villas were erected on sites with previous Belgic occupation. The clearest example of Belgic occupation beneath a later villa is at Hambleden, where plenty of Belgic pottery was found and some of this was clearly associated with a ditch which recent air-photography suggests was part of a rectangular enclosure with rounded corners.[16] Probably in the later first century a small villa was built here, although its original form is uncertain. Belgic pottery has also been recovered from sites at Marlow and at Saunderton where there is also the possibility of late first century villas. At Marlow the evidence is not strong, since the tiles and wall plaster that denote a possible villa site are associated with pottery covering the whole period from late first to mid-fourth century.[17] The evidence from Saunderton is much stronger, for not only do we have at least partial excavation of the villa, but we also have stratified evidence of pre-villa occupation. There is a substantial collection of Belgic pottery from the site, and there is also both samian and coarse-wares of the later first century. Some of this material was found in a pit sealed beneath the excavated building, which was erected in the mid-second century AD. Also in the pit were chalk tesserae, and the contents of a rubbish pit discovered later contained Ashtead-type flue tiles, slabs of Purbeck Marble and several small coloured mosaic tesserae which might also belong to an earlier building than that of the mid-second century.[18] In contrast to these indications of late first century villas, there are six other villa sites in this region where limited evidence suggests the late construction of villas. The most satisfactory evidence is that from Harpsden, where a small winged villa was built in the mid-third century.[19] Limited excavations at Bix and Cuddesdon have both identified stone buildings, the latter with a hypocaust, of similar date, and another late-Roman winged building is reported at Warborough, whilst limited evidence from Headington and

Beckley suggests they may also be no earlier than the third century.[20] Unsatisfactory as all of this evidence is, it suggests that the appearance of villa estates in the western part of the canton took place over a longer period of time than in the Verulamium region. Such first century villas as there may have been were to be found along the Thames or the Icknield Way, on existing lines of communication and on sites previously occupied by Belgic farms. In this respect at least, there is some correspondence between developments here and around Verulamium. Although the evidence is far too slender to say anything about the level of sophistication achieved in the early villas, we can make some comments on the general size and quality of the villas around Dorchester and Alchester on the basis of excavated examples and those known from aerial photographs.

The excavated building at Saunderton is of unusual plan, and there are clear indications from field-walking that another major wing exists, facing the excavated structure. It is possible that Saunderton was a courtyard villa, with a dwelling house of some quality. The mosaic teserae, Purbeck Marble slabs, and fine wall-plaster recovered from a rubbish pit clearly had no place in the excavated outbuilding. The other villas of which we have some knowledge all seem more modest buildings (fig. 29). Two of them, Hambleden and Saunderton Lee,[21] follow the tripartite (or H-plan) design, and three others are of bipartite type with wing rooms projecting only forwards.[22] All five of these buildings, offer broadly the same amount of accommodation, with ten to fourteen rooms and one or two corridors. In this respect they are similar to the majority of villas in the Verulamium region. The quality of accommodation offered, however, may have been somewhat lower, with no bathing facilities to match those at Gadebridge, Park Street, Latimer or High Wycombe. Harpsden, Wheatley and Tingewick[23] had small detached bath houses offering only the basic amenities, and simple integral suites were inserted into Hambledon and probably Saunderton Lee. Only Hambleden and Saunderton have so far yielded evidence for mosaics, the former with one or perhaps two small rooms floored with mosaic in the early fourth century and the

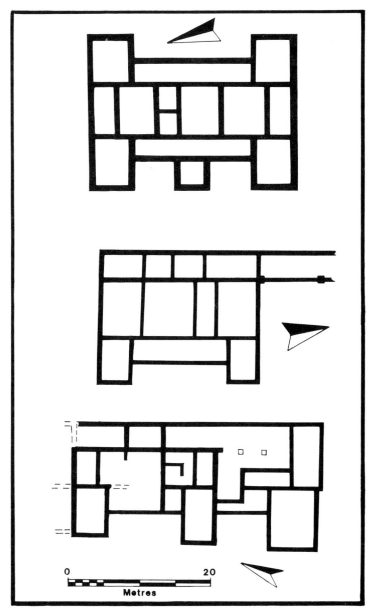

Fig. 29. Villas at Hambleden, Harpsden, and Mill Field.

latter with loose mosaic tesserae in a rubbish dump. The overall impression gained from the villas in the western part of the civitas territory is that they broadly reflect the same level of wealth as the villas around Verulamium, but they show both a later and a less decisive commitment to the Roman life-style.

Villas in the Towcester area

Towcester appears to have been the economic and social focus for a large number of villas, perhaps as many as forty on current evidence, though fewer than half of these have been sampled by excavation. They are found mainly to the south and east of the town, in the upper valley of the Ouse, with smaller numbers in the hill country between the valleys of the Ouse and Nene, and in the upper valley of the Nene itself. Apart from a small group of villas close to Towcester, there are scarcely any known to the west of the town, although there is no obvious explanation for their absence. For whatever reason, the main lines of communication in the area, Watling Street and the road between Alchester and Towcester, also seem to have been much less potent factors in villa distribution than was the case in the region to the south. Barely one in three of the Towcester villas are within three kilometres of one of these roads. The earliest villas in the area stand only a little over two kilometres from Towcester itself, and considerably less distance from each other at Mileoak (Foscote) and Wood Burcote.[24] Both villas are preceded by Belgic occupation, but in both cases this may be of post-conquest date. At Mileoak, Belgic pottery associated with rubble floors suggests a substantial pre-villa building, and at Wood Burcote the villa was preceded by a timber building of late Flavian date associated with Roman pottery. Mileoak villa was probably built around AD 70–80 as a twelve-roomed stone-founded building, but Wood Burcote may not have been constructed until around the turn of the century. Soon after this, a villa may have been established at Piddington, twelve kilometres north-east of Towcester.[25] Further south, in the valley of the Ouse, the earliest villas yet known are those at Bancroft (Bradwell),

Stanton Low, and Deanshanger.[26] The first building at Bancroft was an aisled house erected in the late first or early second century, which was embellished by the addition of a bath-suite and two small rooms in the early-mid second century. When this was destroyed by fire in the late second century, a block of rooms with two-wing rooms was built to replace it. Stanton Low and Deanshanger were constructed in the mid-second century over traces of earlier occupation. At Deanshanger a late first century farmstead with circular huts preceded the villa, and similar huts of early second-century date have been found beneath third century villas at Gayhurst and Stantonbury.[27] It may be that in the upper Ouse valley there was a phase of Romano-British colonisation in the late-first and early-second century with estates established at frequent intervals on both sides of the river. Within two generations several of these were developed from native-style farmsteads into villas. Some villas were established still later, such as Bletchley (Sherwood Drive) and Wymbush, both of which were third century foundations.[28]

There are no earlier remains on these sites, however, to suggest that they developed from earlier native farmsteads, and Wymbush is close enough to the Bancroft villa to encourage speculation that it was the home of a tenant farmer of the larger estate. Broadly contemporary with the building of these two villas was the construction of the first villa at Thenford,[29] over the remains of a late Iron Age occupation and a late first century timber-built farmstead. There is no evidence to suggest continuity of occupation from the late-first to the late-third century and the pattern of development in the hill-country west of Towcester may have been quite different to that in the Ouse valley or in the areas close to the town.

It would be equally wrong to assume that once the villas had been constructed they continued to flourish, with various alterations and additions, into the later fourth century. Mileoak villa seems to have been demolished in the mid-second century, and the first Piddington villa was destroyed by fire towards the end of the century and not replaced until the early third. Bletchley villa was demolished in the early fourth century, perhaps no more than a generation after its construction. Clearly, there are no safe generalisations which can be made about the history of the villas in the Towcester region, except that it is a more varied pattern than that of the villas around Verulamium. Variety is even more apparent when we compare the size and quality of the excavated villas of this region. None of the villas is exceptionally large. Piddington, with at least twenty rooms (fig. 31) may have offered the most accommodation but Bancroft eventually became the most Romanised of the buildings excavated, though not until the mid-fourth century. (fig. 30) Of bi-partite plan, it finally boasted nine main rooms, plus two small bath-suites and a separate service wing to the rear. To one side stood an octagonal shrine, possibly dedicated to Mercury, and beyond that a walled garden area. In the main wing of the house, traces of nine mosaic panels were found, all of geometric design and varying in quality from coarse to fine. Mosaics are not common in the other villas of the region, with single examples known to date from Mileoak, Piddington, Thenford and Nether Heyford, and two from Foxcote, so that their number at Bancroft, together with the provision of a shrine, separate service wing and two small bath suites, must be taken to indicate an owner with highly Romanised tastes if somewhat modest means. Other villas of comparable size and broadly similar quality may have stood at Mursley, Wakefield Lodge, Foxcote and Welton, but in none of these instances do we have sufficient information to be certain. The villas at Mileoak (fig. 31), Stanton Low, Bletchley, Wymbush and Wood Burcote all appear to belong to a single type, though they vary somewhat in size. In each case the dwelling house appears to have been a simple rectangular block without projecting wing rooms, with a corridor providing independent access to the various rooms. Mileoak has the luxury of both front and rear corridors, and with ten rooms and a mosaic is perhaps the most impressive of this group. Stanton Low and Bletchley are both imperfectly known, but the former has a separate bath-house and hypocaust-heated living rooms. The smallest of this group are Wymbush and Wood Burcote,

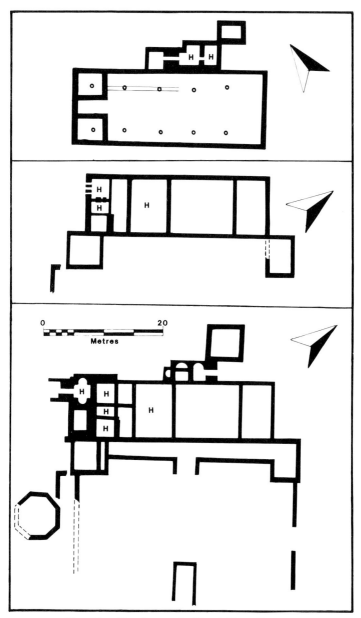

Fig. 30. The Bancroft villa, Milton Keynes.

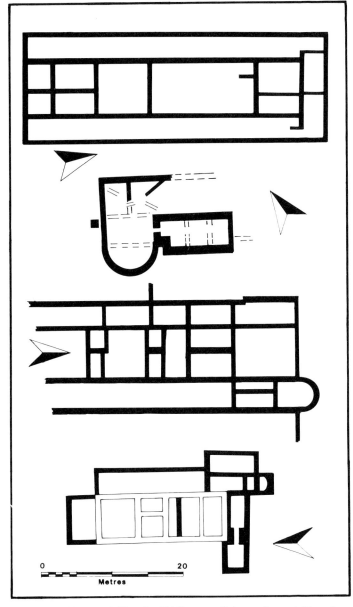

Fig. 31.   Villas at Mileoak, Piddington, Brixworth, and Newnham.

with five and six rooms respectively. The interior furnishings of Wymbush, with opus floors and painted plaster but no hypocausts, tesselated or mosaic floors, match its size, but the situation at Wood Burcote is more of an enigma. Of the four excavated buildings, two may be dwelling houses, but the larger has only four rooms behind a front corridor and the smaller, only three. Painted wall plaster from two rooms of the larger building, and a tesselated floor in the smaller, suggest a modest level of investment in a Romanised home, but they do not provide a context for the stone mouldings, column fragments, and mosaic tesserae found on the site in surface survey. It is possible therefore that the main dwelling house has still to be located here and that the excavated houses belong to labourers or servants. Despite the uncertainties of the evidence, however, the impression which emerges from the villas of the Towcester region is of a greater diversity of size and quality than in either of the areas previously considered.

Villas in the Irchester Area

The concentration of villas in the Irchester area is greater than that in any of the areas previously considered, including that focussed on Verulamium, with about fifty sites identified. Of these, almost half are certain examples, confirmed by partial excavation or air photographs. A glance at the map (fig. 26) shows that they concentrate close to the two Roman roads known to traverse this area, with over half of the sites found within three kilometres of one or other of these roads. It should be noted however that the greatest concentration is along the line of the road which runs from Whilton Lodge (and Watling Street), via Irchester, to Water Newton (and Ermine Street), and that from Northampton eastwards, this road follows very closely the line of the River Nene. These villas may therefore have been located as much to use the river as a means of transport as to use the road. Relatively few villas have so far been located in the dissected hill-country north-west of Irchester.

In view of the abundance of villas in this area, it is

disappointing that we have so little information about either their history or the details of their architecture. The four sites for which a foundation date for the villa can be suggested yield dates ranging from the late first century to the early fourth. All four, however, produce ample evidence of earlier occupation, both Belgic and Romano-British. At Brixworth early Roman occupation is represented by three lengths of ditch and part of a circular timber hut which belonged to a native farmstead of the period c. AD 60–75.[30] This was replaced by a small five roomed stone-founded villa with a timber verandah, of similar size and plan to that at Lockleys. In spite of some rebuilding in the later second century, it was not until the fourth century that the villa was extended and provided with an integral corridor and a small bath-suite. At Newnham, Belgic field-systems and enclosures were followed initially by a first century timber building associated with Romanised pottery.[31] Subsequently three stone buildings were erected, including one which was possibly a dwelling house later converted at least partly into a bath-suite. The date of this and one of the other buildings is not certain, but a third building with seven rooms, floored in cobbles and in pebble-mortar, was probably erected in the mid- or later second century. Similar uncertainty surrounds the chronology of the villa at Ashley, because only the outbuildings seem to have been examined.[32] Fragments of mosaic and a stone column found in the make-up of a cobble floor of around AD 300, however, suggest a villa of the third century or earlier nearby, and second century timber outbuildings are probably to be associated with a contemporary villa. Earlier late Iron Age occupation of the site was marked by ditches and gullies and successive circular timber huts. In contrast to these three sites, and especially Brixworth, the Belgic farmstead at Odell was followed by a lengthy Romano-British occupation of very similar type with circular timber huts remaining in use until the fourth century, when a small timber stone-founded building was erected.[33] It could be argued that this building should not be called a villa, since it has produced no evidence of Roman floor or wall materials. Its foundations were very poorly preserved, however, and it was probably constructed in timber on stone and gravel footings. Nevertheless, in so far as its plan can be recovered, it appears to have had at least five rooms, one of which projects forward rather like a wing-room in a corridor villa. Apart from a common Belgic ancestry which they seem to share, these four sites present a varied picture of villa development in the area to the north-west and south-east of Irchester. Unfortunately we know nothing of the histories of the many villas strung along the Nene Valley on either side of Irchester, although material collected on the site of the Ringstead villa east of Irchester suggests that Belgic occupation was followed by Romanised occupation of the first to third centuries.[34] The weight of the evidence at present available suggests that Odell was an exceptionally late development, but equally we should not assume that Brixworth's first century villa represents the norm.

Amongst the villas whose plan is known from excavation or aerial photographs, there is a scarcity of winged corridor villas, just as there was in the area centred on Towcester. The exceptions are at Newnham, very much on the southern fringe of the area, and at Wollaston. The plan of the building partly excavated at Newnham is difficult to interpret with certainty since the building was badly damaged.[35] Three thick-walled rooms with pillared hypocausts must have been a small bath-suite but the rest of the building looks more like a small winged corridor building with two projecting apsidal rooms, into which the bath-suite had been inserted (fig. 31). If that interpretation is correct, it would have been rather similar in plan in its original state to the villa at Engleton in Staffs. Wollaston, known only from aerial photos, has two projecting wing rooms, a range of four rooms in line, and a front corridor which may have been subdivided at some stage of its history.[36] Neither of these villas is large, and neither has produced evidence of internal furnishings more notable than painted plaster and tesselated floors. The same must be said of the other buildings whose plans are known. The dwelling houses at Ringstead and, in its later phase, Brixworth, appear to be rectangular blocks linked by a corridor running the length of the building. (fig. 31) Little Addington appears from its aerial photograph to be essentially the same though it may have more rooms and outbuildings, and Great Doddington is a rectangular block of five rooms with no corridor, although a verandah supported on timber posts would not necessarily be visible on the air photo.[37] The apparent dwelling house at Raunds is also a rectangular block although forthcoming excavations here may reveal a larger house than that identified on aerial photos at present. In general, these five buildings belong with the four similar villas in the Towcester area, and they are perhaps sufficient in number to suggest that they are representative of most of the villas of the upper Nene and Ouse valleys. We should not assume that larger and wealthier villas were unknown in the Irchester area, however, and there are tantalising hints of their existence. At Higham Ferrers, Moulton and Ashley have been found a Doric capital, a column base and a column shaft respectively, in each case suggesting villas with a higher level of sophistication than anything yet excavated.[38] Ashley has also produced fragments of mosaics, and mosaics are recorded from Raunds (Stanwick) and Weekley too.[39] Nevertheless, the overall picture remains the same, with a large number of comfortable but modest villas, reflecting perhaps the level of sophistication to be found in their urban focus at Irchester.

Villas in the Water Newton Area

Even when due weighting is given for the extra economic and social 'pull' which we believe Durobrivae must have exerted over that provided by Godmanchester to the south and Irchester to the west, the 'catchment' ascribed to Durobrivae shares with that ascribed to Dorchester the distinction of being the smallest in the civitas. In both cases the catchment is distorted by the proximity of the civitas boundary in two directions, although in practice both towns may well have attracted custom and visitors from across those boundaries. Here, however, we are concerned only with villas within the canton of the Catuvellauni, and within the catchment we ascribe to Durobrivae there are about thirty villa sites, of which about two dozen are firm identifications. Relative to the size of the catchment that is a greater number than is found in any other area in the civitas territory, including the catchment of Verulamium itself, although it is only marginally greater than the concentrations in the areas of Irchester and Towcester. To some extent, the density of villas may reflect the amount of archaeological activity in the area ever since the early nineteenth century, but there can be no doubt that the Nene Valley around Durobrivae was a major focus of villa development. Furthermore it can be seen that the villas cluster close to the town itself, with two thirds of the known sites within only eight kilometres of its walls. This is an unusual distribution, the closest parallels to which are perhaps found around Bath and Ilchester in the West Country. One implication of so many villas in so small an area is that some of them, at least, were probably not the centres of agricultural estates, and in some instances in the Nene Valley we have confirmation of this from the excavations.

The relationship between the Nene Valley pottery industry and the villas may be reflected in the chronological development of villas around Durobrivae, for there is little evidence at present for villas which were founded before the later second century. From brief interim reports it is possible that Sacrewell, Helpston and Yarwell villas were established during the second century.[40] Second century timber buildings were replaced by a stone-founded house of the third century at Barnwell, although the nature of the second century structures is not clear.[41] Second century occupation at Orton Longueville was connected with iron-working and the first villa-like structures belong to the third century.[42] At Yarwell (Sulehay), Fotheringhay, and Elton, trial excavations in each case yielded later third and fourth century pottery associated with the villa structures.[43] The great villa complex beneath Castor village was not built before the late third century, and a date of c. AD 300 has recently been proposed for its construction,[44] although it is clearly such an exceptional structure that it may be irrelevant as evidence for the general pattern of development in the area. It may also be argued that the evidence from the aisled barns (or 'basilical buildings') at Barnack and Orton

Longueville (Hall Farm)[45] is irrelevant to villa development, but in each case there are traces of villas nearby which suggest that the barns were probably part of the villa estate. Both Barnack and Hall Farm aisled buildings belong to the mid-third century. The general picture from the villas on the low-lying land close to Durobrivae is therefore one of villa development mainly taking place during the third century, although there may have been some second century foundations. It is difficult to say whether or not it is significant that the only villa from further west in Rockingham Forest, for which a reasonably detailed history is available should reveal a markedly different pattern. Great Weldon villa was built c. AD 70–80 with a central range of rooms, a stone-walled verandah to one side and a timber-post supported verandah on the other.[46] It is broadly comparable therefore to other late first century villas such as Park Street, Lockleys and Brixworth. When it was burnt down at the end of the second century it was soon replaced by a winged-corridor villa, which was extended and improved over the next century and a half.

Great Weldon villa is anomalous in this area not only by reason of its early foundation but also because it is the only genuinely bi-partite villa with wing rooms. It was provided with a main suite of seven rooms, of which the central and largest room was apsidal. A bath suite was developed from one wing, and the construction of three outbuildings and an enclosure wall eventually developed the overall plan into a courtyard villa broadly similar to the villas found immediately around Durobrivae. In several of these villas, the main dwelling house was essentially a rectangular block with a fronting corridor, to which odd rooms were appended. Courtyard walls and outbuildings were used to enclose the area before the dwelling house so that in plan the villas look very impressive structures. In terms of the accommodation they provided, they were in fact rather modest, with between eight and a dozen living rooms, and an impression of somewhat haphazard growth. The classic example is Apethorpe villa, but others include both of the Ailsworth villas, Cotterstock (fig. 32) and the Mill Hill (Castor) villa as revealed by aerial photos.[47] The dwelling

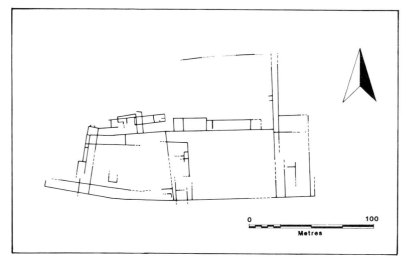

0 ————————————— 100
Metres

Fig. 32. The villa at Cotterstock as seen on aerial photographs.

house at Helpston falls into this group, and there are
indications that it too was developed around a courtyard.[48]
The same development also took place at Hall Farm, but all
of the buildings here appear to be 'outbuildings' in the
sense that no living house with a suite of rooms was
identified.[49] Four of the buildings around the yard were in
fact aisled barns.

Despite its extensive courtyard complex, Hall Farm may
have simply been the working end of an estate centred on
the villa just over one kilometre to the north-west. Other
aisled barns in the area, at Barnack, Werrington and Lynch
Farm can be similarly interpreted, and in each case there
are traces of villa-like structures nearby.[50] The Barnack
(Pilsgate) villa, revealed by aerial photography, is itself a
small and unimpressive structure with just five or six rooms
forming a rectangular block with no visible traces of a
linking corridor.[51] Fotheringhay villa, also known mainly
from aerial photos, may have been broadly similar if slightly
more complex. There are no indications at present that
either was developed into any sort of courtyard
arrangement, and these two villas do seem to represent a
more modest development than those discussed above. Four

of the courtyard villas are known to have possessed mosaics, with two at Apethorpe and Mill Hill, three at Helpston and four at Ailsworth. Great Weldon also boasted four mosaics, and with others at Cotterstock and Longthorpe,[52] the villas in the Durobrivae area provide the largest concentration of villa mosaics in the canton.

This is all the more so if one includes the mosaics from the remains discovered beneath Castor village. This building (or buildings) has to be discussed apart from the other villas since in size alone it is clearly quite exceptional. The remains found by Artis and others in more recent times extend over an area at least 250m × 125m.[53] It is difficult, if not impossible, to interpret them as the remains of a single building, but there is no reason why they cannot have all been part of a single villa complex.[54]

The most recent interpretation of the site is a bold and imaginative reconstruction of the remains at the top of the hill as a single massive building 110m wide with a huge central hall and high flanking wings.[55] The term 'palatial' is applied to this structure, and it is suggested that it may have been built in the later third century as a residence and administrative centre for the Count of the Saxon Shore, or possibly for the commander of the field army in fourth century Britain. This is taking the evidence further than it warrants, but this proposal has emphasised the monumental nature of the building on the top of the hill. If it is a privately owned villa, its owner must have been an extremely wealthy man and almost certainly he would have been involved in the pottery industry carried on in the fields around his residence. We might expect the nearby town of Durobrivae to have benefitted from his patronage.

Villas in the Godmanchester and Braughing Areas

The eastern part of the Catuvellaunian canton is as sparsely occupied by villas as the western. About a dozen known or probable villa sites are identified in the catchments of each of the two towns. They are found mainly in small clusters around not only Braughing and Godmanchester but also around Cambridge and Baldock, suggesting that the social and economic attractions of the former were perhaps little greater than those of the latter towns.

Again there is a paucity of information about the chronological development of the villas in the area. Two villas explored in the nineteenth century, Ickleton and Wendens Ambo,[56] both produced plenty of coins of the late third and fourth centuries, but both excavations also yielded earlier material and there was certainly occupation extending back into the Iron Age at Wendens Ambo. The earliest villa identified by post-war excavations, however, is the small corridor villa at Godmanchester which was built in the early second century, and was extended and improved in the early third century.[57] In contrast, the nearby Huntingdon villa was first constructed in the early third century and only later developed into a winged corridor house.[58] The other villas for which foundation dates can be established all belong to the late third or early fourth century, to judge from the brief interim reports published. These include one at Standon near Braughing, and two on Arbury Road at Cambridge.[59] The latter are both modest structures, and one of them began life in the third century as an aisled building of the type already noted in the Water Newton area. With such a small sample it would be unwise to draw any firm conclusions about the development of villas in this area except to say that some were still being established in the late Roman period.

Thanks to aerial photography we are able to say something about the size of some of the villas for which chronological evidence is lacking. The smallest and simplest villas are those at Arbury Road and the first phase villa at Godmanchester. One of the Arbury Road houses had only four rooms arranged in an L-shape, whilst the other was a converted aisled building to which a front corridor flanked by wing rooms was added to create a more impressive facade. The first Godmanchester villa comprised six small rooms and a front corridor within a simple rectangular block. The main dwelling house at Guilden Morden may have been of essentially the same type, though it certainly possessed more rooms and may have originally had both front and rear corridors.[60] Godmanchester may subsequently have become a winged corridor villa, although that is not certain from the excavated remains, but winged corridor villas are found at Ickleton, Wendens Ambo, and Radwell.[61] Ickleton boasts fifteen rooms with wings projecting forwards and to the rear, and Wendens Ambo has as many rooms but only forward projecting wings. The central room here is much larger than the others and is apsidal, and is clearly the *triclinium* of this house. Huntingdon villa was developed into a winged corridor house, and Radwell too took this form with a central block of rooms, front and rear corridors, and large wing rooms projecting forwards. The interest at Radwell, however, extends beyond the dwelling house to its surroundings. To one side is a second large building, probably for domestic use, and these two buildings are separated by a wall from another group including two very large barn-like structures. All the buildings are arranged to form a huge courtyard complex. A similar complex has been suggested on the basis of field survey work at Ashwell End, and a courtyard villa has also been identified on an aerial photograph at Eynesbury.[62] Although the villas in the area therefore span the range from very small to large, the general impression is that most villas in this region are relatively sophisticated architecturally and compare well with the best from else-where in the canton. This impression is heightened by the evidence that five of the villas possessed mosaic floors,[63] that a sixth (Tempsford) had marble wall veneers,[64] and that even the converted aisled building at Arbury Road produced carved freestone and a fragment of cornice.

Villa estates – summary

Catuvellaunian villas are concentrated heavily in the north and north-west part of the civitas territory for reasons which are not readily apparent. The known distribution may reflect a greater amount of archaeological fieldwork and also the susceptibility of the river gravels to aerial photography, but these factors alone cannot explain it. Another factor may have been the accessibility of water transport in the area, with the Nene and the Ouse providing a cheap and

easy means of moving produce to market centres. In the
Nene Valley there is also the relationship between the villas
and the 'industrial' economy to be considered. Successful
iron and pottery industries may have provided the wealth if
not the impetus for local land-owners to build villas on their
estates.

This biased distribution only became apparent during the
third century, however, and initially the concentration of
villas was around Verulamium, in the old heartland of the
Catuvellaunian kingdom. Here, some villas certainly appear
to have developed from Belgic estates, and there may be
some examples of this continuity around Dorchester and
Towcester too. At the time these estates were seeing the
construction of their first villas, other estates were perhaps
being created for the first time on land previously
unoccupied in the western Chilterns. Something similar
may have happened in the Ouse valley, and in both cases
villas were built a generation or two later. The majority of
the villas in Catuvellaunian territory, however, appear to
belong to the late second – late third century, and this is
particularly true of villas in the Durobrivae area. The
pattern was still being filled-in by new villa foundations in
the early fourth century.

The number of villas built in Catuvellaunian territory
underlines the commitment of the tribes' land-owning class
to their rural estates, and in the late first century this is
particularly demonstrated by the villas around
Verulamium. The quality of their furnishings and amenities
at this time outstrips that of all but the most exceptional
town houses at Verulamium and is far in excess of anything
found in the minor towns in the late first century.
Thereafter, however, the development of villa residences is
rather modest. Most Catuvellaunian villas have between 8
and 15 rooms. In the southern part of the canton winged
corridor plans of either bipartite or tripartite type are the
commonest, but further north and west rectangular blocks
without projecting wing rooms are more frequent. Very few
villas reveal traces of more ambitious planning. In the Nene
Valley around Durobrivae the 'courtyard' villas there are
essentially modest houses with outbuildings arranged to

enclose a yard. The only villas which may have been developed by the provision of deep flanking wings into something approaching the courtyard villas seen in the south and west of England in the fourth century were Tottenhoe, Radwell, Latimer, and possibly Kimble, Saunderton and Eynesbury. Similarly, villa mosaics are relatively scarce in the Catuvellaunian canton. Whereas nearly one hundred villas in the south-west of England, out of a total of about two-hundred and forty, have yielded evidence of mosaics, only thirty of the c. 220 villas in our region have produced such evidence. Architectural embellishments such as cornices, columns, balustrades, and roof finials are known from only a handful of our villas, and sculptures in the round or in relief are almost unknown. The impression is that, for whatever reasons, the villa houses of the Catuvellauni were never developed to the potential that the earliest of them suggested during the late first century and that one might have expected in the territory of one of the most Romanised civitates in the province.

Villages and Farmsteads

Just as most of the people of the civitas of the Catuvellauni lived in the country rather than in towns, so the vast majority who lived in rural settlements were to be found not in villas, but in villages, hamlets and farmsteads. Thanks to aerial photography and increasing field survey work, particularly by local archaeologists, the number of such sites that have been identified has increased rapidly in the past fifty years. In 1975, Taylor was able to demonstrate how the number of known Roman settlements in the Nene Valley had grown from 36 in 1931, to 130 in 1956, and to 434 in 1972.[65] Since that time further aerial photos and survey work have added many new sites to the catalogue, so that the number is now believed to be well in excess of five hundred settlements. The rate of discovery elsewhere has not been so dramatic, but there have been significant increases in the Ouse valley and also on the clays in the Vale of Aylesbury. The problems facing the archaeologist trying to study, sort and analyse these settlements are frankly insurmountable. Apart from the sheer number of sites involved, there is the primary problem of what constitues a 'site'. Taylor's figures for 1972 in the Nene Valley rightly excluded sites known from air photos but undated by subsequent field visits and collection of artifacts; they also excluded pottery scatters unsupported by any other evidence of occupation. Many of the sites excluded in 1972 are now included in the catalogue of sites as new evidence has become available, but equally other discoveries have added many new locations with undated remains or insufficient evidence to proclaim them occupation sites. Even when one considers only the known 'sites' attempts to classify them are doomed to failure because it is impossible to draw the line in many cases between a farmstead and a hamlet, a hamlet and a village, an industrial or craft settlement and a farming village, and so on. Furthermore, many 'sites' merge into one another so that it is difficult to say where one begins and another ends. Beyond these problems are those of chronology; it is often impossible to say on the evidence of air photos and field walking alone which sites were in contemporary occupation. Even if one could solve all these problems, one would be left with a very incomplete distribution pattern due to variations of geology, modern development, and archaeological fieldwork. Finally, very few of these 'native' settlements have been more than partially sampled by excavation, so that our understanding of even selected individual settlements is very poor. All one can do, certainly within the limits of a volume such as this, is to indicate something of the range of settlements in which the vast majority of the Catuvellauni lived throughout the Roman occupation.

We have already seen in the previous chapter that some nucleated settlements, such as Sandy, may have been little more than successful villages in the sense that they lacked the public buildings and specialised functions we associate even with minor towns. It is difficult, however, to place Sandy, and similar settlements such as Baldock, Dunstable, and Bicester in the same category as semi-nucleated agricultural settlements such as Cople in the Ouse valley.[66] The main occupation area here, stretches for about a kilometre alongside an old stream course and contains at least five clusters of enclosures, though small double-ditched lanes appear to divide the area into ten or a dozen 'properties'. Some of the enclosures are so small they can only be occupation areas, garden plots or possibly animal pens. Others are much larger and may have served as paddocks. At least four double-ditched trackways run out from the settlement, roughly at right-angles to it, into the surrounding pasture-land. A rather similar 'village' is known at Fotheringhay in the lower Nene Valley near Durobrivae, and we shall return to that below.[67] Traces of other villages of the same general type can be seen on aerial photos of the Nene Valley, and elsewhere in Northamptonshire they may also be represented by extensive spreads of Roman occupation debris covering areas of between 2 and 8 hectares (5 and 20 acres). Smaller settlements with two to four clusters of enclosures appear to represent hamlets, and they are found in much the same areas. At both Earls Barton and Thorpe Achurch the settlements begin in the Iron Age but are occupied certainly into the first half of the Roman period.[68]

Both settlements have three, perhaps four, groups of enclosures, each of which appears to have an occupation area, garden plots and pens. The enclosures are built either side of a central trackway and both settlements are close to a Roman road. The most numerous settlement type in the valleys of the Welland, Nene, Ouse and Ouzel, however, is the isolated farmstead. Some of these farms, like Great Billing and Tansor,[69] comprise but a single enclosure surrounded by traces of a field system, and some may be totally unenclosed, but many are very similar to the enclosure clusters that we have seen to make up both hamlets and villages. This is seen at Wakerley in the Welland Valley, at Moulton in the hills between the Welland and the Nene, and at Woughton in the valley of the Ouzel for example.[70] Several of these farmsteads have been at least partly excavated and those at Wakerley and Odell, in the valleys of the Welland and the Ouse respectively, may be taken to illustrate not only the similarities shared by these settlements but also the considerable differences that are found from one to another.

The enclosed settlement at Wakerley appears to have been established in the Belgic period before the Roman conquest, the first trapezoidal enclosure being appended by a second similar one shortly before the Roman conquest.[71] In the second enclosure seven circular timber huts were erected, of which up to five could have been in use at one time. Occupation continued in this enclosure for a short period after the conquest, but subsequently an enlarged enclosure was made to the south-east and the focus of activity shifted there. (fig 33) Traces of a circular hut about

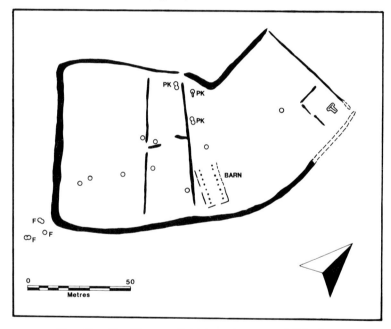

Fig. 33. The Romano-British settlement at Wakerley.

9m in diameter survived in the southern end of the enclosure, and it is possible that amongst the many post-holes discovered are traces of other rectilinear timber buildings. The main enclosure was divided by smaller ditches into four or five areas or yards, and in one of these a timber basilican barn was erected in the late second century. Iron-working was already being undertaken at this time and continued to be an important activity on the farm, but three pottery kilns were also constructed at about the time the barn was built. Corndrying ovens, however, confirm that the settlement was concerned with agriculture and was not purely an industrial site. It is possible that the main living area for those working here in the later first to fourth centuries was to be found about 600m away to the south-west.

At Odell, the focus of occupation remained in the enclosure area from the later Belgic period through to the fourth century, although there was a shift in location from one enclosure area to another.[72] The farm was established at the beginning of the first century AD, with a sub-rectangular or D-shaped enclosure occupied by two circular timber huts, each of which was twice re-built. (fig. 6) These huts were occupied after the Roman conquest and only abandoned in the later first century. At that time, the focus of occupation shifted about 100m to the south, where one or two new timber circular huts were erected. The farming family continued to live in these until the fourth century, when a small villa-like house was erected in timber immediately alongside the earlier houses. Throughout this period the farmhouses had been surrounded by fields and paddocks used for arable and pastoral activities, in connection with which drying ovens and stone-lined wells had been constructed.

The circular huts occupied at both of these sites can be paralleled at many others in the northern part of the canton, at Caldecote, Wood Corner, Overstone and Thorplands, for example.[73] The continued construction of these native style houses throughout the Roman period should come as no surprise when we have already found examples in use alongside villas at Great Doddington, Ringstead and Great Weldon. Similarly, aisled barns like those at Wakerley and Lynch Farm are less substantial versions of the stone barns we have already noted at Werrington, Barnack, and Hall Farm where they are probably outlying buildings of a nearby villa complex. The intermingling of Roman and native architectural forms in the vicinity of many of the villas in and around the valleys of the Welland, Nene and Ouse reflect the strength of the native tradition in this area, to which the hundreds of native villages and farmsteads also attest. In contrast, in the Chilterns around Verulamium there are to date very few traces of 'native' settlements. There are certainly sites known only as surface scatters of material but many of these produce fragments of tile, tesserae and plaster suggestive of villas, and in some cases subsequent excavation has confirmed this. Apart from village-like settlements with an industrial aspect at Cow Roast and Foxholes,[74] there are only a handful of poorly understood sites where cobble, clay or earth floors suggest peasant cottages.[75] Although the Chiltern valleys are much less susceptible to aerial photography than the broad valleys further north, this alone cannot explain the scarcity of 'native' settlements in the Chilterns and we must presume that we are looking at two different patterns of land-holding and settlement. The economic relationships between villas, villages and farms cannot be greatly illuminated by archaeological evidence but some general impressions may emerge by looking at a few selected blocks of landscape rather than individual sites.

Some Catuvellaunian Landscapes

The three areas of landscape chosen for consideration here reveal interesting variations in the pattern of rural settlement, the elements within the pattern, and their relationships. In each case, we shall be attempting to look at settlement as it was in the third century AD. The three areas chosen are the valley of the Bulbourne, west of Verulamium, the environs of Godmanchester in the middle stretches of the Ouse, and the lower Nene valley between Fotheringhay and Wansford. The first area covers about 30 sq. kms. and each of the others about half of this area.

The valley of the Bulbourne is taken as broadly representative of the other Chiltern valleys west of Verulamium, although it differs in two potentially important respects, being the nearest of the valleys to the city, and also being the route taken by Akeman Street as it heads west.[76] Like the other valleys, however, it is rather narrow and steep-sided, and runs generally from north-west to south-east. In the stretch of valley between Kings Langley and Northchurch there were at least three, probably four, villas at Northchurch, Berkhamsted, Boxmoor and Kings Langley, with a further villa in the lower valley of the Gade, which has its confluence with the Bulbourne at Boxmoor. Boxmoor and Northchurch villas were comfortable yet modest houses, but insufficient is known of Berkhamsted and Kings Langley to comment on their size. Gadebridge, though not yet fully developed, was a more impressive house with projecting wings, separate bath-house, and outbuildings constructed to form an enclosed yard in front of the house. About two kilometres north-west of the Northchurch villa an extensive village was established at the site now known as Cow Roast, and this seems to have been involved in iron-working activities. It may have served as a social focus and market centre for labourers from the nearest estates, but though it seems to have been a prosperous settlement there is nothing to suggest it would have provided any attractions for the local land-owners. The estate labourers may have occupied parts of the two outbuildings around the courtyard at Gadebridge, and it is possible that part of a building found about 500m from Boxmoor villa provided accommodation for some of its workers. At Northchurch on the other hand there is no trace of outbuildings suitable for labourers, and it is possible that here and at Berkhamsted, the labourers lived on the hill above the villas. This may account for traces of Roman occupation and building debris at Frithsden and Norcott Hill, in locations unlikely to have been occupied by villas. There is no evidence at present to suggest isolated and independent farmsteads or agricultural villages, nor of extensive field systems associated with the villas. The slopes of the valley are the most likely areas for crop cultivation, and the valley bottoms the probable location of pasture, but modern farming and settlement and the clay with flints which covers all but the valley floor together combine to make detection of buried field boundaries extremely difficult.

Moving from the vicinity of the civitas capital to that of a minor town, Godmanchester, we have already noted earlier the scarcity of villas in this area.[77] Godmanchester is situated on a low gravel island just about the flood level in the middle of the Ouse valley. Alluvium and gravels overlie the thick deposits of boulder clay in the vicinity, so that aerial photography provides some useful information about the environs of the town. A long programme of fieldwork and excavation has enabled a reconstruction of the history of both the town and the surrounding landscape in the Roman period. By the later third century the town may have become a vicus with a local administrative role; it also possessed defences and a market place, and until it was destroyed by fire in the last decade, a *mansio* serving travellers on Ermine Street. Around the town Green has identified areas of infield and outfield on the basis of the density of Roman material, mainly pottery, found on the fields. The infield occupies about 100ha (250 acres) and the outfield about 300ha (750 acres), with the former occupying the best arable, above the 30m contour, and the latter distributed further afield along the gravel terrace and also onto some areas of boulder clay. The infield was cultivated in a series of small fields of between 0.5 and 1.5ha, linked by droveways, but the outfield may have been less tightly organised, except on the heavier damper soils where there are clear traces of lazy-bed cultivation. Pasture-land lay further out, and there were meadows by the river, but pollen samples suggest little woodland in the vicinity of the town. Some of these lowest-lying areas were lost to farming in the third century by flooding, and equally some areas of infield had by then been considerably reduced by the development of cemeteries serving the town. The indication from both excavation within the town and wider field-survey are that most of the infield and outfield areas were farmed from within the town throughout the town's history, as part of a land allotment originating in the Flavian period. By the third century, however, the sole villa established nearby, to the north-east of the town, was a flourishing estate. Aerial photography, survey and excavation have combined to identify an enclosed rectangular area of arable which may have been spade-cultivated rather than ploughed. The labour force needed for this work may have lived in the old villa building when the new and much larger one was built in the third century, or they may have lived in town a little over a kilometre away.

A different pattern again emerges from our third area, in the vicinity of Fotheringhay, five kilometres south-west of Durobrivae.[78] Extensive areas of river gravels on the floor of the Nene provide excellent cropmarks, and they are also found on the limestone and marls of the slightly higher ground. At Fotheringhay Lodge crop-marks reveal a double-ditched trackway which for about 400m is flanked on either side by narrow ditched enclosures. (fig. 34) Roman pottery is found over the whole of the gravel ridge on which this complex sits, and there is little doubt that this is the site of a Roman village. At the south end of the settlement is a stone-founded rectangular house about 36m × 13m built of limestone and with tesselated floors and a tiled roof. A slightly smaller building is situated about 60m to the south-east. Although the detailed chronology of the village and the villa have not yet been established there is no reason to think they are not contemporary, and we appear to have here an example of a villa and its dependent village. The village cemetery appears to lie at the opposite, north-west, end of the settlement, and beyond the village in all directions are fragmentary traces of field-systems. This pattern may be repeated three kilometres further down-stream at Yarwell. A building was partly examined here in 1953 and both its size and a stone capital found in the excavations suggest it is a villa. It may be associated almost certainly with rectilinear enclosures and two droveways seen on aerial photos. Less than 500m to the east begins an extensive scatter of pottery at a point where Artis recorded Roman buildings; on the south-east fringe of the occupation area are traces of a cemetery. The interpretation of this complex of remains as a villa and associated village seems reasonable. A third villa is known about 1.5 kms to the north again, close to the Irchester-Water Newton road, but there are no known traces of a village associated with it. Both south of Fotheringhay villa, and between it and Yarwell to

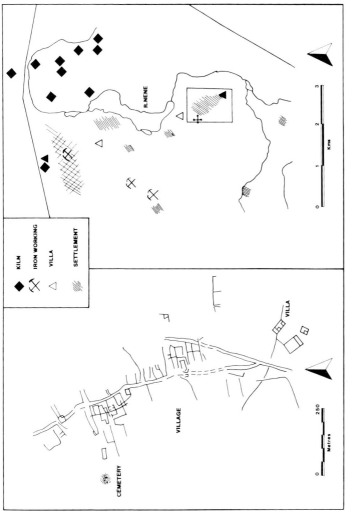

Fig. 34.   Settlement in the Fotheringhay area, lower Nene Valley, and the villa and village at Fotheringhay.

the north, crop-marks and field-walking have revealed further elements certainly or probably, part of the Roman landscape. Small rectangular enclosures, sometimes with traces of a small timber building within them, may represent the sites of farmsteads, possibly operating as tenancies of the villa estates. Fragmentary sections of the trackways which linked them together can be seen too. To the north of Yarwell no such enclosures have been identified, but in Old Sulehay Forest Artis recorded a dozen iron-working sites, and sandwiched as they are between Yarwell villa and that to the north they too seem likely to have been part of a villa estate. Meanwhile, across the river in the loop of the Nene, the Stibbington and Sibson pottery kilns were equally active in the later third century. All of these estates, agricultural and industrial, were within easy reach of Water Newton, and of Ermine Street; they also had the benefit of water transport via the Nene close at hand.

The three small portions of landscape that we have looked at appear to be quite different one from the other. In the Chilterns, villa estates were not only the most prominent component of the rural settlement pattern, but on present evidence they were essentially the only significant form of rural settlement. Villa labour forces lived either at the estate centre or else, perhaps, in isolated buildings within the estate. Around Godmanchester there is evidence for land usage but little for rural settlement. Much of the land around Godmanchester, probably far beyond the limits even of the so-called outfield, was apparently farmed by the townspeople. The labour force for the only villa near to the town on the south side of the Ouse may also have lived in the town. Around Fotheringhay, on the other hand, it appears that substantial agricultural labour forces lived in villages adjacent to the villa residences, and that other farmers, whether holding land or as tenants of the estates, occupied small enclosed farmsteads. Industrial activities may have played a significant part in the villa economies of this area, and in a sense the villas of the lower Nene Valley may represent a microcosm of the economy of the civitas as a whole with a successful blend of industrial and agricultural enterprise.

5

Industry and the Economy

The economy of the civitas of the Catuvellauni was, of course, a part of the economy of the province as a whole, and that in turn was part of the economy of the Roman empire. The empire certainly made economic demands of a civitas such as that of the Catuvellauni in a number of ways, of which the most significant were probably the tax on land and property, and the *annona* or corn levy. There were several other forms of taxation, however, including local taxes which would be used to maintain roads in the civitas territory, and customs dues on goods entering the province from abroad. These taxes all had their effect on both the agricultural and industrial production which formed the backbone of the economy of the civitas.

Agriculture

There can be no doubt that agriculture employed the majority of the people of the civitas during the Roman occupation just as it did in the pre-conquest period. Indeed, the demands of the Roman government to meet the needs of the army of occupation may well have stimulated increased productivity from the land, achieved by a combination of colonisation of new land, marginal improvements in farming methods, and greater powers of coercion. The improvements made to British farming techniques during the Roman occupation have been hotly debated, but cumulatively they should not be lightly dismissed. They included the heavier plough with coulter, two-handled scythes, sophisticated corns-ovens, large rotary mill-stones, high-capacity stone-built granaries, new crops, and new specialisms (such as fish-breeding). We have already seen some evidence for the colonisation of new areas in the previous chapters, with the establishment of estates in the western Chilterns in the later first century as an example. Whether or not the clearance and occupation of areas previously heavily wooded were first initiated after the Roman invasion is more debatable, but certainly the clearance of these areas was continued throughout the Roman period. In particular it is becoming increasingly clear that areas such as Rockingham Forest which until recently were thought to have remained as primary woodland until the 19th century AD were cleared and occupied in the Roman period and only subsequently reverted to woodlands in the period between the fifth and eleventh centuries.[1] All the indications are that, although settlement may have been particularly dense on the river gravels, all parts of the civitas territory were occupied and exploited by agriculture during the Roman period.

Exactly how this vast area was agriculturally exploited it is still impossible to assess on the basis of the archaeological evidence available; the evidence is quite simply too ambiguous, unreliable and above all too little to enable such an assessment to be made. In general terms the agricultural use of the territory can probably be best understood at present by considering its geology and pedology.[2] The area can be divided into three main geological zones, each running broadly east-west; these are, from north to south, the Middle Lias and Cornbrash, the Clays and Gaults, and the Chalk. Deposits of boulder clay are widely spread on the first two zones, and over the Middle Lias and Cornbrash the variety of soils together with river gravels and sands inevitably encourage mixed arable and pastoral farming. The central zone of clays on the other hand are best suited to a pastoral economy, varying from poor ill-drained sheep and cattle pasture in the east to better, richer pastures suitable both for dairy and beef cattle in the west. A band of arable along the foot of the chalk scarp is succeeded by sheep pasture on the scarp itself and along the crest of the Chilterns. On the chalk dip-slope the valley floors contain a variety of soils, but the slopes and hill-tops are covered with clay-with-flints. Cattle pasture is found mainly on the valley floor, and arable fields on the slopes, so that this is another area suitable for mixed farming. Perhaps two-thirds of the civitas territory then naturally favoured mixed farming, and (as elsewhere in Roman Britain) arable farming and pastoralism were practised on the great majority of farms, even where soils and topography encouraged a substantial bias towards one activity or the other. Direct evidence for arable farming is widely but thinly spread and by its nature rarely allows any detailed discussion of an arable economy. The distribution of some seventy corn-ovens, at over thirty sites throughout the area, for example, emphasises that arable farming was widely practised but it tells us nothing of its importance relative to pastoralism at individual farms. In the absence of extensive surviving arable field-systems it is difficult to identify any farms where arable farming may have been of particular importance although the 14 corn-ovens at Hambleden, the building interpreted as a grain-processing unit at Saunderton,[3] a granary at Gorhambury, and the separate mill-building at Wood Burcote might all be taken as pointers in that direction.[4] The long narrow fields seen on aerial photographs at Ashwell[5] suggest that the heavier coulter plough was in use, and this might be related also to the appearance of one-way plough-marks, probably at first century date, at Latimer and Gadebridge.[6] The crops being grown in these fields appear to have been mainly wheat, and especially spelt, to judge from the material found in grain samples discovered at Sandy, Churchill, Godmanchester and Braughing, but barley occurs in small quantities in at least four samples, and oats in another, whilst legumes have been found at Verulamium and Odell.[7] Some legumes may have been grown along with new vegetable and fruit crops in the large enclosures around villas like Ashwell, Islip and Radwell. Market-gardening, though perhaps rather more for home consumption than the market-place, may have become a common-place element in the villa economies of the Catuvellauni, and traces of gardening activity were found within the villa courtyard at Latimer.[8] Equally, many of the small enclosed plots close to dwelling houses at native farmsteads are probably best explained as garden plots rather than stock-pens.

Nevertheless, stock-pens and enclosures are to be seen on many aerial photographs of the Nene and Ouse valleys, and together with the numerous if fragmentary droveways they clearly point to a significant level of pastoral activity in these areas. The stock enclosures characteristic of this activity are associated with both native farms, such as Thorpe Achurch and Odell (first to third centuries), and with villas such as Barnack and Hall Farm, Orton Longueville. Where we have faunal samples available, they suggest that cattle were not only the principal source of meat but that they probably outnumbered sheep. At Lynch Farm, Godmanchester, and Bancroft, cattle represented between 47% and 57% of the animals in the faunal samples, and sheep between 21% and 27%, so that there appears to be no major differences between town-based farming, and that on villa estates and native farms in this area.[9] The samples noted, however, are all third-fourth century ones, and there is some evidence to suggest that in the earlier period the bias towards cattle had not been quite so pronounced. At Godmanchester, for example, the first-early second century sample produced 45% cattle (MNI) as against 57% in the third-fourth century sample, at Towcester in the late 1st-mid 2nd century cattle and sheep appear in roughly equal numbers, and the same pattern is repeated in, the admittedly small, early and late samples from Gadebridge and Latimer in the Chilterns.[10] There is no reason to think that this shift in emphasis was related to climatic changes and it is tempting to suggest that it was a response to the increasing demands of taxation, including taxation in kind to maintain the army, in the later Roman period.

The dominance of sheep in the second century sample from Brixworth, on the other hand, is such that it probably reflects a genuine difference in the pastoral economy of this villa estate situated in the hill country between the valleys of the Nene and Welland.[11] Equally, the Chiltern villas do not seem to have given cattle the same numerical dominance they had in the Ouse and Nene valleys, although the samples from Latimer, Gadebridge, Northchurch and

Boxmoor are all small.[12] Not only are sheep relatively more important here, but pig regularly provide between 20% and 30% of the sample. This may partly reflect the continued influence of the pre-Roman economy in the area; at Skeleton Green, for example, the late Belgic sample yielded figures of pig 36%, cattle 28% and sheep 26%.[13] It may also indicate that the upper slopes of the Chilterns were still wooded, since there is no evidence of intensive pig-rearing in sties and little available land in the valley bottoms that could be spared for pigs. In pastoralism, as in the broader farming economy, the Chiltern villa estates seems to epitomise the 'mixed' economy.

Neither in the Chilterns or elsewhere is there much sign of agricultural specialisation. It has been suggested that the combination of many corn ovens and a faunal sample allegedly dominated by horse and cattle at Hambleden point to an economy geared to specialised corn, beef and leather production for the army, but no details of the faunal sample have ever been published.[14] Specialisation on a much more modest scale is represented by the fish-pond at Lynch Farm,[15] but in the Nene Valley specialisation for the majority of land owners may have meant industrial rather than agricultural activity.

Pottery Manufacture

The Nene Valley potteries are but one of three major pottery industries to be found in the canton of the Catuvellauni, with others located around Oxford and between Verulamium and London. In addition there were other kilns in Herts, Bucks, Bedfordshire and the upper Nene Valley which contributed to the local supplies of pottery for rural and urban settlements alike. (fig. 35)

Of the major potteries, those south of Verulamium are the earliest. Peacock regards the Brockley Hill-Radlett-Aldenham complex as a nucleated urban industry centred on Verulamium,[16] but the kilns are spread over a distance of twenty kilometres and essentially a ribbon development along Watling Street rather than a true nucleation. Further-

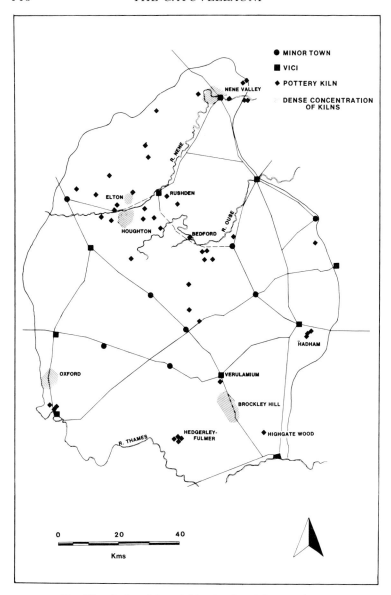

Fig. 35.   Industrial activities in the civitas territory.

more the potteries nearest Verulamium, including those inside the town and by the London Gate as well as the Munden kiln, are rather later than the kilns at Brockley Hill-Radlett and they did not specialise in mortaria manufacture in the same way as the Brockley Hill potteries. The principal concentration of major potteries is along a five kilometre length of Watling Street, and there can be little doubt in view of the wide distribution of the products, that much of the pottery was carried to London for shipment to other parts of the province. Despite much patient work by local archaeologists we still have a very patchy picture of the pottery works – lengths of ditches and trackways, cobbled yards, clay pits and puddling pits, and more than a dozen kilns at Brockley Hill itself.[17] The earliest kilns were in use in the 60's when Albinus, Oastrius and Secundus were producing mortaria and between this time and the mid-second century when production came to an end at least another dozen named mortaria manufacturers are known to have worked here. Several of them operated kilns at Brockley Hill and Radlett, and in the case of the most prolific of all mortaria manufacturers – Albinus – we know that when he died or retired, his son Matugenus carried on the business. Other Brockley Hill potters such as a G Attius Marinus were less successful here and moved on to establish new mortaria kilns at Mancetter/Hartshill in Warwickshire in the early second century. The success of these kilns may have been one of the most potent factors in the decline of the Brockley Hill industry from the Hadrianic period. We still do not understand how the Brockley Hill/Radlett potteries were organised. Brockley Hill was known as Sulloniacis in the Roman period, which implies that it was, initially at least, an estate belonging to a man named Sullonios or his family.[18] He may have rented out plots of land to the various potters who worked here, and who one assumes probably came originally from the continent; the potters' names are a mixture of Roman (Castus, Marinus, Secundus) and Celtic (Doinus, Sollus, Moricamulus). Whatever the precise organisation at the kilns, the venture was hugely successful for sixty or seventy years, with the kilns supplying the bulk of mortaria found in northern

Britain in the first century, and also penetrating the Welsh market.[19]

As the Brockley Hill potteries went into decline, those of the lower Nene Valley were just beginning. Although the Nene Valley kilns produced mortaria they yielded a far wider range of products than the Brockley Hill kilns and the two events are probably only marginally connected. Certainly, the Mancetter-Hartshill kilns took over the mortarium trade. The earliest kilns in the lower Nene Valley were those at Longthorpe, built close to the legionary vexillation fortress whose needs they served.[20] Over thirty kilns were built and used here during the occupation of the fortress from c. AD 50 to around AD 65. They produced a standard range of domestic forms – flagons, narrow-necked jars, beakers, bowls and dishes – in buff and grey wares. However, large storage jars in calcite-gritted ware, found both in the fortress and at the kilns, seems not to have been produced in the Longthorpe kilns but to have been the product of another local pottery as yet undiscovered. Significantly, when the garrison moved away in the mid-60's, the kiln site reverted to agricultural use and there is no reason to think that this successful but short-lived venture was in any direct way ancestral to the Nene Valley pottery industry of the period c. 150–400. Indeed, the origins of that industry are still obscure and debated. It has long been argued that the scale of the industry, its technology and its products are best explained by assuming it was established by entrepreneurs from the continent, and from Germania Inferior in particular where colour-coated white-bodied wares were already being produced.[21] This still seems the most likely source of inspiration for the colour-coated industry, although we should not exclude the possibility that it was founded by Britons, possibly migrating (in the same way as the mortaria manufacturers) from Colchester where colour-coated products were being made. The Nene Valley industry, however, produced not only colour-coated wares but also grey wares, and there is a strong case for believing that the potters who produced the first Nene Valley grey wares in the mid-second century had moved to the Water Newton area from much nearer at hand,

either the upper Nene Valley or the Ouse valley.[22] Grey
wares had been manufactured in these areas for decades
before the earliest known Nene Valley production began at
Hall Farm and Normangate Field in the period c. AD
125–150. On present evidence it is possible to envisage a
two-stage development of the Nene Valley potteries, with
grey wares being produced from the period around AD 130
and the subsequent arrival of colour-coated technology and
potters two or three decades later. The date at which
colour-coated production began is still uncertain; the earliest excavated kilns producing it are probably no earlier than
the late second century, but colour-coated ware found in the
Antonine fire deposit of c. AD 155 at Verulamium is
thought likely to be from the Nene Valley, so that
production may have begun no later than c. AD 150.
Although single workshops certainly produced both colour-
coated and grey wares during the third century, it is
therefore possible to argue that the Nene Valley industry
centred on Water Newton was begun by local potters
producing grey ware in the Hadrianic period, and that their
success, together with the size of the local market, the clay
resources, and the availability of water transport, attracted
the colour-coated producers to the area shortly after.

Certainly the two products were not in major competition
with one another.[23] The grey wares were used for the
manufacturers of domestic pottery for the local market,
producing the same basic range of vessels as the earlier
Longthorpe kilns, and dozens of other local pottery
industries all over the province. The colour-coated
production, in contrast, was concentrated on a limited range
of specialised products, particularly beakers. (fig. 36) In the
third century 'hunt cups' and barbotine decorated beakers
were in high demand over much of the province, and the
so-called 'Castor box' was also in vogue. It was only in the
fourth century that grey ware production declined as
colour-coated fabrics were used with much greater frequency for forms such as the dish, bowl and flagon. By this
time, too, the Nene Valley kilns were producing quantities
of 'imitation samian' in a white fabric covered with a
colour-coat varying from red to orange-brown and in forms

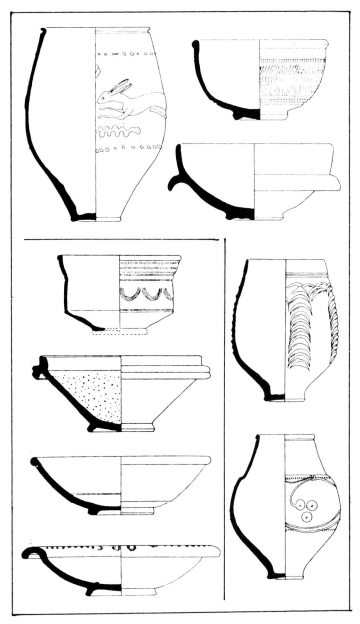

Fig. 36. Nene Valley and Oxford wares.

copying samian forms 31, 36, 37, 38 and 45. Although this was essentially a late-third and fourth century initiative, matching those of the Oxfordshire and New Forest kilns, it is interesting to note that an early example of a British kiln trying to break into the former 'samian market' was located at Stanground, near Peterborough, and produced imitations of forms 36 and 37 in the early third century.[24] This rapid response to the decline of samian production in Gaul reflects well on the commercial acumen of the Nene Valley potters, even though in this instance they may have underestimated the amount of samian still available in storage and in circulation.

Although about eighty individual kilns have been discovered and excavated in Water Newton area, we still know remarkably little about the way in which the industry was organised. This is partly because the majority of the kilns were excavated by Artis in the early nineteenth century and we have insufficient information about what he found and in particular about the relationships between kilns and adjacent buildings and other features. It also reflects the fact that even today, most pottery kilns are excavated as isolated structures rather than as elements of a much larger unit. Two areas where workshops as well as kilns have been excavated are at Stibbington and in Normangate Field, Castor. Artis uncovered eight rectangular buildings in Normangate Field, mostly with a single large room or workshop, together with kilns, clay heaps and a well;[25] he recorded no traces of property boundaries, and there is nothing in the apparently haphazard arrangement of buildings and other structures to indicate individual 'factories'. Aerial photographs, on the other hand, reveal many ditched enclosures, served either by Ermine Street or two minor roads which join it. Recent excavations have added some useful details to the picture.[26] The earliest Roman activity here, in the mid-second century, may have been the production of grey wares in bonfires and clamps by potters who actually lived not here but in Durobrivae. Kilns and permanent buildings of stone and timber begin to appear by the late second century. One group, set back from Ermine Street and served by a

droveway or lane, comprises three circular buildings, one
with a tesselated floor, and a rectangular barn, converted by
the addition of a portico, apse and tesselated floor into
something more sophisticated. It has been suggested that
these may be shrines on the analogy of the circular temples
not far to the west of Durobrivae at Brigstock and
Collyweston. The absence of shrine furniture of any kind
and the location of four such structures in the middle of an
industrial area, however, suggest that they may equally well
have been the homes of potters working here. A circular hut
with tesselated floor certainly served a domestic and craft
function at Great Weldon villa, only 5 kms north-west of the
Brigstock temples. Such buildings were certainly not
extravagant for the potters who operated in Normangate
Field if we are to judge from the burial found in a small
mausoleum on the other side of the lane; amongst this
lady's jewellery were a silver brooch and gold and silver
ear-rings. If the lane acted as a property boundary, she may
have been associated with the pottery workshop to the south
alongside Ermine Street. (fig. 37) This building, an aisled
barn about 22m x 12m, was flanked on one side by a pit and
on the other by a kiln and appears to form a workshop unit,
though other kilns and pits should be expected nearby.
Further east, aerial photographs reveal a series of
substantial stone buildings which may belong to further
similar units. Whether such workshops and the plots in
which they stood were independently owned or were part of
a single large enterprise is uncertain, though it has been
suggested that the villa at Castor overlooking Normangate
Field was built on the proceeds of the pottery industry there
by a single successful businessman. A third possibility is
that Normangate Field was owned by a single land-owner
who leased-out plots to potters who then erected their own
workshops and kilns and worked for themselves. This seems
the more likely of the three alternatives.

A similar situation may have existed in the Sibson-
Stibbington area, on the land which lay in the bend of the
Nene. Third and fourth century kilns are numerous here,
and Wild excavated a workshop unit similar to that found in
Normangate Field.[27] The workshop building, about 12m

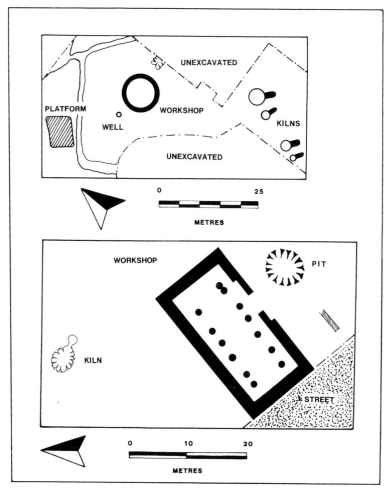

Fig. 37.   Pottery workshops at Normangate Field, Castor (bottom) and at Churchill, Oxon. (top)

long and half as wide, was of timber on stone foundations and contained four tanks for clay. Outside were a well and a pit, and two kilns of typical Nene Valley type with tongue-shaped pedestal and fire-bars. One kiln produced domestic grey-wares and the other colour-coated flagons, boxes and dishes as well as mortaria and 'imitation samian', so that by this time certainly, single small workshops were producing the whole range of Nene Valley wares. Kilns previously excavated at Stibbington revealed a similar range of products and like other Nene Valley kilns they were large enough to fire up to 500 pots in a single operation, an indication of the scale and success of the industry perhaps, even at a time when it was facing competition from the Oxford potteries on the other side of the civitas territory. (fig. 38)

Fig. 38.   An abandoned kiln at Water Newton.

As in the Nene Valley, the earliest kilns in the Oxford region date to soon after the Roman conquest and they are short-lived and have little or nothing to do with later development of a major pottery industry in the area. The kilns at Cassington and Hanborough are both on the west of the Cherwell, and are well away from the main focus of the Oxford kilns in the suburbs of Oxford itself.[28] The late first century kilns at Overdale are also west of the Cherwell, and it is not until the early second century that kilns appear at Sandford and Littlemore, and also further south at Dorchester, within the Catuvellaunian canton. There was continued expansion of the industrial area at Oxford into Cowley and Churchill, and in the late third century new kilns were developed both to the north, at Headington, and to the south at Baldon.[29] This picture of progressive extension of the production areas is matched by increasing quantities of Oxfordshire Ware on both urban and rural sites, and by the extension of its market area in the late 3rd and 4th centuries.

The initial success of the Oxford kilns was relatively local, though some vessels reached Verulamium to the east and Gloucester to the west, and was based on a range of products which included mortaria, flagons and imitations of samian forms. (fig. 36) The distinctive mortaria in a white fabric with a pink core and multi-coloured translucent quartzite grits found a ready market in the southern part of the canton following the demise of the Brockley Hill industry, and eventually came to dominate the mortaria market in the southern half of the province as a whole. It was not until the later third century, however, that the Oxford kilns developed other products which ensured a major share of the market for table wares. The red colour-coated wares were developed as an alternative to the Nene Valley and New Forest 'imitation samian', and like those wares they were used to manufacture a range of shapes taken from the samian repertoire, notably forms 31R, 36, 37, 38 and 45. Decoration was by roulette, stamped rosettes, and white paint. Alongside this popular fabric the kilns produced white ware decorated in red paint known as 'parchment ware'; it was used mainly to manufacture wall-sided bowls with moulded rims and carination, although small jars and occasionally platters were also made in the fabric. Unlike the Nene Valley, where individual workshops seem to have made both grey wares and colour-coated wares, the parchment wares were manufactured only in the northern potteries and the colour-coated 'imitation samian' only in the central and southern workshops.

The organisation of the Oxfordshire kilns is as poorly

understood as that of the Nene Valley potteries. Young has argued that the sudden and substantial expansion of the industry in the mid-3rd century can only be explained by the intervention of new entrepreneurs who recognised that the combination of good clay sources, existing expertise, and good communications made this area an obvious one on which to base a new industry aimed at the now wide-open market for home-produced table-wares.[30] Fulford, on the other hand, believes that late Roman rural pottery industries including Oxford may have been created in response to the increasing burden of taxation on urban facilities.[31] There is no way in which useful light can be thrown on the problem, but there is no evidence from the Oxford kiln sites of wealthy entrepreneurs living in the immediate area in the way that we find well-appointed villas close to the Nene Valley kilns. If such men were directly involved in the Oxford kilns, they must have lived at Alchester or Dorchester, or possibly in villas like Islip, some miles from the pottery fields. Alternatively, as Young suggests, the impetus may have come from businessmen or merchants who made bulk purchases of the products and ensured their wide dispersal and marketing. Certainly the little evidence available from the potteries themselves suggests that individual units were small, with one or two buildings used as workshops and home, and a few kilns. The most recent unit excavated, at Churchill, proved to consist of a circular workshop with a cobbled floor and small T-shaped drying oven, a well, a working platform, and four kilns, all enclosed within an area drained by ditches.[32] (fig. 37) On present evidence, the great Oxford potteries were made up of a series of such units; they were linked by a common range of products and a common marketing network, but there is no reason on present evidence to suppose that they were linked in any closer and more formal relationship.

The extent to which the individual units which made up the Oxford potteries were different to the workshops of the smaller potteries operating within the canton is open to debate. At a glance, the unit just described at Churchill is similar to that excavated at Highgate Wood in north

London, yet the demand for Oxford wares was such that we have no difficulty in assuming that the Churchill potter was essentially a full-time specialist. At Highgate a careful appraisal of the evidence suggests that the potters here worked not only part-time but very intermittently, and the same may be true of some of the other local potteries such as those at Fulmer-Hedgerley in south Bucks, at Bromleyhall Farm (Herts), at Souldrop and Eastcotts (Beds), and at many sites in the upper Nene Valley. The market for many of the wares produced by these kilns was extremely localised and therefore small, and the amount of potting activity must have been correspondingly limited. It is impossible in the space available to do justice to these small industries but a few points of particular interest may be noted.

The Highgate Wood potteries, which are probably representative of several potteries operating in the north London area, produced grey wares in the native tradition between c. AD 50–AD 100, and rather finer grey wares in the following half century.[33] However, careful study of the excavated material suggests that it represents little more than six months work, and that potting here was therefore a part-time activity which took place in short bursts at widely spaced intervals. Altogether the site yielded remains of ten kilns, as well as pits, a circular hut and drainage ditches, and it should serve as a useful reminder that the remains of several kilns and other features need not document a specialist pottery industry. It may well be that the widely spread kilns producing Bedfordshire grey wares operated in a not dissimilar fashion, although excavation of the production sites has not been extensive enough to allow a clear picture of the activity on them.[34] The discovery of a corn-drying oven, querns and possible granary on the site of the kilns producing 'Clapham shelly ware' might suggest that potting was here an adjunct of farming, but the pottery production began in the first century and the agricultural remains belong to the second century.[35] The demise of the Clapham kilns may have ensured the continued production of the Harrold kilns, also producing 'shelly ware' from the later first century, and continuing to do so until the fourth century, but again the nine or ten kilns in which this production occurred may well have operated on a part-time and intermittent basis.[36]

This is less likely for the kilns which cluster in the parishes of Brafield, Great Houghton and Little Houghton in the upper Nene Valley. Even though there has been little exploration of these remains, the kiln sites are so numerous that they must indicate an important local industry which operated on a regular if part-time basis producing second century grey wares.[37] The same may probably be said for the kilns across the river at Ecton, where it is reported that over 60 kiln sites can be identified.[38] The most interesting aspect of the upper Nene Valley potteries, however, is the insight they provide into the beginnings of the Romano-British industry. Potteries of the mid-first century AD are known at several sites including, Weekley, Far Cotton, Hardingstone and Rushden.[39] At Far Cotton and Hardingstone the pottery was produced in the native tradition, though the Hardingstone products included some which were hand-made but wheel-finished. At Rushden on the other hand, an existing native settlement and industry was initially taken over by potters producing exotic fabrics and shapes who must surely have followed the army to the area.[40] After a short period production reverted to wares in the Belgic tradition which were produced in large quantities and with increasing signs of Roman influence, until the period around AD 70, after which production fell away rapidly and was continued thereafter on a much reduced scale. A similar reduction was noticed at Hardingstone and Weekley, and it may relate to the final removal of the military markets from the south-east midlands. The rapid rise and considerable production of these kilns, together with the signs of increasing Romanisation of their wares and the brief appearance of foreign potters at Rushden, all reflect the impact of the Roman army and conquest on the native pottery industry.

Iron Production

Whether or not the invasion had the same initial impact on

iron production is less clear, but the requirements of the
army would have been followed by those of town and
country as the development of roads, towns, and agriculture
got under way. The principal source of iron within the
civitas territory was in the north where carbonate ores occur
in sedimentary deposits. These were exploited in the Iron
Age, and they appear to have been utilised throughout the
Roman period too. Although the mineral resources of the
province were at the disposal of the government, there is no
evidence to suggest the government's active involvement in
the iron industry in the canton apart from small-scale
working in the works depot at Longthorpe.[41] Otherwise iron
working seems to have been left very much to the initiative
of the local land-owners and entrepreneurs. In many cases,
therefore, iron-working was but one element in the economy
of a settlement which largely depended on farming for its
livelihood. This is true of native settlements such as
Caldecote, Cottingham, Gretton and Quinton, as well as
villas like Great Weldon.[42] It is clear, however, that some
rural settlements were essentially based on an industrial
economy producing pottery or iron or both. The settlements
producing pottery in the Houghton-Brafield area, for example, also worked iron,[43] and iron-working was a significant
activity in the area close to Water Newton which we have
already seen to have been a major pottery-producing area.
Across the river from the Stibbington-Sibson kilns are traces
of extensive iron-working in the parish of Nassington.[44] (fig.
34) Artis recorded four Roman iron-working sites here and
recent discoveries include a small anvil found in a spread of
slag situated on an outcrop of Ironstone. At Sacrewell only
three kilometres to the north-east a villa was replaced by an
iron-working establishment in the fourth century.[45] Around
the demolished villa buildings, half a dozen bowl-furnaces,
a roasting furnace and a shaft furnace were discovered,
associated with dumps of slag and charcoal. Together with
evidence from Barnack to the north and from Normangate
Field to the east, these new discoveries suggest that iron-
working made a significant and possibly increasing
contribution to the economy of the Durobrivae area, and it
is interesting to note that the figure of Vulcan, patron of

smiths and ironworkers, appears on several Nene Valley beakers.

What is still uncertain is whether or not nucleated iron-working settlements were established in the region in the Roman period, and if so how they came into existence. One possible settlement of this sort is suspected in the northern part of Weekley Hall Wood, Geddington, where several areas of iron-working have been identified by the discovery of pits, ditches, slag, and remains of furnaces.[46] But the spread of remains to the south and to the east suggests an area of intensive exploitation rather than a nucleated settlement. A much stronger candidate is the settlement at Ashton, 18 kms to the east, where excavations have revealed a fragment of a nucleated settlement covering up to 15ha (37 acres).[47] The regularised settlement with a central street and lanes running off at right-angles was established some time in the later second century. Remains of nine or ten rectangular buildings have so far been recovered, mostly large one-roomed structures of workshop type. Hearths set in their floors and the large quantities of hammer-scale found indicate that smithing activities were carried out in several of these buildings. Building 1, first excavated, is a particularly well-documented smithy, with at least five furnaces, one of which was associated with a smith's hammer and mower's anvil. A quenching tank stood to one side, and another tank stood outside the building. At present, however, the evidence points to a settlement mainly concerned with smithing activities, and smelted iron was presumably brought here from the more scattered, iron-working settlements such as Geddington and Nassington, where smelting seems to have been the main activity. For this reason we should not too readily assume that Ashton was a settlement with an economy based essentially on iron-working. Away from the main street timber and stone buildings are found less regularly placed, and evidence of industrial activity is less. The excavations along the main street may have simply exposed a small industrial quarter of a settlement which was mainly concerned with agriculture. Certainly the beginnings of the settlement, in the earlier first century, seem to have been associated with an agricultural settlement of some importance, although two small pottery kilns of this pre-Roman phase indicate some craft activity. About AD 50/60 an extensive series of ditches seems to have been laid out and to have divided the settlement area into a series of plots or enclosures; later the ditches were replaced by fences. There is at least the possibility that this activity and the subsequent development of the settlement was initiated and controlled by a single land-owner. Apart from the regularity of layout, the discovery of a column fragment and two lead 'baptismal' tanks in two wells on the site suggests the proximity of a building of much greater sophistication than the industrial buildings and the presence of a wealthy Romanised family in the fourth century AD if not earlier.

It is possible that the settlement at the Cow Roast near Northchurch is similar to that at Ashton, in some respects.[48] Like Ashton it appears to have been first occupied in the late Belgic era, and to have been in continued occupation until the late third century. Military metalwork from the site suggests that there may have been some brief involvement with the requirements of the army in the mid-first century, but otherwise the settlement is clearly a civilian one. Chalk floors and postholes belonging to timber buildings are the main structural remains, but apart from nine wells there are also herring-bone floor tiles, and box-tiles as well as roof tiles, and these suggest one or more masonry buildings nearby. Iron-working debris was found in the occupation levels, as well as two bowl-furnaces, but a further six furnaces were found just 400m away, used from the mid-first to the late-third century and almost certainly part of the same roadside settlement. The settlement is only a kilometre from the Northchurch villa, whilst a hypocaust was recently found only 300m from the main concentration of iron furnaces and may belong to either a well-appointed house or a bath-house. Although the settlement is not as regular in its layout as Ashton and the majority of its buildings are less substantial, it appears to be a nucleated roadside settlement in which iron-working played an important role and which may be connected with a nearby villa and its estate. One other site in the Verulamium area where iron-working was an important element of the economy was Foxholes Farm near Hertford.[49] The settlement may extend over 10 ha (25 acres), but the degree to which it is nucleated is uncertain. In the fourth century, however, iron appears to have been smelted and worked on the site in quantity; over forty bowl furnaces and roasting ovens have been excavated, associated with crucible fragments. The discovery of four corn-ovens, however, emphasise that the settlement had an agricultural as well as an industrial base. At present we have no indications as to the nature of the buildings which made up the settlement.

Building Materials

In the southern part of the civitas territory most of the stone buildings were constructed of flint and mortar, and in the northern region of limestone. The extent to which the extraction and use of either material was commercial is unknown, but most rural settlements and villas presumably acquired local materials for themselves. The only building stone which appears to have been quarried for commercial purposes was Barnack rag-stone, quarried to the north of Durobrivae and used at Water Newton, Cambridge and Godmanchester as well as Verulamium.[50] West of Barnack, Collyweston slate was also quarried for roofing tiles and again it was widely used in the northern part of the canton and also reached the Verulamium area.[51] Despite the availability of water transport, however, building stone and roof slates were expensive items to trade over any distance and in addition to utilising local flint, the southern part of the civitas territory manufactured its own clay roofing and hypocaust box tiles. More than a dozen tile kilns are known in the canton, and they are heavily concentrated south of the Ouse. Tile kilns at Aldenham and Edgware lie at the northern and southern fringes of the Brockley Hill potteries and may have been constructed to supply tiles to Verulamium and London as well as nearby farmsteads and villas.[52] Similarly, the kilns at Netherwild and Park Street (fig. 39) may have been producing not just for estate consumption but for Verulamium.[53] At Netherwild several

Fig. 39. The early fourth century tile kiln at Park Street.

kilns in the mid-second century were manufacturing roof and flue tiles which would have been in current demand in the rebuilding activity following the Antonine fire. Similarly, the Park Street kiln was built early in the fourth century when demand in Verulamium was stimulated by rebuilding and new building work in the early years of the reign of Constantine. The range of products produced here – bonding tiles, tegulae, imbreces, flue tiles and square pilae pieces – is notably wide, and the appearance of a simple stamp with the monogram M is perhaps suggestive of the intention to market the tiles and not use them only in rebuilding on the villa estate itself. A third example of tile kilns geared to the needs of a nearby town may be the cluster of kilns four kilometres south-east of Braughing, near Little Hadham.[54] There must be other tileries still to be found close to several of the minor towns in the canton, however, and Verulamium must certainly have been served by extensive tileries which probably stood very close to the town. It must also have had lime-kilns working nearby, and it has been suggested that the chalk-pits dug at Gadebridge villa may have been for lime production to meet the needs not only of the estate but also of other nearby villas or Verulamium itself.[55] Lime-kilns found in the canton all seem too isolated to have been built for mainly commercial reasons, and they were probably constructed to facilitate building work nearby. The Newnham and Helpston kilns may have served the needs of their respective villas, and those at Wellingborough must have manufactured lime for use in building stone dwellings in the extensive settlement there.[56]

The embellishment of substantial buildings in both town and country appears to have been partly served by crafts which were centred on Durobrivae. The most notable of these, though possibly a short-lived enterprise, was the Durobrivan school of mosaicists.[57] Dated broadly between c. AD 350–380, the mosaics of this school are almost exclusively geometric and are noted for their imaginative use of the swastika-peltae and patterns of lozenges. (fig. 40) They appear to have been produced mainly for villa-owners, and the twenty or so sites which have yielded mosaics attributed to this school are found clustered in Northants, Lincolnshire and Leicestershire, with the distribution centred around Water Newton. Whether the mosaicists were actually based in the town is uncertain, although Artis did excavate a building there with one room which was being used as a mosaicists workshop, with heaps of sorted tesserae still lying on the floor.

A century before the Durobrivan mosaic school was established, the town may have seen the establishment of a mason's workshop.[58] Blagg has identified such a workshop on the basis of capitals with beads and indented fillets and with unusually short cyma mouldings. Examples have been found at Yarwell, Chesterton and Titchmarsh, and an outlying example at Hadstock in Essex, some 40kms from Water Newton. Architectural mouldings rarely survive in situ, having been robbed and re-used in a way that cannot be applied to mosaic floors, so that the small number of surviving examples so far noted may be misleading as to the significance of this workshop. The absence of suitable sources of nearby stone precluded Verulamium from developing such workshops, but it does seem to have been

Fig. 40. A Durobrivan mosaic from Great Staughton.

involved in the early development of the mosaic industry.[59] The distinctive 'nine-panel' mosaics of the Colchester-Verulamium school include some notable examples from the city itself, and although the school may have served Colchester at a time earlier than it provided mosaics for Verulamium, it seems likely that a workshop must have existed at Verulamium in the later second century. This is particularly so in view of the western 'outliers' of the group at North Leigh and Cirencester. It is still uncertain whether

there were two related workshops, in Colchester and
Verulamium, or whether a single workshop may have
moved its operations from the former to the latter, but the
Verulamium workshop seems to have survived into the third
century.

Marketing and Trade

The development of mosaic schools at Verulamium and
Durobrivae illustrates just one aspect of the relationship
between the towns and the rural settlements in the civitas,
with the towns in this instance providing a service for the
rural estates. The relationship between town and country in
Roman Britain as a whole has been the focus of much
discussion in recent years.[60] One view of the relationship
sees the towns as parasites living off the country, and this
has been developed further to envisage an administered
market in the first two centuries of the Roman occupation,
in which the civitas capitals monopolised trade and marketing both within and without the civitas. A corollary of
this model is that most minor towns were late developments
and that exceptions to that rule would be found not around
the tribal boundaries but mid-way between the civitas
capital and the edge of the canton. Equally, coinage would
scarcely circulate outside the capital since all trade and
marketing was deliberately channelled through it. The
extent to which coinage was of any importance in the
economy in the first to third centuries has indeed been
challenged, and it has been suggested that the economy was
essentially embedded in social relationships and operated
on the basis of reciprocity, redistribution and fixed price
transactions. It follows from this that 'market forces' were
unimportant and that self-regulating markets were
unknown during this period. It is possible to refute these
arguments in general terms as well as by particular
reference to the civitas of the Catuvellauni. The fora and
market halls not only at Verulamium but at other civitas
capitals were clearly built to act as public market places,
and at Wroxeter there is clear evidence that the forum was
being used for that purpose when it was destroyed by fire in

the mid-second century.[61] That these markets were self-regulating is surely demonstrated both by the *annona*, which enabled the state to operate outside the freemarket to ensure its corn supplies, and by Diocletian's edict which attempted to fix prices specifically to constrain the free-market. It is significant that the measure failed abysmally.

If we look briefly at marketing and the role of the small towns in the civitas of the Catuvellauni we can see too that there is little reason to envisage the operation of an 'administered market' in the canton. The distribution of the products of the three major potteries, for example, was clearly mainly undertaken by means of water transport, via the Thames and the Nene initially, to a series of nodal points found both within and without the civitas.[62] There is no reason whatsoever to suppose that even the mortaria of the Brockley Hill potteries were all exported through Verulamium, as opposed to being transported and channelled directly through London. The same would obviously apply to the products of the Barnack and Collyweston stone quarries which are mainly distributed only in the northern part of the canton. Even in the countryside well away from Verulamium, marketing of pottery was almost certainly undertaken mainly through market centres rather than through direct exchange between potter and client. Hodder has demonstrated this for potteries elsewhere in southern England, and there are pointers in this direction from studies of Bedfordshire 'grey wares'.[63] Equally, if we try and look at the problem from the opposite direction – that of products imported from elsewhere in the canton, from other civitas areas, and from other provinces, we arrive at a similar conclusion. We may take the example of Quinton, 75kms north-west of Verulamium, and 10kms west of Towcester, a small native settlement occupied up until the middle of the second century.[64] The pottery its occupants acquired was drawn from local sources such as the kilns at Ecton and Houghton, from kilns slightly further afield such as Harrold and the lower Nene Valley, and from more distant potteries such as Brockley Hill and Mancetter. In addition they obtained samian in moderate quantities and other imported materials ranging from Niedermendig querns, to north Italian bronze and glass. Such a wide-ranging selection of material must have been acquired through a market centre, and that centre was surely Towcester, not Verulamium. The presence of a flourishing small town at Towcester in the later first and second centuries is not an isolated phenomenon, and we saw in chapter three that all of the towns which we believe may have become vici were established no later than the Hadrianic period and most of them in the Flavian era. This situation is very different to that which should occur in an 'administered market' system, and the contrast is enhanced by the location of the seven towns along the periphery of the civitas territory. This distribution is clearly related to marketing factors[65] and emphasises that these minor towns not only existed but that they developed mainly to provide market facilities at a distance from the civitas capital. There is thus little reason to envisage an administered market system operating in the civitas of the Catuvellauni at any time from the Flavian period onward, nor is there any reason to think that reciprocity or redistribution played a significant part in exchange. The scarcity of coinage of the first and second century is explicable in other ways, such as the activity of the government in continually calling in early coinage and minting new debased coinage in its place, and occasionally chance reveals sites where some indication of the circulation of first and second century coinage has survived. The site of Gadebridge villa for example has produced about forty coins of the period and there is nothing to suggest that either the villa or its economy were in any way anomalous in the late first and second centuries.[65] At the same time, there is little doubt that many of the minor towns were at their most prosperous during the early decades of the fourth century, at which time they appear to have fulfilled a variety of social and administrative roles as well as economic ones.

6

The late Fourth and Fifth Centuries

From the middle of the fourth century onward, Britain was forcibly and repeatedly reminded that it did not exist in either a political or a geographical vacuum. Both the politics of the Roman Empire and the social and economic turbulence of western and northern Europe intruded upon, and interrupted, the normal course of events in Britain, and stimulated the process of change in this province as elsewhere. Attacks on the south-east coast of Britain by raiders from across the North Sea had become sufficiently severe by the late third century for military bases at Reculver in Kent and Brancaster in Norfolk to be supplemented by seven or eight new coastal forts.[1] These provided a defensive screen for the south-eastern quarter of the province which seems to have worked well until the middle of the fourth century. In AD 367, however, the west, north and south-east frontiers all came under attack at the same time and the defensive screen in the south-east was by-passed or overwhelmed. By the time Theodosius arrived with an army to restore the situation, the London area was infested with raiders according to our main source, the historian Ammianus Marcellinus.[2] The southern part of the Catuvellaunian canton we must therefore expect to have been directly affected by the raid of 367, though there is no reliable evidence for it amongst excavated sites in the area. A fire which destroyed part of the Park Street villa during the 360's and was followed by its abandonment might be linked to the events of AD 367–9 but it is more likely to have been the victim of accident.[3] Equally, traces of the restoration of cities to which Ammianus twice refers are difficult to detect in the towns of the civitas. The two known bastions and associated towers at Verulamium were said by Wheeler to be an integral part of the city wall, and all the available evidence suggests that this is correct.[4] They must therefore date no later than the late 3rd century, and in our view perhaps forty-fifty years earlier, and cannot be associated with other defensive bastions of the mid-fourth century often attributed to Theodosius. The seven rectangular bastions known around part of the defensive circuit at Durobrivae are undated. This leaves only a single fan-shaped tower at Godmanchester as possible evidence for the strengthening of the town defences in c. AD 369. The tower is built over the earlier defensive ditch and accompanied by a new wide ditch of fourth century type.[5] Furthermore, the unusual fan-shaped tower is paralleled by four fourth-century corner towers 50kms. to the north at Ancaster.[6] Presumably other towers existed at Godmanchester and have either been destroyed or remain to be found. Mid-late fourth century towers elsewhere in Britain take a variety of forms and the difference between that at Godmanchester and those at Water Newton need not imply that the latter cannot belong to the same period of defensive activity as the former. Certainly Durobrivae was in a relatively exposed position to attacks on the east coast and if new additions to defences were expected anywhere it would be here. If, as seems likely, the bastions on city walls were intended to take artillery (catapults), then it follows that small detachments of troops must have been garrisoned in the towns in order to maintain and operate the weapons. Whether such units would have been drawn from the regular garrison of the province, drafted or recruited from local peoples, or brought into the province from elsewhere is an open question.

Within fifteen years, however, any supplementation of the British garrison which may have taken place in 369 was reversed by the activities of Magnus Maximus. Maximus commanded troops in Britain and in AD 383 usurped the throne. He led an army, which must have included part of the British garrison, to the continent where he held sway until his defeat in AD 388. A decade later an expedition organised by the general Stilicho was sent to stiffen the defences of the province, but it has been argued that its main purpose was to reorganise the diminished garrison in such a way that more troops could be withdrawn to defend Italy itself. Whatever the intention in 397–8, three years later Stilicho was taking troops from Britain to fight on the continent. The inability of Rome to defend the province led to the army in Britain electing its own emperors in AD 406, the second of whom was a *municeps* – a city councillor – revealing how local men of wealth and influence could occupy positions of power, albeit by the agreement of the army. Within months he was replaced by a soldier, Constantine, who in order to head off a potentially devastating attack on Britain by Germanic tribesmen, led an army to Gaul. In his initial objective he was successful, but there can have been few if any troops left in Britain by now and in AD 409 the British decided that they must look to their own defence and administration. The Roman administrators were ejected, and although Constantine was subsequently defeated and killed, there is no indication that Rome ever reclaimed the province. Indeed, in AD 410, Honorius effectively recognised the independence of Britain by telling the civitates they must look to their own defence. For the civitates of south-eastern England this meant primarily that they must be prepared to repulse raids by Saxons and Franks. Although both the historical and archaeological evidence for Saxon raids and settlements in southern and eastern England is confused and confusing, there is little doubt that raids continued through the following decades and that by the mid-fifth century Saxons were settling in Britain. Although our concern is with the civitas of the Catuvellauni, it is therefore essential that we briefly consider the evidence for Saxon settlement within the civitas territory by the mid-fifth century.

Saxon Settlement

One source of evidence which can be firmly set on one side as irrelevant is the so-called Romano-Saxon pottery. This ware, which usually combines a Romano-British fabric and

form with bossed or stamped decoration similar to that on
Saxon pottery, cannot be the result of the fusion of the two
ceramic traditions following Saxon settlement because it
appears far too early in the archaeological record. The
Water Newton coin hoard of c. AD 350 was buried in a bowl
of this ware, and it seems to have been manufactured at
both Harston (Cambs) and Much Hadham (Herts) from the
early fourth century if not earlier, along with other Romano-
British wares.[7] Nevertheless, Romano-Saxon pottery is
interesting as perhaps the earliest of several possible mani-
festations of Germanic influence in the culture of fourth
century Britain.[8] The most controversial of these are the
bronze belt-pieces dating from the mid-fourth to early-fifth
century, found mainly in southern England and the
midlands, including several locations in the territory of the
Catuvellauni. When the group was initially identified it was
suggested that they belonged not only to military units but
specifically to Germanic ones,[9] and they therefore provided
evidence for the disposition of Germanic 'irregulars' – *laeti*,
foederati or *gentiles* – in late fourth century Britain.
Subsequent research has revealed that such buckles were
worn by regular units of the Roman army and cannot
therefore be taken as indicators of the presence of Germanic
troops alone.[10] Whether or not such buckles were also
acquired and worn by civilians is more open to debate, but
their primary military associations remain certain.

Two burials from Dorchester on Thames, one male and
the other female, include buckles of this group, and the
male was accompanied by a full range of belt pieces and had
clearly been buried with the complete belt.[11] In this instance
it is generally agreed that we have the burial of a late fourth
century soldier and almost certainly an officer. It is possible
that he was on secondment at Dorchester, just as Marcus
Varius Severus had been in earlier times, but it is also
possible that he commanded a small force of irregular
auxiliaries (*gentiles*). Unlike most Romano-British settlements, Dorchester saw a marked rise in the amount of
coinage in circulation in the reign of Theodosius (AD
379–95), which might be related to the presence of a
military garrison. At present, however, we have no good

evidence for any other local garrisons in the civitas territory, and more particularly nothing to suggest the presence of Saxon *laeti* like those settled at Mucking in the Thames estuary.[12] On present evidence, therefore, the first Saxon settlers in the canton of the Catuvellauni are those found in pagan Saxon cemeteries and settlements rather than in Romano-British ones.

The date at which the earliest of these cemeteries were in use is still disputed. There are at least three such cemeteries which have produced 'Luton' brooches which continental evidence dates to the late fourth-early fifth century. Two of these are in Bedfordshire, at Kempston and Luton, and the third in Oxfordshire at Berinsfield.[13] The earliest pottery in each cemetery is ascribed to the early-mid fifth century, but in each case material of the later fifth and sixth centuries is present in much greater quantities, and it is possible to argue that the brooches are occasional 'heirlooms' deposited long after their period of manufacture. The discovery of an early-mid fifth century belt-plate in an otherwise sixth century cemetery at Bishopstone in Bucks lends some support to this view.[14] However, in support of an early fifth century date for these burials one can point to other cemeteries where the pottery includes several examples of that period, including Cambridge and Sandy, and to the occupation site at Marholm, north of Water Newton, which yielded another example of a 'Luton' brooch. A group of burials at Ashwell (Slip End) is also of great interest since alongside early Saxon pottery were late Roman vessels; unless one assumes that the vessels had been robbed from earlier Roman burials it would be difficult to see them surviving in use much beyond the first quarter of the fifth century.[15] Equally at Orton Hall near Water Newton the early Saxon pottery included a mortarium made in Saxon fabric and bi-conical vase in Roman fabric, neatly suggesting a mixing and fusing of cultural traditions.[16] The evidence from Orton Hall is the more impressive because the early Saxon settlement here, with grubenhauser, one or more rectangular timber-frame buildings and various pits, is carefully sited around and between the Roman buildings rather than in or over them. (fig. 41) The implication

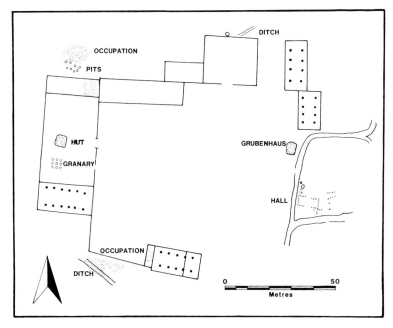

Fig. 41.   Orton Hall Farm – Roman buildings and pagan Saxon remains.

appears to be that the timber Romano-British buildings were still standing and some at least may still have been used by the first Saxon settlers. The fact that the Saxon occupation must have followed close on the Romano-British one is underlined by the re-cutting of Romano-British ditches *after* Saxon pottery had begun to accumulate in the fill, implying that there was continuity in the use of the ditch system and that the gap between Roman and Saxon use of the ditch must have been very short. A fine Frisian-style bone comb places Saxon occupation no later than the early/mid-fifth century, and it cannot be pushed any later since the latest material marking Saxon abandonment of the site belongs in the early sixth. Into broadly the same period may be placed another example of a Romano-British ditch system retained in use by early Saxon settlers at Caldecote, and the Saxon settlement and cemetery at Walton near Aylesbury, with both metalwork and pottery dating from the early fifth century. Preliminary study of finds from the Saxon settlement of grubenhauser and four-post structures at Pennyland, Milton Keynes, suggests that this settlement too might be an early foundation.[17] There seems to be sufficient early 5th century Saxon material to suggest that Saxons were arriving in the region and settling there during the first two or three decades of the fifth century. It remains true, however, that the majority of the Saxon cemeteries and settlements in the canton date from the late fifth or early sixth century, and that it is not until that period that the Saxons appear to have become a major element in the local population. We may also recall that it was not until AD 571, according to the Anglo-Saxon Chronicle, that Cutha fought the Britons and captured the villages of Limbury (by Luton), Aylesbury, Benson and Eynsham. This brief piece of history emphasises not only the continued presence in the late sixth century of Britons and British settlements, but also the continued bias of Saxon settlement and activity to the clay lands north of the Chilterns. All of the sites yielding evidence of early Saxon occupation that we have considered are either on the clay lands in the centre of the canton or in the lower Nene Valley. There is no doubt that the Saxons also moved along the Thames Valley to the Oxford area, but at present there is no evidence that they moved into the Chiltern valleys of Bucks and Herts before the late sixth century AD. We should also note that until the Chronicle entry of AD 571 there is nothing in the historical or archaeological record to suggest that Saxon settlement in the canton of the Catuvellauni was other than a peaceful and gradual process.

Rural settlements

Given the evidence of a slow and gradual Saxon infiltration into the canton, we should expect to find that Roman-British rural settlements at least continued in occupation with few signs of change until at least the mid-fifth century and in some areas much longer. Unfortunately, the withdrawal of Roman troops and administration induced a decline in the commercial economy of the province which saw the end of coinage, the collapse of major industries, and the gradual breakdown of communications and market systems. As a result, after c. AD 400 there was little material getting into circulation which provides any means of dating associated structures and occupations. This problem is particularly acute on 'native' sites which were further removed from the monetary economy and acquired fewer imported objects than the villas, and where datable artifacts are in any case relatively few in numbers. Yet because these settlements were less dependent on market facilities and on the continued availability of Roman technology and expertise to maintain their buildings and equipment, it is precisely these settlements that we would expect to be maintained for longest. There are scattered indications to confirm that occupation was maintained at least until the circulation of coinage ceased, with coins of Arcadius and Honorius found on settlement sites from Duston, Huntingdon, Aston and Ware.[18] The industrial settlement at Foxholes was also using coins at least to c. 390, and at the Cow Roast industrial site there were over thirty coins of AD 388 or later, suggesting a particularly active economy here in the last decade of the fourth century at least.[19] At some of these sites, Saxon occupation may have followed. At Foxholes, an interesting settlement of two grubenhauser, two long buildings and two square ones was constructed nearby, its inhabitants using a mixture of coarse grass-tempered ware and residual late Roman pottery.[20] Grass-tempered pottery turned up in the latest levels at Ware too, and we have already noted the evidence for continuity of the use of the ditch systems at Orton Hall and Caldecote. But the implications of these various scraps of evidence may well be different and should be treated with some caution. Whereas the evidence at Caldecote and Orton Hall suggests Romano-British farms surviving into the first quarter of the fifth century and then being rapidly superseded or transformed into Saxon ones, the grass-tempered pottery at Ware is small in quantity and does not herald a major Saxon occupation of the site; nor can it be dated closely or even firmly attributed to Saxon settlers. At Foxholes we cannot directly connect the Romano-British and Saxon occupations, and again the grass-tempered ware is not closely dated. The dangers of assuming continuity where Roman-British and pagan Saxon material occur on the same site has been emphasised by Kennett in relation to the settlement at Duston,[21] and all we can safely say is that on some sites evidence survives to indicate that rural farms and settlements were operating normally at the beginning of the fifth century.

When we turn to the villas, the picture in the north of the canton is broadly similar to that from the 'native' settlements, but perhaps because the decay and decline of a Romanised, stone-founded building leaves more permanent traces than that of a timber one, we are able to trace the process in more detail in a few cases. In the northern part of the canton there are several villas which appear to have continued in occupation until the end of the fourth century at least, and some of these produce evidence which suggests that up until at least c. 370–380 they were being maintained as well-furnished residences. At Thenford, for example, a farm building was converted into residential accommodation in the mid-fourth century and provided with six rooms, one of which boasted a mosaic floor.[22] A bath-suite was built, and underwent two extensions before it was finally demolished. How long the villa house and bath-suite were in use is uncertain, but the latest coins in the courtyard levels belong to Arcadius so that the estate was certainly working at the close of the fourth century. At Great Weldon, the rebuilding of a barn destroyed by fire in the middle of the century was followed by a series of alterations to the bath-suite of the villa.[23] Although baths appear to have been modified and repaired more frequently than other parts of villas, four phases of development after c. AD 350 argue for the continued use and maintenance of the bath-suite at Great Weldon into the last decade or two of the century. The Durobrivan mosaics at Great Weldon also belong in the second half of the fourth century, and it is likely that those at Castor and Nether Hayford do too, since the floruit of the school seems to be broadly c. AD 350–380. The Bancroft mosaics have been placed marginally earlier (c. AD 340), but Denton confirms that the school was still active post AD

370. The foundation and activity of a mosaic school in the region from c. AD 350 in itself says much for the buoyancy of both rural and urban settlement there in the period c. 350–380. On the other hand some decline in the quality of life in the villas is indicated by examples like Sacrewell and Bancroft. In the previous chapter it was noted that the villa house at Sacrewell was abandoned and probably demolished in the later fourth century and the site was then given over to iron-working.[24] Nothing so dramatic can be seen at Bancroft, but in two of the mosaic-floored rooms, open hearths were built directly on the floors, suggesting that the days of elegant living were past.[25] In one case, the hearth was laid after the tesserae had come loose from the floor and been cleared away, so that a date very late in the fourth century or later is probable. Coins again attest occupation certainly to the end of the century, and it was probably much later that two shallow graves were dug into the villa and Saxon pottery arrived on site. The same may be true of Saxon remains found on the sites of Brixworth and Walton villas too, but here there is in each case evidence to suggest that the villa was not used as a cemetery but for occupation. At both sites Romano-British occupation runs at least to the last quarter of the fourth century, and possibly to c. AD 400. At Brixworth, ten post-holes cut through the floor of room V and associated with two sherds of early Saxon pottery suggest that the walls of the building may still have been standing when the Saxon settlers took occupation of the site.[26] At Walton this is less likely, since an early Saxon brooch was found in the debris of a collapsed wall, and the Saxon occupiers appear to have cleared up debris, dug new ditches and then re-occupied the site.[27] There is nothing at any of these three sites to suggest continuity of occupation from Romano-British villa to Saxon farm. As far as the limited evidence can be interpreted, then, the villas in the northern part of the civitas territory reveal a similar pattern to that of native settlements in the same area. Between c. AD 350 and 380, villas and farmsteads alike were still thriving and even seeing some investment of effort and perhaps capital. Thereafter, though some villas were no longer properly maintained and began a slide into archi-

tectural decay, villa estates and farmsteads alike continued to function at the very least until coins were going out of circulation. A few farms like Orton Hall and Caldecote may soon have passed into Saxon hands, but others, and in particular villa buildings only reveal traces of Saxon occupation or use of the site much later.

This pattern is very different to that which can be identified in the Chilterns around Verulamium. The first and most striking difference, which can have no connection with Saxon settlers, is the state of the villas after c. AD 350. Of ten excavated villas, five or six were either abandoned or drastically reduced by the 350's. At High Wycombe and Harpsden there is nothing to suggest any activity at the sites after c. AD 350.[28] The same may be true of Welwyn (Rectory) where the floor levels contained six coins of Constantine I and nothing later, but later occupation without coins may have been overlooked.[29] Boxmoor and Gadebridge were also abandoned by c. AD 350 and AD 355 respectively, but in each case there is evidence of later occupation to which we will need to return shortly. Similarly, Latimer was drastically reduced in size at a time unlikely to be later than AD 350 and probably somewhat earlier, but occupation of a debased form continued and was followed by further occupation nearby.[30] The early demise of these villas, which had been amongst the earliest Romanised estates in Britain, is both surprising and incapable of any easy explanation. If they were really abandoned or severely curtailed in the period c. 350–355 it would be tempting to relate their decline to the confiscatory activities of Paulus, 'the Chain,' following the collapse of Magnentius' usurpation. But the picture is probably more complex than this. Boxmoor had been reduced in size at the beginning of the fourth century, several decades before it was abandoned. At High Wycombe the house had seen no improvements or structural maintenance since the early 3rd century, but the bath-house had been extended c. AD 325. Latimer was probably reduced in size before rather than after AD 350, and Gadebridge was abruptly abandoned and some of its buildings were deliberately demolished c. AD 355. Spread over several decades, but accelerating perhaps in the middle of the century, this pattern of the architectural decline of the villas is perhaps best explained in terms of a return to Verulamium by some of the estate owners who had previously occupied the villa residences. The abandonment of Park Street in the 360's after just two of its rooms had been destroyed by fire is probably a reflection of this same trend.

It is important to note, however, that the decline and even abandonment of the villas does not signal the end of Romano-British occupation on these sites. Continued use of the site at Boxmoor is indicated by several coins of the later fourth century through to Arcadius and by the discovery of a coin minted no earlier than AD 388 sealed beneath a trampled clay surface in room 6. Some sort of occupation by people who still used and acquired coins c. AD 400 seems certain.[31] At Latimer, the abandonment of the northern half of the main wing in the mid-fourth century was followed by a slow period of decline. Lumps of tesselated floor and broken floor tiles were ripped out of the now disused rear corridor and used to make alterations to the baths. Later, the south wing and most southerly rooms of the west wing were also abandoned and occupation reduced to just two rooms, a section of front corridor, a linking corridor and the baths. In these rooms the tesselated floors were poorly repaired with odd tesserae and even with lumps of tile, and attempts were made to repair patches of wall with old roof tiles. Then the baths were abandoned and used as a rubbish tip, leaving the occupants of a villa which once boasted nearly twenty rooms and a large bath suite using just two rooms and two short stretches of corridor. It is difficult to say how long this process of decline and contraction took before the villa was finally abandoned altogether, but pottery from the excavations of these rooms in 1910–12 includes types and fabrics of the later fourth century.[32] At Gadebridge, as at Boxmoor, coinage still circulated after the villa house was so abruptly abandoned c. AD 355. Occupation was now concentrated in one of the existing stone-founded outbuildings to the north of the old house. This was a simple, two-roomed hut about 8.5m x 5m. The inner room had plastered walls but no other notable fea-

tures, whilst the outer had an oven, cist, lined pit and other
small pits in the floor surface. (fig. 42) There were about a
dozen coins in the occupation debris on the floor, including
five of the post-367 period. The latest coin, minted AD
388–402, confirms that occupation continued until the end
of the century, but it could well have continued much
longer.[33] Finally, we should note the evidence from the villa
at Totternhoe, below the Chiltern scarp. Here too, there was
a period of gradual decline in the later fourth century, with
tesselated floors patched in plain mortar, and in one case
eventually overlain by a much rougher floor of mortar, flint
and tile suggesting that a living room may have been given
over to some working function. When the west wing of the
villa caught fire it was not re-occupied or rebuilt, and
eventually, as at Gadebridge, occupation shifted from the
villa building to a cottage built over, and partly from the
remains of, the old gate-house of the villa. (fig. 42) Although
the dating of this sequence is uncertain, it appears to begin
post AD 370, so that the building and occupation of the
cottage may well have taken place in the early fifth
century.[34] In each of these four villas, therefore, we have
evidence of occupation continuing until at least the end of
the fourth century and probably beyond it. It is clearly
occupation of a very different kind to that seen on the same
sites a century earlier, and the term 'squatter' occupation is
often used to describe it. This is probably a misleading term
however, with its implication of outsiders occupying
buildings left empty by others. It is altogether more likely
that we are looking at the remains of occupation by farm
bailiffs or foremen, who were expected to still run the
estates after the owners had transferred their households
back to Verulamium. What is much less certain is how long
the estates continued to function, and at what point they
disintegrated entirely. In the absence of datable artifacts
this is an impossible problem to solve, but at Latimer some
impression of an answer may have emerged.[35]

When the last rooms of the villa were finally abandoned
there may have been a short period when the site was
unoccupied, but new buildings were erected about 50m east
of the main wing shortly after. Alongside the decaying

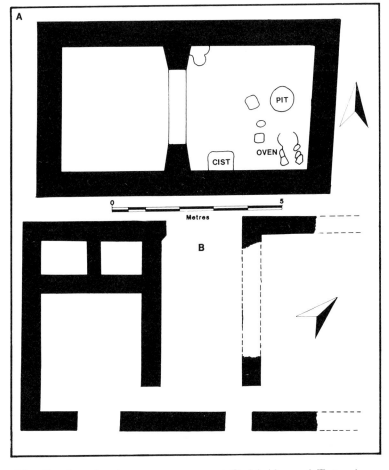

Fig. 42.   Late fourth century cottages at Gadebridge and Totternhoe.

courtyard wall of the villa two timber structures were
erected. (fig. 43) One was 16m × 3.5m, with walls stood on
sleeper beams in shallow trenches and the roof supported
by pairs of timber posts set alongside the walls. This
unusual arrangement suggests some form of cruck-roof, or
possibly an A-frame arrangement. Immediately south of
this building on the same alignment a smaller structure,
about 6m × 3.5m was erected on a framework of timber

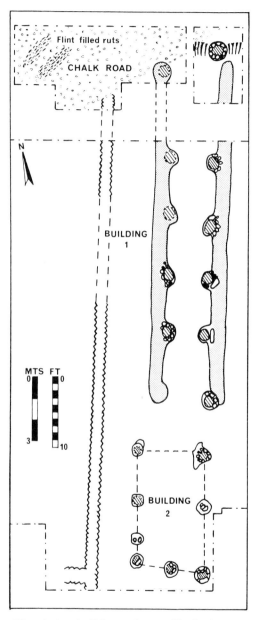

Fig. 43. The timber buildings of post-villa I phase at Latimer.

posts, while to the north of the long building a chalk-surfaced roadway was laid over the demolished remains of the courtyard wall and gatehouse. Post-holes in both buildings were re-cut, presumably to take replacement posts, before the two buildings were eventually abandoned and demolished. A number of animal burials were then made in this area, while new structures were built a little to the west. The most interesting of these, which appears to have been a dwelling house, was a timber building 6m × 5m. (fig. 44) Sill-beams were placed on a flint and tile foundation and there are traces of internal partitions. The floor was of compacted soil and pebbles, with a re-surfacing by the doorway on the south side of the building. On the floor were the remains of six broken pottery vessels, all of Romano-British type but of debased fabric and manufacture, and a few personal items such as a bronze pennanular ring and a bone pin. Possibly while this building was still in occupation the site of the long building and its companion was levelled and a new light-weight timber outbuilding was constructed as a barn or something similar. In time, this too was demolished and flint and tile rubble, presumably taken from the collapsed walls and roof of the long abandoned villa, was used to make two rectangular platforms which appear to be the bases of two small buildings constructed on sill-beams. One was 10m × 2.3m, and was so narrow it can only have been a storebuilding or workshed, but the other was 12m × 4.5m and may have been a living house. There were variations in the density of the rubble base suggestive of internal partitions, with possibly one large room, two small ones, and an entrance corridor. This remarkable sequence of three or four phases of late-fourth and fifth century occupation at Latimer suggests that villa estates could and did continue to function in the Chilterns to a late date. How late is difficult to judge, but there are three possible pointers. One is the appearance of Romano-British pots of simple type on the floor of the building of post-villa phase 2. It is generally thought that Romano-British potteries had ceased production by about AD 425, so that these vessels are unlikely to have been deposited later than c. AD 450 at the

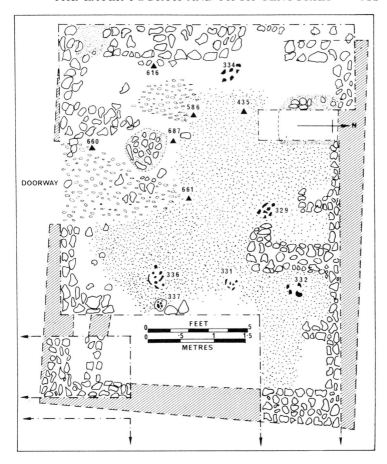

Fig. 44.   The foundations of the post-villa II phase at Latimer.

very latest, and could have been deposited much earlier. In
the make-up of the rubble base of the last phase building
was a very worn coin tentatively identified as an issue of
Honorius. If the identification was correct, then post-villa
phase 4 must have begun well into the fifth century at the
earliest. Finally, there are a dozen sherds of hand-made
grass-marked pottery found in post-villa phase 2–4 levels.
We have noted similar pottery in fifth century deposits at
Ware and Foxholes, and it is found much more widely (and

usually in small quantities) elsewhere in southern England. Along with the other evidence, and the estimations we can make for the length of use of the various buildings, it is difficult to conclude that the final post-villa buildings at Latimer were constructed much, if anything, before the mid-fifth century. We might reasonably expect other estates to have been farmed and occupied to a similar period but we should perhaps note that the post-villa occupation at Latimer is not entirely Romano-British in character. The long cruck or A-frame building of post-villa 1 is not yet paralleled in Roman Britain and its nearest, though by no means close, parallels are to be found in the low countries in the fourth century AD.[36] A fragment of cauldron chain from the building has north European parallels,[37] and the grass-marked pottery might be associated with continental users.[37] There is thus a real possibility that at Latimer the estate changed hands when the villa was finally abandoned and that its continued productivity was due not to the efforts of Romano-Britons but of settlers from the continent.

The towns

Whilst the continued exploitation and settlement of the countryside was to be expected, if only because subsistence needs demanded it, the maintenance of town life beyond the final Roman withdrawal from Britain in the first decade of the fifth century should not be assumed. Todd has argued that after AD 409 there was no role left for either the *civitas* or its *ordo*, since their prime functions in tax-gathering, administration of Roman law, and similar activities – were no longer required.[38] Equally, the economic system which needed towns and cities and on which towns and cities in turn depended was in rapid decline if it had not already collapsed. Coinage was effectively no longer entering Britain after c. 402 and had probably ceased to circulate altogether as a means of exchange by AD 425. The major potteries, including the Nene Valley and Oxford kilns had ceased production during the same period,[39] probably due to the collapse of the marketing system on which they depended, and possibly affected also by a deteriorating communications network.[40] In this context, the collapse of the towns might be expected to occur sooner rather than later. One factor perhaps working in favour of the continued maintenance of the Roman order and of town-life was the strength of the Christian church in Britain at this time. It is generally agreed that the church found much of its support amongst the wealthier and more Romanised elements of the population, and the interests of church, civitas and town may have been largely identical in the early fifth century. The strength of the church in the civitas of the Catuvellauni is not easy to judge, but significantly perhaps the evidence that does exist is concentrated around Water Newton and Verulamium.

The Water Newton hoard of Christian silverware, containing one gold and twenty seven silver objects, dates to the first half of the fourth century and was almost certainly removed from a sanctuary and buried for safe-keeping at a time of crisis.[41] Although opinions vary, there is no good reason to assume that the treasure, found inside the Roman town, was actually in transit from somewhere else when the crisis arose. The most economic explanation of its location is that it came from a Christian building in Durobrivae itself. There is other evidence pointing to a Christian element in the population of the area at this time, including a lead plug from Marholm, 6kms to the north, bearing both Khi-Rho and Alpha-Omega graffiti.[42] From Ashton, 10kms to the south-west of the town, come two lead 'baptismal' tanks, one decorated with the Khi-Rho monogram, and a well ordered cemetery of east-west burials without grave goods which may well be a Christian burial ground. Other uninscribed examples of the lead tanks come from near Huntingdon and the vicinity of Cambridge.[43] Scattered though these finds are, they are cumulatively an impressive testimony to an active Christian presence in the Water Newton area in the fourth century AD. There is nothing as impressive or decisive in the archaeological record from Verulamium. A basilical building of unusual design and uncertain date found in the southern corner of the town might be a church but the case is, and will remain, unproven.[44] The same must be said of a building with an

apse found associated with fourth century pottery and a
cemetery outside the London Gate.[45] Its tesselated floor
suggests it was not a workshop or barn, and it could well be
a cemetery chapel, but distinctively Christian material is
lacking. Fortunately the evidence for a Christian church at
Verulamium does not rest on this evidence, but on the
martyrdom of St. Alban and the account of a visit to his
shrine by St. Germanus in the fifth century.[46]

In view of the evidence for an active Christian community
in the area of Durobrivae in the fourth century, it is
particularly regrettable that we know little or nothing about
the town itself in the late fourth and early fifth century.
Instead we have to turn to the nearest neighbouring town,
Godmanchester, to get some impression of town life in the
north of the civitas in this period. The picture at Godmanchester is not an impressive one.[47] Sometime after AD
367 the 'basilica', as well as the ruins of the fire-destroyed
mansio, was robbed of its masonry, most probably to
facilitate the rapid re-modelling of the defences and
construction of external bastions or towers. The only public
building still functioning in Godmanchester may now have
been the rebuilt shrine to Abandinus, which continued in
use into the late fourth century. It is possible that the north
end of the mansio baths, which had been put back into
service earlier in the fourth century, also served as a public
facility, and this was maintained in use until at least the end
of the fourth century. Here and elsewhere in the town
timber-framed cottages were still being constructed in the
later fourth century, the latest of them producing coins to c.
AD 390. Associated drying-racks and storage bins suggest
that the pattern of small town life here was really little
changed since the late first century, whatever may have
happened to the modest public buildings the town had once
possessed. It is possible that some of these cottages,
including the two in the vicinity of the ruined mansio, were
occupied not by Romano-Britons but by Saxons. Saxon
pottery was recovered in the soil overlying the disturbed
remains of the huts, and on the east side of the town a
fenced enclosure yielded Saxon as well as late Roman
pottery from the foundation trench. There seems little

doubt that Saxons arrived and settled in Godmanchester in the early fifth century and on present evidence they did so without immediately changing the character of the existing town in any significant way. This agrees well with the sort of picture which emerged of the early Saxon settlement at Orton Hall less than 30kms to the north, and close to Durobrivae.

On the far side of the canton at Dorchester a different pattern of events emerges but the overall impression is broadly similar.[48] The town was still thriving in the late fourth century to judge from the quantity of Theodosian coinage recovered from the site, and at least two stone-founded buildings were first erected in this period. It is possible that these features are both connected with the late-Roman military burial we discussed earlier and that Dorchester was given a small military garrison in the late fourth century. There is no reason to assume that if such a garrison existed it was comprised of barbarian troops, and more particularly Saxons. Saxon settlers did arrive in the Dorchester area, probably via the Thames, before the mid-fifth century however, and they subsequently appear inside the walls of Dorchester. Grubenhauser are found built alongside Roman streets and there appears to have been a transition between the mid-fifth and early sixth century from a declining Romano-British town to a well-ordered Saxon settlement still utilising the Roman street system. On both the eastern and western fringes of the civitas, then, we can see urban communities still existing at the end of the fourth century and still acquiring and using coinage at that time. We have no evidence of a sudden or dramatic change in their fortunes, but in each case we can detect the arrival of Saxon settlers in the community during the course of the fifth century. The impact of their cultural traditions, together with the breakdown of the Romano-British exchange and communications network, inevitably led to a change in the character of the settlements, but the change was a gradual one taking place over many decades.

What then of the civitas capital itself? The series of excavations by Professor Frere allow us to answer the question with some confidence.[49] We have no knowledge of the late history of the forum and basilica, but three public buildings at least were still in active use in the last decade of the fourth century. From the uppermost levels of the market hall came two coins of Maximus (c. 383–388), and from the theatre-temple a dozen coins of the House of Theodosius; the temple was actually re-modelled sometime after AD 379. The adjacent theatre was apparently abandoned and used as a rubbish dump at a date which cannot be earlier than c. AD 380–390 and may well be rather later. Furthermore, its closure and the re-orientation of the temple may reflect, as Frere suggests, not the collapse of urban life or even cultured tastes at Verulamium but simply the increasing pressure to abandon pagan cults in the later fourth century.[50] The most significant feature of the theatre excavations is the quantity of coinage recovered from the post-AD 380 rubbish tip. Over 900 coins came from the tip itself, another 1300 from the overlying levels of debris, and another 1500 from the superficial levels over this. Although there were only 38 coins of the House of Theodosius in this total of over 3700 coins, there can be little doubt that many of the coins were still being used for market activity in the last decade or so of the fourth century. Taken together with the evidence for the continued use of the market hall at this time it is difficult to avoid the conclusion that Verulamium still acted as a thriving market centre at the close of the fourth century.

Private commercial activity certainly continued in the shops on the Watling Street frontage close to the market and theatre until at least the last quarter of the fourth century, but the clearest signs of private prosperity and confidence in the late fourth century come from three private houses excavated by Frere. One of these, in insula XXII, survived only as a fragment but it demonstrates the construction of a substantial building with opus floors at a date which must be very late in the fourth century – it was built over a house with an attractively decorated cellar which was itself not erected before about AD 360. The second house, which lay behind the shops in insula XIV, was excavated in its entirety. It was probably built no earlier than c. AD 380, and was a simple but comfortable home.

(fig. 45) At one end was a work-room with oven and a stoke-hole for the hypocaust which heated a small living room with an opus floor and plain white wall-plaster. Next to the latter was a still smaller room with a tesselated floor, and beyond this a large room with a gravel floor and open hearth. A verandah or corridor ran down one side of the building and was floored with tesserae. One of its walls had been decorated with ornate painted plaster. Despite the building's modest proportions it provides examples of all those Roman furnishings which we expect to find in a well-appointed Romano-British town-house – hypocaust, opus and tesselated floors, and decorated wall plaster. This building was in use for some time, for the floor and stokehole in room 2 were both renewed and the verandah floor was eventually patched with various materials – opus, chalk and tile reminiscent of the front corridor at Latimer villa. Occupation can hardly have lasted less than twenty years, yet the building was not then abandoned but re-modelled. Its four original rooms now became two large ones, and a wing-room was added and provided with a hypocaust. The smaller of the two main rooms was given a tesselated floor and the larger retained a kitchen area with chalk floor at one end but was provided with a tesselated floor with a small mosaic panel at the other. This room, at least, also had painted plaster on its walls. This phase of occupation can hardly begin before AD 400 and it says much for the strength and resilience of urban life at Verulamium at this time that mosaic floors were not only in demand but were capable of being laid at such a late date. The quality of workmanship was not high, to judge from the subsequent break-up of the pavement, but its period of wear and the re-flooring of the kitchen area no less than four times carries the occupation of this house into the middle of the fifth century, at the earliest. Even after the house was finally abandoned there are signs of continued activity on the site.

The area of late occupation in insulae XXII and XIV are linked by a third house discovered in insulae XXVII. This building is the most impressive of the three, with three wings around a central court, twenty-two ground-floor

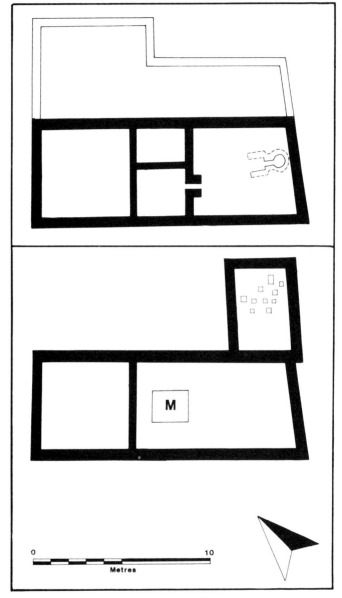

Fig. 45.   The two phases of the late fourth century house in insula XIV
at Verulamium (top, phase 1; bottom phase 2).

rooms, and well-built walls on good foundations; it reveals
the work of skilled builders and it was not constructed until
c. AD 380 at the earliest. (fig. 46) Six of its rooms and its

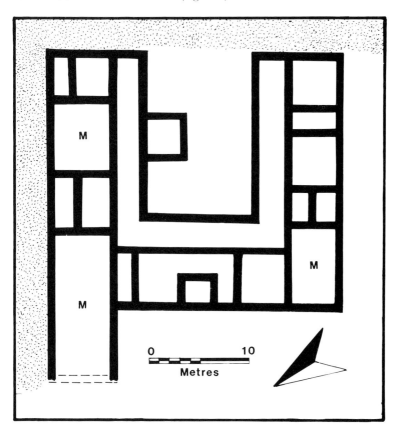

Fig. 46.   The late fourth century house in insula XXVII at Verulamium.

main corridor had tesselated floors and one room had an
attractive mosaic with a central flower-design. (fig. 47)
Later, possibly around AD 400, two corner rooms were both
extended and provided with new mosaic floors; from one
room came evidence of elaborate plaster mouldings too. The
northern of the rooms may have been extended to form a
small hall about 12m long, with the mosaic extending over

Fig. 47.   A late fourth century mosaic from insula XXVII, Verulamium.

the whole of this area. The creation of such a room and such a floor at a date which can hardly be before AD 400 and may well be rather later amply confirms the picture suggested by the buildings in insulae XXII and XIV. As it moved into the fifth century, the community at Verulamium was still in every sense a Romano-British one with a firm commitment to urban life.

A change in circumstances seems to be indicated by the next phase of activity in the house, since the smaller of the new mosaics was now destroyed and a very large corn-oven inserted in its place. Since the mosaic had been repaired before this happened, the change is unlikely to be before c. AD 430; the complete absence of coins in associated levels would support such a date. Subsequently the corn-dryer was partly re-built, before both it and the house were finally abandoned. A date of c. AD 435/40 is a reasonable guess as to when this happened; it could hardly be much earlier, but might be later. What brought about the abandonment of such a fine house we cannot say, but it was not the collapse of the urban community or even the urban authority. This much is proved by subsequent activity on the site. Overlying the abandoned house a large buttressed barn was built, with tiles robbed from some earlier Roman structure. It measured nearly 40m × c. 16m and was of such size and capacity it might well have been built by the community for public use; the safe storage of agricultural produce may have been its purpose, but we should be careful of reading too dramatic a story into its construction. It was built no earlier than about AD 440 and, due to underlying pits affecting its foundations, it may have lasted no more than ten to twenty years. Yet when it was abandoned perhaps c. AD 450–460, it was replaced by a still more surprising if less imposing feature – a water main. Across the foundations of the barn ran a Roman timber water main, its pipe sections joined by iron collars. This simple structure clearly carries at least three significant implications for our picture of Romano-British Verulamium in the later fifth century. The first is that the skills and technology of Roman hydraulic engineering were still available at that period. The second is that the Roman aqueduct which served Verulamium must have been maintained up to this time. Thirdly, the pipe-line argues strongly that the municipal authorities at Verulamium were still functioning in the later fifth century AD. How far beyond the walls of Verulamium their authority now carried is impossible to say; it may well have counted for nothing in the Vale of Aylesbury and beyond,[52] but in the valleys around Verulamium it may still have held sway and may have continued to do so for decades to come. The Saxons finally appear at Verulamium in the years either side of AD 600, but even then they are found only in the cemetery beyond its walls.[53]

Notes and References

References to British journals use the abbreviations recommended by the Council for British Archaeology, which are those of the American Standards Association (list Z39, 5–1963, revised 1966). Other abbreviations used are:

CBA   Council for British Archaeology
PRN   Public Record Number
RCHM   Royal Commission on Historical Monuments (England)
RIB   R. Collingwood and R.P. Wright *Roman Inscriptions in Britain*, i
           (Oxford 1965)
VCH   *Victoria County History*

1. TRIBAL TERRITORY AND THE PRE-ROMAN IRON AGE.

1. Drury *1963*.
2. Wheeler *1936*.
3. Dyer *1973*, 182, 188.
4. Thompson *1979*, Saunders C *1982*.
5. Hawkes *1980*.
6. Goodburn *1981*, 127, Partridge *1981*, 353–4.
7. Allen *1967*.
8. Peacock *1971*.
9. Dunnett *1975*, 11.
10. Hodder *1977*.
11. Thompson *1982*.
12. Todd *1981*, 33.
13. Rodwell *1976*, 276.
14. Webster *1980*, 49.
15. Todd *1981*, 48.
16. Frere *1978*, 61, Webster *1980*, 67.
17. Allen *1976*.
18. Henig *1972*.

19. Partridge *1981*, 152–203.
20. Muckelroy et al *1978*.
21. Stead *1975*.
22. Dunnett *1975*, 15–27.
23. Wheeler *1936*.
24. Saunders *1982*.
25. Hunn *1980*.
26. Neal *1978*, Grew *1980*, 374, fig 11.
27. Frere *1983*, 30–32.
28. Partridge *1981*, 32–35.
29. Rodwell *1976*, 247.
30. Partridge *1981*, 355.
31. Partridge *1982*.
32. Saunders and Havercroft *1982*.
33. Rowley *1975*, 115.
34. Rook *1968*, Rook et al *1982*.
35. Rook *1970*.
36. Stead *1968*, *1975*, 127, Frere *1984*a, 304.
37. O'Neil *1945*.
38. Branigan *1968*.
39. Simco *1984*, 14.
40. Dix *1980*.
41. Jackson and Ambrose *1978*.
42. Dallas *1975*.
43. Wild *1973*.
44. Pryor *1975*.
45. Mackreth and O'Neil *1980*.
46. *RIB* 1962.
47. Wacher *1974*, 91.
48. Rodwell *1975*, 90–94.
49. Rivet *1964*, 134.
50. Rivet *1964*, 146, Todd *1973*, 14–15.
51. Dunnett *1975*, 28–9.
52. Dunnett *1975*, 86.

2. HISTORY: AD 43–367

1. Dio Cassius, ix, 19–22.
2. Dunnett *1975*, 32–44.
3. Webster *1980*, 122.
4. Anthony *1970*.
5. Frere *1983*, 37–9.
6. Frere *1972*, 118–46.
7. Green *1975*, 185.
8. Rankov *1982*, 363.
9. Webster *1980*, 155.
10. Branigan *1978*.

11. Woodfield *1971*.
12. Rowley *1975*, 118; Hargreaves *1978*, suggests a road alignment can be identified leading to the east gate of a fort.
13. Rowley, *1975*, 122.
14. Goodburn *1976*, 338–9; Farley *1981*.
15. Frere *1978*, 86–100, Todd *1981*, 78–88.
16. Frere and St Joseph *1974*.
17. Frere *1983*, 44–9.
18. Frere *1983*, 105–7.
19. Frere *1972*, 5–23.
20. Walthew *1978*, 343–4.
21. Wilson *1975*, 258, *VCH* 1914, 130.
22. Tacitus *Annals* XIV, 33.
23. Frere *1983*, 26–28.
24. Frere and St Joseph *1974*, 16–17.
25. Rodwell *1972*, 291–3.
26. Tacitus *Annals* XIV, 38.
27. Woodfield *1971*.
28. Marsden *1980*, 36–9; Dunnett *1975*, 70.
29. Wacher *1974*, 204.
30. Frere *1983*, 69–72.
31. Tacitus *Agricola*, 21.
32. Saunders *1961*, Neal *1974*, 8–9, 88.
33. Branigan *1973*, 49–50.
34. Frere *1983*, 16, 34–35.
35. Lewis *1966*, 67–69.
36. Frere *1983*, 36–37.
37. Marsden *1980*, 120; Maloney and Hobley *1983*, 104.
38. Wheeler *1936*, 62.
39. Frere *1983*, 46.
40. Frere *1983*, 34–35.
41. Wheeler *1936*, p.1. XXII, section C-D.
42. Wacher, *1974*, 122–23.
43. Wheeler *1936*, 195–97, fig. 35.
44. Frere *1983*, 36.
45. Wacher *1974*, 75; Frere *1978*, 285; Salway *1981*, 218, 261–5. Frere *1984* now argues they precede the governorship of Albinus, and perhaps date c. 185–190; Todd *1981*, 164–5.
46. Frere *1984* argues forcefully for a single, Imperial initiative, Hartley *1983*, for a more widespread process.
47. Stevens *1952*. Wacher, *1974* 408, has persuasively dealt with objections to this interpretation put forward by Bogaers, *1967*.
48. RIB 2235.
49. Mackreth *1979*.
50. Tomlin *1983*.
51. Frere *1983*, 75–82.
52. Frere *1983*, 244–52.
53. Frere *1983*, 133–141.

54. Wheeler *1936*, 28.
55. Frere *1983*, 15.
56. Summarised in Branigan *1973*, 75.
57. See for example the comments in Todd *1976*, 117–9, and Hingley *1982*.
58. Summarised in Branigan *1973*, 126–8.

3. COMMUNICATIONS AND URBAN SETTLEMENT

1. Simco *1984*, 66–9.
2. Goodburn *1979*, 306; Green *1975*, 185; Wild *1974*.
3. supra p.
4. Parnum and Cotton *1983*, 318f.
5. Green *1975*, 185; Branigan *1968*, 136.
6. Goodburn *1976*, 335; Lambrick *1980*, 45.
7. Branigan *1968*, 136.
8. Viatores *1964*, 68–70; Wilson *1972*, 327.
9. Goodburn *1976*, 335.
10. RIB. 2235, 2238.
11. Simco *1984*, 78–9.
12. On all these points, see Rivet and Smith *1979*, 497–99.
13. RIB 1962 'Civitate Catuvellaunorum'.
14. Wheeler *1936*, 63–73.
15. Frere *1983*, 55–74.
16. VCH *Herts* IV, 132.
17. Richardson, *1944*. There are traces of a substantial timber building beneath the late Flavian *mucellum* which would possibly have been an earlier wooden market hall.
18. Wheeler *1936*, 131–33.
19. Muckelroy *1976*, 179.
20. Wacher *1974*, 207.
21. Wheeler *1936*, 113–20.
22. Wheeler *1936*, 76, pl. XXVI, pl. DCIIIA.
23. Frere *1983*, 80–1.
24. Kenyon *1934*, 213–61.
25. see Morris *1968*, 2.
26. Frere *1983*, 12, suggests the baths may have been in insula XVIII.
27. Frere *1983*, 105–7.
28. see houses excavated by Wheeler in insula III (houses A, B, C); Wheeler *1936*, 93–4, pl. XXVIII, and house XXVII 2D, excavated by Frere *1983*, 197, fig. 79.
29. Frere *1983* 161–76, 237–41.
30. Wheeler *1936*, 104–5. This interpretation is not without problems, however, and in particular rooms 6 and 7 look very much like a large triclinium.
31. e.g. buildings VIII, 1–3, 1, 1–2, III, 1.
32. Wheeler *1936*, 91, p.1. XCIX, A.

33. Frere *1983*, 121, insula XVIII.
34. Frere *1983*, 14.
35. Johnson, S *1975* for discussion of the term vicus. Although Isidor (7th century AD) claimed that *vici* had no walls; some continental *vici* did and the walled towns under discussion here could certainly not all have been *civitas* capitals. Note the term may have been applied particularly in the 1st-2nd centuries; after the building of walls in the 3rd century *vici* may often have been called *castra*.
36. Johnson, S *1975*, and especially 79.
37. VCH *Northants* I, 169f; Mackereth *1979*; Blagg 1981; Artis *1828*.
38. *RIB* 231.
39. Green *1975*; Goodburn *1976*, 340, *1979*, 300–1; Rankov 1982, 363.
40. Partridge *1975*, *1981*, *1982a*.
41. VCH *Northants* I, 178–84; RCHM *Northants* II, 91–6; *RIB* 233; Wilson *1975a*, 11, pl. VIa; Hall and Nickerson *1968*; Knight *1968*; Rankov *1982*, 366; Woodfield, P *1978*, 81–86. Cowley and Foard *1979*, fig. 5.
42. VCH *Northants* I, 184–6; Wilson *1975*, 255; Goodburn *1976*, 335; Frere *1977*, 399; Woodfield, P *1978*, 77–85; Brain and Alexander 1982; Woodfield, C *1978*; Frere *1984a*, 300; Lambrick *1980*.
43. Rowley *1975*; Wilson *1975*, 256; Wilson *1975a*, 11, pl. V1b.
44. Rowley *1975*; VCH *Oxon* I, 281–8, Frere *1962*.
45. Rivet *1975*, 113.
46. Alexander *1975*; Goodburn *1976*, 340, *1979*, 346–7; Browne 1974.
47. VCH *Northants* I, 186–7; RCHM *Northants* III, 150–2; Wilson *1972*, 325, *1974*, 296.
48. VCH *Bucks* II, 5; Manning *1972*, 235; Wilson *1970*, 288; *1971*, 268; personal communication from M. Farley.
49. Matthews *1981*; Simco *1984*, 101–3.
50. Mathews *1981*, 46–8.
51. *RIB* 230.
52. Johnson *1975*; Simco *1984*, 114–6.
53. Wilson *1971*, 269; Stead *1975*.
54. Goodburn *1976*, 351; Gentry, Ivens and McClean *1977*; Sheldon and Schaaf *1978*.
55. Crouch *1976*, *1978*, Crouch and Shanks *1984*.
56. Reports in *Trans. London Middlesex Archaeol. Soc.* 10 (1951), 173–4: 17 (1954), 173f, 23 (1973), 148–59, 24 (1974), 85–110, 26 (1975), 267–77, 27 (1976), 206–227.
57. Goodburn *1976*, 338–9; *1978*, 444; Reece *1982*.
58. Goodburn *1976*, 339.
59. *Dix* 1983.
60. RCHM *Northants* II, xlv–xlvii, 102–3: RCHM *Northants* III, 152–3; RCHM *Northants*, I, 54–5, 98–9.

4. RURAL SETTLEMENT

1. Ward Perkins *1938*; O'Neal *1945*, Saunders *1961*.

2. Webster *1969*, 243–6.
3. Grew *1980*, Neal *1978*.
4. Branigan *1978*.
5. Neal *1974*, 7–9, Neal *1976*, 57–9.
6. Neal *1976*, 6.
7. Branigan *1971; 1968, 1972*.
8. Northchurch (supra n. 6), Amersham Bury End, Shardloes; Kings Langley has also been examined and reported on for the first time.
9. Rankov *1982*, 369; Millard *1956*.
10. Branigan *1971*; VCH Herts IV, 163, Branigan *1967*, 142–5; Hartley *1959*.
11. Selkirk *1971*. Rook suggests the intriguing possibility of foreign ownership of this villa, see Rook, Walker and Dunstan *1984*.
12. The later first century mosaics from Fishbourne and Eccles are generally considered to be exceptional.
13. Branigan *1973*, 75–77; Neal *1976*, 11, 68.
14. Neal *1976*, pl. 37 a–b; Neal *1978*, 52.
15. Branigan *1971*, 86; Neal *1974*, 75–6, 98.
16. Cocks *1922*; Farley *1983*.
17. *VCH Bucks* II (1980), 9; Bucks County Mus. Rep. *1966*, 12.
18. Ashcroft *1939*; Branigan *1969*. There is additional material, including a large piece of a fine butt-beaker excavated by the late Jack Head from the same silo-cutting described in Branigan *1969*.
19. Rivers-Moore, *1951*.
20. Oxford County Museum PRN 2866, 2867; PRN 3422, 8553–6; VCH *Oxford* I, 320–21.
21. St. Joseph *1965*, 88, pl. XIII, 2.
22. Frere and St. Joseph *1983*, 196; Farley *1983*; Harpsden, supra n. 19.
23. Roundell *1863*; Rivers-Moore *1951*.
24. Grey & Draper *1978*; Turland *1977*.
25. Friendship-Taylor and Woodfield *1981*.
26. Wilson *1974*, 436, *1975*, 257, Goodburn *1976*, 337, Barnbrook *1979*, Zeepvat *1984*, Williams *1984*; Jones *1981; J. Roman Studs* 48 (1958), 140–1, Wilson *1973*, 293.
27. Wilson *1971*, 268.
28. Green, M. *1974*; Zeepvat *1980*.
29. Wilson *1972*, 325, *1974*, 434.
30. Woods, *1970*.
31. Simco *1984*, 26–7.
32. RCHM *Northants* II, 1; Wilson *1971*, 266.
33. Dix *1979*.
34. RCHM *Northants* I, 83,
35. supra n. 30.
36. RCHM *Northants* II, 176; Wilson *1974*, 253.
37. RCHM *Northants* I, 3, fig. 75; Wilson *1974*, 255, pl. XXIIB.
38. Higham Ferrers RCHM *Northants* I, 54–55; Moore 1974; Ashley, supra n. 31.
39. VCH *Northants* I, 194.

40. Challands *1974*; 1975; RCHM *Northants* I, 114.
41. RCHM *Northants* I, 13; Hadman and Upex *1974*.
42. RCHM *Peterborough* 29.
43. RCHM *Northants* I, 114; 40; Wilson *1971*, 264.
44. RCHM *Peterborough* 24–5; Wild *1978*, 69.
45. Simpson *1966*, 23; Mackreth *1976*, 1977.
46. I am greatly indebted to Dr. D.J. Smith for discussing the details of the Great Weldon villa with me in advance of his publication of the excavations. see also RCHM *Northants* II, 164.
47. RCHM *Northants* I, 8–10, fig. 21; *Peterborough*, 17, figs, 5, 6; 25, fig. 11.
48. supra n. 39.
49. supra n. 44.
50. Barnack supra n. 44; *J. Roman Studs* 53 (1963), 135; Wild *1973*a.
51. Wilson *1974*a, pl. XXIVa.
52. RCHM *Northants* I, 32; *Peterborough*, 10.
53. Wild *1978*, 67–9.
54. Wild *ibid*; Hartley *1972*, 7.
55. Mackreth *1984*.
56. Neville *1849*; VCH *Essex* III (1963), 199, pl. 29B.
57. Frend *1968*.
58. Green, H. *1975*, 206.
59. VCH *Herts* IV (1908), 164; Wilson *1973*, 299; *J. Roman Studs* 56 (1966), 209; 57 (1967), 189; RCHM *Cambridge City* I (1959), 6–7.
60. St. Joseph *1973*, 245, pl. XVIII, 2.
61. supra n. 55; Wilson 1974a, pl. XXVII.
62. Wilson *1971*, 268–9; CBA Grp 7 *Bull Archaeol Discoveries* 8 (1961), 1.
63. Godmanchester, Standon, Eyeworth (Simco *1984*, 104), Youngsbury and probably Ickleton.
64. Simco *1984*, 119.
65. Taylor *1975*, 113.
66. Simco *1984*, 32, 122, G278.
67. RCHM *Northants* I, 40–2, fig. 52.
68. RCHM *Northants* II, 40–1, fig. 42; I, 94, fig. 101; Windell *1981*.
69. Taylor *1975*, pl. 7a; RCHM *Northants* I, 93, fig. 99.
70. Jackson and Ambrose *1978*; RCHM *Northants* II, III, fig. 105; Wilson *1974*, 437.
71. Jackson and Ambrose *1978*.
72. Dix *1979*, *1981*.
73. Petchley *1979*; Goodburn *1976*, 338; Williams, 1976; Hunter & Mynard 1977.
74. Goodburn *1976*, 338–9.
75. Partridge *1975*, 152; J. Roman Studs 46 (1956), 138; Cauvain *1978*.
76. A useful survey of sites and references for the Bulbourne Valley can be found in Neal *1976*, 132–3.
77. Green *1975*, 190–1; *1978*.
78. RCHM *Northants* I, 40–2, fig. 50; 67–9; 114–5, fig. 121.

5. INDUSTRY AND THE ECONOMY

1. RCHM *Northants* II, xliv.
2. Dury *1963*, 69–73, 127–8.
3. Cocks *1922*; Branigan *1969*.
4. Grew *1980*, fig. 12 centre; Turland *1977*, 218.
5. Frere and St Joseph *1983*, 189–91.
6. Branigan *1971*, 60, fig. 14, 1, pl. III; Neal *1974*, 42, fig. 22.
7. Simco *1984*, 115; Green *1975*, 191; monk *1981*; Helbeck *1952*, 229; Goodburn *1978*, 442.
8. Branigan *1971*, 184, fig. 14, H and M. Note also the occurrence of carrot, parsnip, celery and several herbs in the plant remains from Lonthorpe and Fengate, Wilson G, *1978*.
9. Green *1975*, 191, fig. 8; King *1978*, 219, table 4, 33.
10. Harcourt *1974*; Hamilton *1971*; Lambrick *1980*, 105ff.
11. King *1978*, 219, table 4, 38.
12. supra n. 10; Gebbels *1976*.
13. Ashdown and Evans *1981*.
14. Appelbaum *1966*, 102–3.
15. Wild *1973*, fig. 10.
16. Peacock *1982*, 101.
17. Castle *1972; 1973*; Saunders and Havercroft *1977*.
18. Rivet and Smith *1981*, 463.
19. Hartley *1973*, 42.
20. Wilson, M *1974*; Dannell *1975*.
21. Hartley *1972*, 21.
22. Howe, Perrin and Mackreth *1982*, 6–7.
23. Howe, Perrin and Mackreth *1982* for a good general description of forms and fabric.
24. Dannell *1973*.
25. Artis *1828*.
26. Dannell *1974*.
27. Wild *1973b*.
28. Atkinson *1948*; Case and Sturdy *1960*, 133.
29. Young *1977*, 231–41.
30. Young *1973*, 108.
31. Fulford *1975*, 130.
32. Young 1972, 211.
33. Brown and Sheldon *1974*.
34. Simco *1984*, 97, G15; 100, 103, G79; 108, G132.
35. Tilson *1973*.
36. Brown *1969*.
37. RCHM *Northants* II, 7, 84, 86–7, and personal communication from R. Friendship-Taylor.
38. RCHM *Northants* II, 47; Johnston *1969*.
39. Wilson D, *1971*, 266–7; Grew *1980*, 372; Woods *1969; 1984*.
40. Woods *1984*; see also Woods *1974* for a description and discussion of the early surface-kilns with movable pedestals at these sites.

41. Todd and Cleland *1976*.
42. RCHM *Northants* II, 26; Friendship-Taylor *1979; J. Roman Studs* 45 (1955), 135.
43. RCHM *Northants* II, 7.
44. Challands *1979*; RCHM *Northants* I, 68.
45. Challands *1974*.
46. RCHM *Northants* II, 50.
47. Hadman and Upex *1975*; Dix *1984*; Hadman *1984*.
48. Wilson D, *1975*, 257; Goodburn *1976*, 338–9, 444.
49. Goodburn *1976*, 339.
50. Todd *1973*, 111–2.
51. Williams *1971*, 178.
52. VCH *Herts* IV, 148; Grew *1980*, 381.
53. *J Roman Studs* 53 (1963), 136; 56 (1966) 209, Rawlins *1970*.
54. *J Roman Studs* 58 (1968), 194; Wilson D, *1970*, 289; *1972*, 330.
55. Neal *1974*, 83–7, 100.
56. Simco *1984*, 97; Challands *1976*; Foster, Harper and Watkins *1977*, 63–65.
57. Smith *1984*, 372–3; *1969*, 107–9.
58. Blagg *1981*.
59. Smith *1975*, 276–9, 288.
60. Hingeley *1982*; Hodder *1979*; Reece *1979*; Gillam and Greene *1981*.
61. Webster G, *1975*, 43.
62. Hodder *1974*.
63. Hodder *1974*; Simco *1984*, 40, reporting on P. Aird's study of Beds Grey Wares.
64. Friendship-Taylor *1974*, *1979*.
65. Hodder and Hassall *1971*; Hodder *1975*.
66. Curnow *1974*.

6. THE LATE FOURTH AND FIFTH CENTURIES

1. Johnson, S *1976*, 96f.
2. Ammianus Marcellinus xxvii, 8; xxviii, 3; for a new and controversial interpretation of the events of 367, see Bartholomew *1984*.
3. O'Neill *1945*, 56f.
4. Wheeler *1936*, 59–63.
5. Green *1975*, 206–7, fig. 14.
6. Todd *1975*, 217, figs 5–7.
7. Wilson D, *1970*, 289; Goodburn *1978*, 447; Kennett *1983*.
8. note also the hybrid shoes excavated mid-4th century deposits at Lynch Farm, Orton Longueville, Swann and Metcalfe *1975*.
9. Hawkes and Dunning *1961*.
10. e.g. Simpson *1976*.
11. Kirk and Leeds *1954*.

12. Dunnett *1975*, 138–40; Kennett *1983a*, suggests that one of the male burials at Kempston may be compared with the Dorchester burials.
13. Rutherford-Davis *1982*, pl. IVa; Miles pers. comm.
14. Head, *1955*, 92–93.
15. Goodburn *1976*, 340.
16. Mackreth *1978*, 219.
17. Webster L *1979*, 235, Farley *1976*.
18. Kennett *1977*; Wilson D, *1975* 251; Rook and Henig 1981; Goodburn *1979*, 306–7.
19. Reece *1982*; Goodburn *1976* 339.
20. Selkirk *1975*.
21. Kennett *1977*.
22. Wilson D, *1974*, 434.
23. *J Roman Studs* 44 (1954) 93; 45 (1955) 135; 46 (1956) 133–4; 47 (1957) 213–4.
24. Challands *1974*.
25. Goodburn *1976* 337; Barnbrook *1979*.
26. Woods *1972*; Woods *1970*, fig. 1.
27. Wilson D. *1974* 433; Jones *1974*.
28. Hartley B. *1959* 242; Rivers-Moore *1951*.
29. VCH *Herts* IV, 170–1.
30. Neal *1976*, 71; *1974* 75–6; Branigan *1971* 172.
31. Neal *1976*, 71; VCH *Herts* IV, 154–5.
32. Branigan *1971* 86–9, 172–3.
33. Neal *1974* 58–9.
34. Mathews *1964*, 61–4.
35. Branigan *1971* 89–99, 173–75.
36. Van Es *1967*.
37. see comments by Mrs. Fenwick in Branigan *1971* 155.
38. Todd *1981* 245.
39. Young *1973* 112.
40. Note, for example, that rubbish was accumulating on Ermine Street at Godmanchester in the late 4th century.
41. Painter *1977*.
42. Hall and Martin *1980*.
43. Guy *1977*, *1981*, for lead tanks; Frere *1984a* 350, fig. 17. The case for a Christian cemetery is strengthened by the discovery of other less organised contemporary burials with grave goods.
44. Wheeler *1936*, 122–3, pl. XXXV.
45. Anthony *1968*, 49–50.
46. Morris *1968*; Bede *History of the English Church and People* xviii.
47. Green *1975*, 206–8; Goodburn *1976* 333–4; Rankov *1982*, 363.
48. Frere *1966*; Rowley *1973*.
49. Frere *1972*, 110–12; *1983*.
50. Frere *1983*, 21.
51. Frere *1983*; Arnold *1984* appears to have noted only one of the three late houses, and to ignore the implications of four mosaics laid post-AD. 380, for the strength of Romano-British urban traditions at

Verulamium at the close of the fourth century.
52. Rutherford-Davis *1982*, argues for an extensive British Kingdom based on Verulamium and extending well north of the Chiltern scarp, but the evidence is not strong enough to support this view.
53. Stead *1969*.

Bibliography

Alexander, J., (1975), 'The development of urban communities: The evidence of Cambridge and Great Chesterford', in Rodwell, W., and Rowley, T., (eds) *Small Towns of Roman Britain* (Oxford), 103–9.

Allen, D., (1967), 'Celtic coins from the Romano-British temple at Harlow' *Brit. Numis. J.* xxxvi, 1–7.

Allen, D., (1976), 'Did Adminius strike coins?', *Britannia* vii, 96–100.

Anthony, I., (1970), 'Excavations in Verulam Hill Fields, St Albans, 1963–4', *Herts Archaeol.* ii, 9–50.

Anthony, I., (1970a), 'St Michaels, St Albans, Excavations 1966', *Herts Archaeol.* ii, 51–61.

Applebaum, S., (1966), 'Peasant economy and types of agriculture', in Thomas, C., (ed) *Rural Settlement in Roman Britain* (London), 99–107.

Arnold, C., (1984), *Roman Britain to Saxon England* (London)

Artis, E., (1828), *The Durobrivae of Antoninus* (London)

Ashcroft, D., (1939), 'Report on the excavation of a Romano-British villa at Saunderton, Bucks.', *Rec. Buckinghamshire* xiii, 398–426.

Ashdown, R., and Evans, C., (1981), 'Animal Bones. Part I: Mammalian bones' in Partridge *1981*, 205–35.

Atkinson, R.J.C., (1948), 'Archaeological Notes' *Oxoniensia* xiii, 66–7.

Barnbrook, I., (1979), 'Bancroft Roman Villa' *CBA Grp 9 Newsletter* ix, 67–76.

Bartholomew, P., (1984) 'Fourth Century Saxons', *Britannia* xv, 169–186.

Blagg, T., (1981), 'Architectural patronage in the western provinces of the Roman Empire in the third century' in King, A., and Henig, M., (eds) *The Roman West in the 3rd Century* (Oxford).

Branigan, K., (1967) 'The distribution and development of Romano-British occupation in the Chess Valley' *Rec. Buckinghamshire* xviii, 136–49.

Branigan, K., (1968) 'Romano-British rural settlement in the western Chilterns' *Archaeol. J.* cxxiv, 129–59.

Branigan, K., (1969) 'The Romano-British villa at Saunderton reconsidered' *Rec. Buckinghamshire* xviii, 261–76.

Branigan, K., (1971) *Latimer* (Bristol).

Branigan, K., (1972) 'Verulamium and the Chiltern villas' in Ucko, P., et al (eds) *Man, Settlement and Urbanism* (London), 851–6.

Branigan, K., (1973) *Town and Country: Verulamium and the Roman Chilterns* (Bourne End).

Branigan, K., (1978) 'Britain after Boudicca' *Archaeol. Cambrensis* cxxvi, 53–9.

Branigan, K., (1982) 'Celtic Farm to Roman Villa' in Miles, D., (ed) *The Romano-British Countryside* (Oxford), 81–96.

Brown, A., (1969) 'Excavations at Harrold, Beds., 1969' *Wolverton Hist J* 1970, 1618.

Brown, A., and Sheldon, H., (1974) 'Highgate Wood: The pottery and its production' *London Archaeol.* ii, 222–31.

Brown, A. and Woodfield, C. (1983), 'Excavations at Towcester, Northamptonshire: The Alchester Road Suburb', *Northants Archaeol.* xviii, 43–140.

Brown, D., (1974) 'An archaeological gazeteer of the city of Cambridge' *Proc. Cambs. Antiq. Soc.* lxv, 16–22.

Case, H., and Sturdy, D. (1960), 'Archaeological Notes' *Oxoniensia* xxv, 131–6.

Castle, S., (1972), 'A Kiln of the Potter Doinus' *Archaeol J.* cxxix, 69–88.

Castle, S., (1973), 'Trial Excavations at Brockley Hill, pt. 2' *London Archaeol* ii, 78–83.

Cauvain, S and P., (1978), 'A Romano-British site at Micklefield, High Wycombe' *Rec. Buckinghamshire* xx, 528–34.

Challands, A., (1974) 'A Roman Industrial Site and Villa at Sacrewell' *Durobrivae* ii, 13–16.

Challands, A., (1975) 'The Roman villa at Helpston' *Durobrivae* iii, 22–3.

Challands, A., (1976) 'A Roman lime-kiln at Helpston' *Durobrivae* iv, 22–3.

Challands, A., (1979) 'Roman ironworking and an anvil from Nassington' *Durobrivae* vii, 21–2.

Cocks, A., (1922) 'A Romano-British homestead in the Hambleden Valley' *Archaeologia* lxxi, 141–198.

Cowley, D., and Foard, G., (1979) 'Aerial archaeology in Northamptonshire' *Northamptonshire Archaeol.* xiv, 91–7.

Crickmore, D., (1984) *Romano-British Urban Defences* (Oxford).

Crouch, K., (1976) 'The archaeology of Staines and the excavation at Elmsleigh House' *Trans. London and Middlesex Archaeol. Soc.* xxvii, 71–134.

Crouch, K., (1978) 'New thoughts on Roman Staines' *London Archaeol.* iii, 180–6.

Crouch, K and Shanks, S. (1984) *Excavations in Staines, 1975–76* (London)

Curnow, P., (1974) 'The coins' in Neal, D., *1974*, 101–122.

Dallas, C., (1975) 'A Belgic farmstead at Orton Longueville' *Durobrivae* iii, 26–7.

Dannell, G., (1973), 'The Potter Indixivixus' in Detsicas, A., (ed) *Current Research in Romano-British Coarse Pottery* (London), 139–42.

Dannell, G., (1974), 'Roman Industry in Normangate Field, Castor' *Durobrivae* ii, 7–9.

Dannell, G., (1975), 'Longthorpe 1974' *Durobrivae* iii, 18–20.

Dix, B., (1979) 'Odell: A River Valley Farm' *Current Archaeol.* lxvi, 215–8.

Dix, B., (1980) 'Excavations at Harrold Pit, Odell. 1974–80. A preliminary report' *Bedfordshire Archaeol. J.* xiv, 15–18.

Dix, B., (1981) 'The Romano-British farmstead at Odell and its setting. . .' *Landscape History* iii, 17–26.

Dix, B., (1984), 'Ashton Roman Town; Archaeological Rescue Excavations' *Durobrivae* ix, 26–7.

Drury, G., (1963), *The East Midlands and the Peak* (London).

Dunnett, R., (1975), *The Trinovantes* (London).

Dyer, J., (1973) *Southern England: An Archaeological Guide* (London).

Farley, M., (1976) Saxon and Medieval Walton, Aylesbury, Bucks. Excavations 1973–4' *Rec. Buckinghamshire* xx, 153–290.

Farley, M., (1981) 'A late Iron Age and Roman site at Walton Court, Aylesbury' *Rec. Buckinghamshire* xxiii, 51–75.

Farley, M., (1982) 'Archaeological notes from Bucks County Museum', *Rec. Buckinghamshire*, xxiv, 171–5.

Farley, M., (1983) 'The villa at Mill End, Hambleden, Bucks . . .' *Britannia* xiv, 256–9.

Foster, P., Harper, R., and Watkins, S., (1977) 'An Iron Age and Romano-British Settlement at Hardwick Park . . .' *Northamptonshire Archaeol.* xii, 55–96.

Frend, W., (1968) 'A Roman farm settlement at Godmanchester' *Proc. Cambs. Archaeol. Soc.* lix, 19–43.

Frere, S.S., (1962) 'Excavations at Dorchester on Thames' *Archaeol. J.* cxix, 114–49.

Frere, S.S., (1966) 'The end of towns in Roman Britain' in Wacher, J., (ed) *The Civitas Capitals of Roman Britain* (Leicester), 87–100

Frere, S.S., (1972) *Verulamium Excavations. I.* (London).

Frere, S.S., (1977) 'Roman Britain in 1976 (i)' *Britannia* viii, 356–425.

Frere, S.S., (1978) *Britannia* (London).

Frere, S.S., (1983) *Verulamium Excavations II* (London)

Frere, S.S., (1984) 'British urban defences in earthwork' *Britannia* xv, 63–74.

Frere, S.S., (1984a) 'Roman Britain in 1983, i' *Britannia* xv, 266–332.

Frere, S.S., (1984b) *Verulamium Excavations III* (Oxford).

Frere, S.S., and St. Joseph, J., (1974) 'The Roman fortress at Longthorpe' *Britannia* v, 1–129.

Frere, S.S., and St. Joseph, J., (1983) *Roman Britain from the Air* (Cambridge)

Friendship- Taylor, R., (1974) 'The excavation of the Belgic and Romano-British settlement at Quinton, Northants, 1971–2' *J. Northamptonshire Mus.* xi, 3–59.

Friendship-Taylor, R., (1979) 'The excavation of the Belgic and Romano-British settlement at Quinton, Northants, 1973–8' *J. Northamptonshire Mus.* xiii, 2–176.

Friendship-Taylor, R. and E., and Woodfield, C. and P., (1981) 'Piddington Villa 1979/80' *CBA Grp 9 Newsletter* xi, 33–5.

Fulford, M., (1975) *New Forest Pottery* (Oxford)

Fulford, M., (1977) 'The location of Romano-British pottery kilns:

institutional trade and the market' in Dore. J., and Greene, K., (eds) *Roman Pottery Studies in Britain and Beyond.*

Gebbels, A., (1976) 'Animal bones' in Neal, D., (1976), 48–51; 106, 110.

Gentrey, A., Ivens, J., and McClean, H., (1977) 'Excavations at Lincoln Rd., Enfield, 1974–1976' *Trans. London Middlesex Archaeol Soc.* xxviii, 101–89.

Gillam, J., and Greene, K., (1981) 'Roman pottery and the economy' in Anderson, S. and A. (eds) *Roman Pottery Research in Britain and North West Europe* (Oxford), 1–25.

Goodburn, R., (1976) 'Roman Britain in 1975, i.' *Britannia* vii, 291–377.

Goodburn, R., (1978) 'Roman Britain in 1977, i.' *Britannia* ix, 403–472.

Goodburn, R., (1979) 'Roman Britain in 1978, i.' *Britannia* x, 267–338.

Goodburn, R., (1981) 'The Celtic coins' in Partridge, C. (1981), 121–9.

Gowing, C., (1971) 'Archaeological Notes from the Bucks County Museum' *Rec. Buckinghamshire* xix, 92–95.

Green, C., and Draper, J., (1978) 'The Mileoak Roman villa, Handley, Towcester' *Northamptonshire Archaeol.* xiii, 28–66.

Green, H.M., (1975) 'Roman Godmanchester' in Rodwell, W., and Rowley, T., (eds) *Small Towns of Roman Britain* (Oxford), 183–210.

Green, H.M., (1978), 'A villa estate at Godmanchester' in Todd, M. (ed) *Studies in The Romano-British Villa* (Leicester), 103–16.

Green, M., (1974), 'Excavations at Sherwood Drive' *Milton Keynes J* iii, 14–22.

Grew, F., (1980) 'Roman Britain in 1979, i' *Britannia* xi, 346-402.

Guy, C., (1977), 'The lead tank from Ashton' *Durobrivae* v, 10–11.

Guy, C., (1981), 'Roman circular lead tanks in Britain' *Britannia* xii, 271–6.

Hadman, J., (1984) 'Ashton 1979–82' *Durobrivae* ix, 28–30.

Hadman, J. and Upex, S., (1974) 'The Roman villa at North Lodge, Barnwell, 1973' *Durobrivae* ii, 27–8.

Hadman, J. and Upex, S., (1975) 'The Roman settlement at Ashton, near Oundle' *Durobrivae* ii, 13–15.

Hall, D. and Martin, P., (1980) 'Fieldwork survey of the Soke of Peterborough' *Durobrivae* viii, 13.

Hall, D. and Nickerson, N., (1968) 'Excavations at Irchester 1962–3' *Archaeol J* cxxiv, 65–99.

Hamilton, R. (1971) 'Animal Remains' in Branigan (1971), 163–6.

Harcourt, R., (1974) 'Animal Bones' in Neal (1974), 256–61.

Hargreaves, G et al (1978) 'Dorchester, Oxfordshire' *CBA Grp 9 Newsletter* viii, 5–7.

Hartley, B., (1959) 'A Romano-British villa at High Wycombe' *Rec. Buckinghamshire* xvi, 227–57.

Hartley. B., (1972) *Notes on the Roman Pottery Industry in the Nene Valley* (Peterborough).

Hartley, B., (1983) 'The enclosure of Romano-British towns in the second century AD' in Hartley, B. and Wacher, J. (eds) *Rome and Her Northern Provinces* (Gloucester).

Hartley, K., (1973) 'The marketing and distribution of mortaria' in

Detsicas, A. (ed) *Current Research in Romano-British Coarse Pottery* (London), 39–51.

Hassall, M. and Tomlin, R., (1983) 'Roman Britain in 1982, ii. '*Britannia* xiv, 336–56'

Hawkes, C., (1980) 'Caesar's Britain. An oppidum for Cassivellaunus' *Antiquity* liv, 138–9.

Hawkes, S. and Dunning, G., (1961) 'Soldiers and settlers in Britain, 4th to 5th centuries' *Medieval Archaeol.* v, 1–70.

Head, J., (1955) *Early Man in South Buckinghamshire* (Bristol).

Helbaek, H. (1952), 'Early crops in southern England' *Proc. Prehist. Soc.* xviii, 194–233.

Henig, M., (1972), 'The origin of some ancient British coin types' *Britannia* iii, 209–23.

Hingley, R., (1982) 'The structure of Roman imperialism and the consequences of imperialism on the development of a peripheral province' in Miles, D. (ed) *The Romano-British Countryside* (Oxford), 17–52.

Hodder, I., (1974) 'Some marketing models for Romano-British coarse pottery', *Britannia* v, 340–59.

Hodder, I., (1975) 'The spatial distribution of Romano-British small towns' in Rodwell, W. and Rowley, T., *Small Towns of Roman Britain* (Oxford), 67–74.

Hodder, I., (1977) 'Some new directions in spatial analysis' in Clarke, D. (ed), *Spatial Archaeology* (London), 223–352.

Hodder, I., (1979) 'Pre-Roman and Romano-British tribal economies' in Burnham, B. and Johnson, C., (eds) *Invasion and Response: The Case of Roman Britain* (Oxford), 189–96.

Hodder, I. and Hassall, M., (1971) 'Non-random spacing of Romano-British walled towns' *Man* vi, 391–407.

Howe, M., Perrin, J. and Mackreth, D., (1982) *Roman Pottery from the Nene Valley: A Guide* (Peterborough)

Hunn, J., (1980) 'The earthworks of Prae Wood: An interim account' *Britannia* xi, 21–30.

Hunter, R. and Mynard, D., (1977) 'Excavations at Thorplands near Northampton' *Northamptonshire Archaeol.* xii, 97–154.

Jackson, D., (1979) 'Roman ironworking at Bulwick and Greeton' *Northamptonshire Archaeol.* xiv, 31–7.

Jackson, D. and Ambrose, T., (1978) 'Excavations at Wakerley, Northants, 1972–75' *Britannia* ix, 115–242.

Johnson, S., (1975) 'Vici in Lowland Britain' in Rodwell, W. and Rowley, T. (eds) *Small Towns of Roman Britain* (Oxford), 75–84.

Johnson, S., (1976) *The Roman Forts of the Saxon Shore* (London).

Johnston, D., (1969) 'Romano-British pottery kilns near Northampton' *Antiq. J.* xlix, 75–97.

Johnston, D., (1975) 'Sandy' in Rodwell, W. and Rowley, T. (eds) *Small Towns of Roman Britain* (Oxford), 225–31.

Jones, M., (1981) 'Tegula mould stamps from Stanton Low, Bucks.' *Antiq. J* lxi, 335–6.

Jones, R., (1974) 'Walton' *Northamptonshire Archaeol.* ix, 97–100.

Kennett, D., (1977) 'Duston and Discontinuity' *CBA Grp 9 Newsletter* vii, 13–14.

Kennett, D., (1983) 'Romano-Saxon Pottery: a critical note' *Bedfordshire Archaeol.* xvi, 87–88.

Kennett, D., (1983a) 'The earliest male grave at Kempston' *Bedfordshire Archaeol.* xvi, 88–91.

Kenyon, K., (1934) 'The Roman theatre at Verulamium, St Albans' *Archaeologia* lxxxiv, 213–61.

King, A., (1978) 'A comparative survey of bone assemblages from Roman sites in Britain' *Bull. Inst. Archaeol. London* xv, 207–232.

Kirk, J and Leeds, E. (1954) 'Three early Saxon graves from Dorchester' *Oxoniensia* xviii, 63–76

Knight, J., (1968) 'Excavations at the Roman town of Irchester, 1962–3' *Archaeol. J.* cxxiv, 100–28.

Lambrick, G., (1980) 'Excavations in Park St., Towcester' *Northamptonshire Archaeol,* xv, 35–118.

Lewis, M., (1966) *Temples in Roman Britain* (Cambridge).

Luff, (1982) *A Zoo-archaeological study of the Roman North-West Provinces* (Oxford).

Mackreth, D., (1976) 'Hall Farm, Orton Longueville' *Durobrivae* iv, 24–5.

Mackreth, D., (1977) 'Orton Hall Farm – the Saxon connection' *Durobrivae* v, 20–21.

Mackreth, D., (1978) 'Orton Hall Farm, Peterborough: a Roman and Saxon Settlement' in Todd, M. (ed) *Studies in the Romano-British Villa* (Leicester) 209–223.

Mackreth, D., (1979) 'Durobrivae' *Durobrivae* vii, 19–21.

Mackreth, D., (1984) 'Castor' *Durobrivae* ix, 22–25.

Mackreth, D., and O'Neill, F. (1980) 'Werrington: an Iron Age and Roman site' *Durobrivae* viii, 23–5.

Maloney, J., and Hobley, B., (1983) (eds) *Roman Urban Defences in the West* (London).

Manning, W., (1972) 'Iron-Work Hoards in Iron Age and Roman Britain' *Britannia* iii, 224–50.

Marsden, P. (1980) *Roman London* (London).

Matthews, C.L., (1964) *Ancient Dunstable* (Dunstable).

Mathews, C.L., (1981) (A Romano-British Inhumation Cemetery at Dunstable' *Bedfordshire Archaeol. J.* xv, 1–74.

Millard, A., (1956) 'Interim report on excavations of a Roman building at Moor Park' tract published by Merchants Taylors School.

Monk, M., (1981) 'Carbonized cereal grains from building vii' in Partridge (1981), 204–5.

Moore, N., (1974) 'Moulton' *Northamptonshire Archaeol.* ix, 91.

Morris, J., (1968) 'The date of St. Alban' *Hertfordshire Archaeol.* i (1968), 1–8.

Muckelroy, K., (1976) 'Enclosed ambulatories in Romano-Celtic temples in Britain' *Britannia* vii, 173–91.

Muckelroy, K., et al (1978) 'A pre-Roman coin from Canterbury' *Proc. Prehist. Soc.* xliv, 439–44.

Neal, D.S., (1974) *The Excavation of a Roman Villa in Gadebridge Park* (London).

Neal, D.S., (1976) 'The excavation of three Roman buildings in the Bulbourne valley' *Hertfordshire Archaeol.* iv, 1–135.

Neal, D.S., (1978) 'The growth and decline of villas in the Verulamium area' in Todd, M. (ed) *Studies in the Romano-British Villa* (Leicester) 33–58.

Neal, D.S., (1983) 'Unusual buildings at Wood Lane End, Hemel Hempstead' *Britannia* xiv, 73–87.

Neal, D.S., (1984) 'A Sanctuary at Wood Lane, End, Hemel Hempstead' *Britannia* xv, 193–216.

Neville, R., (1849) 'Memoirs on Roman remains and villas discovered at Ickleton and Chesterford' *Archaeol. J.* vi, 14–26.

O'Neill, H., (1945) 'The Roman villa at Park Street' *Archaeol. J.* cii, 21–110.

Painter, K., (1977) *The Water Newton Early Christian Treasure* (London).

Parnum, A., and Cotton, J. (1983) 'Recent work in Brentford . . . 1974–82' *London Archaeol* iv, 318–25.

Partridge, C., (1975) 'Braughing' in Rodwell, W. and Rowley, T. (eds) *Small Towns of Roman Britain* (Oxford), 139–57.

Partridge, C., (1981) *Skeleton Green* (London).

Partridge, C., (1982) 'Graffiti from Skeleton Green' *Britannia* xiii, 325–6.

Partridge, C., (1982a) 'Braughing; Wickham Kennels 1982' *Hertfordshire Archaeol.* viii, 40-59.

Peacock, D., (1971) 'Roman amphorae in pre-Roman Britain' in Jesson, M. and Hill, D. (eds) *The Iron Age and its Hillforts* (Southampton), 161–88.

Peacock, D., (1982) *Pottery in the Roman World* (London).

Petchley, M., (1979) 'Caldecote' *CBA Grp 9 Newsletter* ix, 63–67.

Pryor, F., (1976) 'Fengate 1975' *Durobrivae* iv, 10–12.

Rankov, N., (1982) 'Roman Britain in 1981, i.' *Britannia* xiii, 328–95.

Rawlins, B., (1970) 'A Roman tile kiln at Park St. near St Albans' *Hertfordshire Archaeol.* ii, 62–6.

Reece, R. (1979), 'Roman Monetary Impact' in Burnham, B., and Johnson, C. (eds). *Invasion and Response: The Case of Roman Britain* (Oxford), 211–17.

Reece, R., (1982) 'The coins from the Cow Roast, Herts; a commentary' *Hertfordshire Archaeol.* viii, 60–6.

Richardson, K., (1944) 'Report on excavations at Verulamium, insula XVIII, 1938' *Archaeologia* xc, 81–126.

Rivers-Moore, C., (1951) 'Further excavations in the Roman house at Harpsden Wood, Henley-on-Thames' *Oxoniensia* xvi, 23–7.

Rivet, A.L.F., (1964) *Town and Country in Roman Britain* (London).

Rivet, A.L.F., (1975) 'The classification of minor towns and related settlements' in Rodwell, W., and Rowley, T. (eds) *Small Towns of Roman Britain* (Oxford), 111–14.

Rivet, A.L.F. and Smith, C. (1979) *The Place-Names of Roman Britain* (London).

Rodwell, W., (1972) 'The Roman fort at Great Chesterford, Essex' *Britannia* iii, 291–3.

Rodwell, W., (1975) 'Milestones, civic territories and the Antonine Itinerary' *Britannia* vi, 76–101.

Rodwell, W., (1976) 'Coinage, oppida and the rise of Belgic power in south-east Britain' in Cunliffe, B., and Rowley, T. (eds) *Oppida: The Beginnings of Urbanization in Barbarian Europe* (Oxford), 181–366.

Rook, A., (1968) 'Investigation of a Belgic occupation site at Crookhams, Welwyn Garden City' *Hertfordshire Archaeol.* i, 51–65.

Rook, A., (1970) 'Investigation of a Belgic site at Grubs Barn, Welwyn Garden City' *Hertfordshire Archaeol.* ii, 31–6.

Rook, A., and Henig, M., (1981) 'A bronze cockerel from a late Romano-British context at Ashton, Herts' *Antiq. J.* lxi, 356–7.

Rook, A., Walker, S., and Denston, C. (1984) 'A Roman mausoleum and associated marble sarcophagus and burial from Welwyn' *Britannia* xv, 143–62.

Rook, A., et al (1982) 'An Iron Age bronze mirror from Aston, Herts.' *Antiq. J.* lxii, 18–34.

Roundell, H., (1863), 'Account of Roman foundations and other antiquities discovered in 1860–62 at Tingewick' *Rec. Buckinghamshire* iii, 33–5.

Rowley, T., (1973) 'Early Saxon settlements in Dorchester on Thames' in Rowley, T (ed) *Anglo-Saxon Settlement and Landscape* (Oxford), 42–50.

Rowley, T., (1975) 'The Roman towns of Oxfordshire' in Rodwell, W., and Rowley, T., (eds) *Small Towns of Roman Britain* (Oxford), 115–124.

Rutherford-Davis, K., (1982) *Britons and Saxons* (Chichester).

St. Joseph, J., (1973) 'Air reconnaisance in Roman Britain 1969–72' *J. Roman Studs.* lxiii, 214–46.

Salway, P., (1981) *Roman Britain* (Oxford).

Saunders, A., (1961) 'Excavations at Park Street, 1954–7' *Archaeol. J.* cxviii, 100–35.

Saunders, C., (1982) 'Some thoughts on the oppida at Wheathampstead and Verulamium' *Hertfordshire Archaeol.* viii, 31–9.

Saunders, C. and Havercroft, A., (1977) 'A kiln of the potter Oastrius.' *Hertfordshire Archaeol.* v, 109–56.

Saunders, C., and Havercroft, A., (1982) 'Excavations on the line of the Wheathampstead By-Pass, 1974 and 1977' *Hertfordshire Archaeol.* vii, 11–31.

Selkirk, A., (1971) 'Dickets Mead, Lockleys' *Current Archaeol.* xxvii, 106–9.

Selkirk, A., (1975) 'A corn-dryer at Foxholes' *Current Archaeol.* lii, 152–3.

Sheldon, H. and Schaaf, L. (1978), 'A survey of Roman sites in Greater London' in Bird, J. et al (eds) *Collectiana Londinienses* (London), 59–88.

Simco, A., (1984) *Survey of Bedfordshire. The Roman Period* (Bedford).

Simpson, C., (1976) 'Belt-buckles and strap ends of the Later Roman Empire' *Britannia* vii, 192–223.

Simpson, W.G., (1966) 'Romano-British settlement on the Welland gravels' in Thomas, C. (ed) *Rural Settlement in Roman Britain* (London), 15–25.

Smith, D.J., (1969) 'The mosaic pavements' in Rivet, A.L.F. (ed) *The Roman Villa in Britain* (London), 71–125

Smith, D.J., (1975) 'Roman mosaics in Britain before the fourth century' in Picard, A. and J. (eds) *La Mosaique Greco-Romaine. II* (Paris), 269–90.

Smith, D.J., (1984) 'Roman mosaics in Britain: A synthesis' in R. Farioli Campanati (ed) *IIIrd Colloquio Internazionale sul Mosaico Antico* (Ravenna) 357–80.

Stead, I., (1967) 'A La Tene III burial at Welwyn Garden City' *Archaeologia* ci, 1–62.

Stead, I., (1968) 'A La Tene III burial at the Tene, Baldock, Herts' *Antiq. J.* xlviii, 306

Stead, I., (1969) 'Verulamium, 1966–8' *Antiquity* xliii, 45–52.

Stead, I., (1975) 'Baldock' in Rodwell, W. and Rowley, T. (eds) *Small Towns of Roman Britain* (Oxford), 125–9.

Stevens, C.E., (1952) 'The Roman name of Ilchester' *Proc. Somerset Archaeol. Natur. Hist. Soc.* xcvi, 188–92.

Swann, J., and Metcalfe, A., (1975) 'Roman leather shoes from Lynch Farm *'Durobrivae* iii, 24–5.

Taylor, C., (1975) 'Roman settlement in the Nene Valley: the impact of recent archaeology' in Fowler, P. (ed) *Recent Work in Rural Archaeology* (Bradford on Aveon), 107–20.

Taylor, M., (1956) 'Roman Britain in 1955, i.' *J. Roman Studs.* xcvi, 119–46.

Thompson, I., (1979) 'Wheathampstead revisited' *Bull. Inst. Archaeol. Univ. London* xvi, 159–85.

Thompson, I., (1982) *Grog Tempered Pottery of South East England* (Oxford).

Tilson, P., (1973) 'A Belgic and Romano-British site at Bromham' *Bedfordshire Archaeol* viii, 23–66.

Todd, J., and Cleland, J. (1976) 'Roman Ironworking at Longthorpe' *Durobrivae* iv, 19.

Todd, M., (1973) *The Coritani* (London).

Todd, M., (1975) 'Margidunum and Ancaster' in Rodwell, W. and Rowley, T. (eds) *Small Towns of Roman Britain* (Oxford), 211–223.

Todd, M., (1976) 'The Vici of western England' in Branigan, K., and Fowler, P. (eds) *The Roman West Country* (Newton Abbott), 99–119.

Todd, M., (1981) *Roman Britain: 55 BC – AD 400.* (London).

Tomlin, R. (1983) 'Non Coritani sed Corieltauvi' *Antiq. J.* liii, 353–4.

Turland, R., (1977) 'Towcester-Wood Burcote' *Northamptonshire Archaeol.* xii, 218–23.

Van Es, W., (1967) 'Wijster: a native village beyond the imperial frontier. 150–425 AD.' *Palaeohistoria* xi, 1–595.

Wacher, J., (1974) *The Towns of Roman Britain* (London).

Walthew, C., (1978) 'Property boundaries and the size of building plots in Roman towns' *Britannia* ix, 335–50.

Ward-Perkins, J., (1938) 'The Roman villa at Lockleys, Welwyn' *Antiq. J.* xviii, 339–76.

Webster, G., (1969) 'The future of villa studies' in Rivet, A.L.F. (ed) *The Roman Villa in Britain* (London), 217–49.

Webster, G., (1975) *The Cornovii* (London).

Webster, G., (1980) *The Roman Invasion of Britain* (London).

Webster, L., (1979) 'Medieval Britain in 1978' *Medieval Archaeol.* xxiii, 234–8.

Wheeler, R.E.M. (1936) *Verulamium: A Belgic and Two Roman Cities* (London).

Wild, J.P., (1973) 'Longthorpe: An essay in continuity' *Durobrivae* i, 7–10.

Wild, J.P., (1973a) 'The Roman fishpond at Lynch Farm' *Durobrivae* i, 20–21.

Wild, J.P., (1973b) 'A fourth century potters workshop and kilns at Stibbington, Peterborough' in Detsicas A. (ed) *Current Research in Romano-British Coarse Pottery* (London), 135–7.

Wild, J.P., (1974) 'Roman settlement in the lower Nene valley' *Archaeol J.* cxxxi, 140–70

Wild, J.P., (1978) 'Villas in the lower Nene valley' in Todd, M. (cd) *Studies in the Romano-British villa.* (Leicester), 59–69.

Williams, J., (1976) 'Excavations on a Roman site at Overstone' *Northamptonshire Archaeol.* xi, 100–33.

Williams, R., (1982) 'Pennyland' *CBA Grp. 9 Newsletter*, xii, 73–8.

Williams, R., (1984) 'Bancroft mausoleum' *South Midlands Archaeol.* xiv, 21–6.

Wilson, D.R., (1970) 'Roman Britain in 1969, i' *Britannia* i, 269–305.

Wilson, D.R., (1971) 'Roman Britain in 1970, i' *Britannia* ii, 242–88.

Wilson, D.R., (1973) 'Roman Britain in 1972, i' *Britannia* iv, 271–323.

Wilson, D.R., (1974) 'Roman Britain in 1973, i' *Britannia* v, 397–460.

Wilson, D.R., (1974a) 'Romano-British villas from the air' *Britannia* v, 251–61.

Wilson, D.R., (1975) 'Roman Britain in 1974, i' *Britannia* vi, 221–283.

Wilson, D.R., (1975a) 'The small towns of Roman Britain from the air' in Rodwell, W. and Rowley, T. (eds) *Small Towns of Roman Britain* (Oxford), 9–49.

Wilson, G. (1978) 'Early plants in the Nene Valley: an interim report' *Durobrivae* vi, 17–18.

Wilson, M. (1974) 'The other pottery' in Frere and St Joseph (1974), 96–111.

Windell, D., (1981) 'Earls Barton; Clay Lane' *CBA Grp 9 Newsletter* xi, 20–22.

Woodfield, C., (1977) 'A Roman military site at Magiovinium' *Rec. Buckinghamshire* xx, 384–99.

Woodfield, C., (1978) 'Towcester' *Northamptonshire Archaeol* xiii, 184.

Woodfield, P., (1978) 'Roman architectural masonry from Northants' *Northamptonshire Archaeol.* xiii, 67–86.

Woods, P., (1969) *Excavations at Hardingstone, Northants* (Northampton).

Woods, P., (1970) *Brixworth I.* (Northampton)

Woods, P., (1972) 'Brixworth, Northants' *CBA Grp. 9 Newsletter* ii, 9–10.

Woods, P., (1974) 'Types of Late Belgic and early Romano-British pottery kilns in the Nene Valley' *Britannia* v, 262–81.

Woods, P., and Hastings, B., (1984) *Rushden: The Early Fine Wares* (Northampton).

Young, C., (1972) 'The Oxford Potteries' *Current Archaeol.* xxxi, 209–211.

Young, C., (1973) 'The pottery industry of the Oxford region' in Detsicas, A., (ed) *Current Research in Romano-British Coarse Pottery* (London), 105–15

Young, C., (1977) *Oxfordshire Roman Pottery* (Oxford)

Zeepvat, R., (1980) 'Wymbush Roman farmstead' *CBA Grp. 9 Newsletter* x, 60–64.

Zeepvat, R., (1983) 'Stantonbury villa excavation' *South Midlands Archaeology* xiii, 49–52.

Zeepvat, R., (1984) 'Bancroft villa' *South Midlands Archaeology* xiv, 16–21.

Index

Hambleden, villa, 59, 111, 112, 143
Hardingstone, kiln, 158
Harlow, temple, 29
Harpsden, villa, 111, 112, 179
Harrold, kilns, 157, 167
Harston, kilns, 172
Headington, kilns, 155
   villa, 111
Hedsor, settlement 64
Helpston, lime kiln, 164
   villa, 123, 125, 126
Higham Ferrers, settlement, 98, villa?, 122
Highgate Wood, kilns, 157
High Wycombe, villa, 60, 105, 109, 110, 179
Hodder, I. 5, 167
Huntingdon, villa, 127, 128, 176

Ickleton, villa, 127, 128
Irchester, fort? 37
   town 56, 89, 119
Iron-working, 98, 140, 158–62
Islip, villa, 143, 156

Johnson, S. 82

Kempton, 173
Kettering, settlement, 98
Kimble, villa, 130,
Kings Langley, villa, 105, 136

Latimer, villa, 59, 60, 105, 109, 110, 130, 143, 179, 180
Lime kilns, post-villa occupation, 181–6, 163–4
Little Addington, villa, 121
Little Brickhill, fort? 35, 44
Little Hadham, kilns, 163
Little Houghton, settlement, 98
Littlemore, kilns, 155
Lockleys, Belgic farm, 23, 104
   villa 104, 108, 109
Longthorpe, Belgic farm, 26
   vexillation fortress 38, 42, 44, 159
   villa? 126
Luton brooches, 173

Lynch Farm, barn, 125, 134, 144
   fish-pond, 145

Magnentius 60, 110, 179
Marholm, 173, 187
Marketing, 48, 71, 97, 166–68, 186, 190
Marlow, villa?, 111
Maximus, Magnus, 170, 190
Mercury, 73, 116
Mileoak, villa, 48, 114, 115, 116
Moor Park, villa, 105
Mosaic production, 164–6
Moulton Park, Belgic farm, 25
   villa, 122
Much Hadham, kiln, 172
Muckelroy, K. 73
Munden, kiln, 147
Mursley, villa, 116

Nassington, 159, 160
Neal, D. 95
Nene Valley potteries, 123, 148–54, 186
Nether Heyford, villa, 116, 177
Netherwild, kilns, 162
Newnham, villa, 25, 120, 121, 164
Normangate Field, kilns, 149;52, 159
Northchurch, fort? 37,
   villa 105, 109, 136, 144, 161
Norton, settlement, 98

Odell, Belgic farm, 24–25, 120
   farm, 120, 134, 143, 144
   villa? 120
Orton Longueville, Belgic farm, 26
   Hall Farm villa, 123, 125, 134, 144, 173
   Saxon occupation, 173–4, 176
Overstone, settlement, 134
Oxfordshire potteries, 154–56, 186

Panshanger, Welwyn-burial, 22
Park Street, Belgic farm 23, 43, 104
   villa 48, 59, 104, 106, 109, 110, 162–3, 169, 180
Partridge, C. 4, 5, 19, 20
Paulus, 60, 179
Peacock, D. 5